ALCOHOL, YOUTH AND THE STATE

SOCIAL ANALYSIS
A Series in the Social Sciences
Edited by Richard Scase, University of Kent

Beyond Class Images:
Explorations in the Structure of
Social Consciousness
Howard H. Davis

Fundamental Concepts and the
Sociological Enterprise
C.C. Harris

Urban Planning in a Capitalist Society
Gwyneth Kirk

The State in Western Europe
Edited by Richard Scase

Autonomy and Control at the Workplace:
Contexts for Job Redesign
Edited by John E. Kelly and Chris W. Clegg

The Entrepreneurial Middle Class
Richard Scase and Robert Goffee

Capitalism, the State and Industrial Relations:
The Case of Britain
Dominic Strinati

Alcohol, Youth and the State

NICHOLAS DORN

CROOM HELM
London & Canberra

Croom Helm Ltd, Provident House, Burrell Row,
Beckenham, Kent BR3 1AT
Croom Helm Australia, PO Box 391, Manuka,
ACT 2603, Australia

British Library Cataloguing in Publication Data

Dorn, Nicholas
Alcohol youth and the state.
1. Alcohol and youth--Great Britain
I. Title
306.4 HV5135

ISBN 0-7099-0243-3

Printed and bound in Great Britain by
Biddles Ltd, Guildford and King's Lynn

CONTENTS

PREFACE

This book originated in a study, funded by the Health Education Council, of youthful drinking practices. The funding was motivated partly by increasing government interest in alcohol-related problems and in the possibilities for 'prevention', and partly by press depictions of these problems, in which 'teenage alcoholism' was becoming a familiar motif. It was against this background that the study was intended to generate information or strategies that might be useful in health and social policy generally, and in health education in particular. Viewing this situation from a position informed by the sociology of social problems, it seemed clear to me that a comprehensive study with practical implications must necessarily engage both dimensions of 'the problem' – not only the vicissitudes of youthful drinking practices and their meanings to those involved, but also the nature and origins of social reaction. These two areas of enquiry take up parts I and II of the study, whilst part III takes up some of the implications. The research has proved to be a useful resource in the writing (with Bente Nortoft) and revision of the *Health Careers* teachers' manual which, I hope, goes some way towards meeting the needs of practitioners in health and social education in schools, colleges, training schemes, youth work, community education projects and the media. My key proposition (underlying the research study and manual) is that acquiring an understanding of health-related 'social problems' is a form of education about 'working life'.

A study such as this leaves as many outstanding debts as it does unsolved problems. I am grateful to all those employers, teachers and others in Servicetown, my case study area, who helped me with my fieldwork. Special thanks to John and Lily. I received critical support from John Auld (Middlesex Polytechnic), Alan Beatty (Institute of Education), Steve Box (Kent University), Dick Scase (Kent University), and Nigel South (Institute for the Study of Drug Dependence, London). The latter read the whole thing through, yawning copiously. Peter Schiøler at the Danish Ministry of Education and Jasper Woodcock at the Institute for the Study of Drug Dependence managed to combine nagging and encouragement. I am also indebted to the library staff at I.S.D.D., at the L.S.E., and at the University of London, and to Ray Johnson at the Medical Council on Alcoholism. Kathy Cohn, Karolina Frey and Susan Marrows typed the various versions of the manuscript, not without justifiable complaint. First and last, of course, I am grateful to the original sponsors, without whom this study would not have been started, and also very grateful to my employing institution, the Institute for the Study of Drug Dependence, for putting a roof over the project. None of these agencies or individuals is, of course, responsible for what follows.

Leafing through the pages at proof stage I felt regret over four remaining problems. These are – my relative neglect of the Weberian sociological tradition (a point for which I am indebted to Bill Tyler); the unevenness with which sexual divisions are theorised throughout the work; also the inadequate treatment of ethnicity (mention of which is restricted to asides to the white-centred argument); and the extent to which things may have changed since the fieldwork was done in the late 1970s. I leave it to the reader to reflect on the extent of reconstruction that might be required for a definitive study of 'alcohol-related problems'.

London, 1983

INTRODUCTION

This study addresses itself to three substantive questions; what are the historical origins of contemporary concerns about youthful drinking; how can drinking practices within particular strata of working class youth be understood; and what general implications may be drawn for the development of health and social education touching upon youthful drinking? The answers to these questions depend upon the form of social analysis adopted, and this introduction outlines a sociological perspective that is applied in the following chapters.

Youth, Drink and Indiscipline: a new moral panic

During the last few years, a 'moral panic' has arisen about teenage drinking, which is characterised as a specific aspect of a more general breakdown in the good order of society.[1] The quality of this panic is well illustrated by the following press report, taken from the International Herald Tribune of 24th November 1980, which neatly summarises concerns voiced in the English and Scottish press during the late 1970s:

> *Rising Crime Disturbs Britain's Air of Civility, Homicides Double, Muggings Soar: Experts Blame Unemployment, Teenage Drinking.* For generations, Britain has been regarded as one of the world's safest countries, a model of civility, with quiet streets and a largely unarmed police force. But in recent months police officers and sociologists have been alarmed by increasing violence . . .[2]

In this and other media accounts teenage drinking is placed firmly within the context of social indisicipline. Statistical evidence that the police are arresting increasing numbers of young people for drink-related offences is deployed within this context:

> *Drink blamed for vandalism, theft and assaults.* THE BATTLE TO SAVE BRITAIN'S BOOZING KIDS. The crisis of Britain's

> tipsy teenagers was revealed this week in shock Government figures. Booze-related offences are up a startling 10 per cent since 1976 (i.e. in the year 1976-7). (Daily Mirror, 14 November 1980)

It is indeed the case that findings of guilt for offences of drunkenness have increased in England and Wales over the past decade, and that the increase is sharpest in the 18-21 year old group (Home Office, 1978). Trends in such statistics, interpreted within a framework of concern over youth and social indiscipline, tend to give a certain impression of both the quantitative and qualitative aspects of youth drinking; the impression is given that the 'the problem' is increasing in size, and is one in which youthful drinking and public disorder are closely linked.[3]

Press reports based on official statistics have been supplemented more recently by the Government's own attempts to stimulate public debate about 'alcohol problems' generally, and youthful drinking in particular.

> DRINKING SENSIBLY
> The growing problem of alcohol misuse was highlighted today by Norman Fowler, Secretary of State for Social Services, speaking at the publication of the DHSS Booklet 'Drinking Sensibly'... "The aim of this booklet is not to stop people drinking but to encourage more sensible attitudes towards use of alcohol. The purpose is to widen understanding of the problems that can be caused... Above all, prevention depends on better understanding of the issues and the will to face up to them." (DHSS *Press Release,* 14th December 1981)

Drinking Sensibly is one of a series of planned 'discussion documents' prepared by the Health Departments of England and Wales, Scotland and Northern Ireland. It has chapters on the effects of alcohol misuse, education, the law, tax and price disincentives, early identification and help, and prevention. The booklet poses the dilemma that:

> Government controls capable of effectively influencing the minority who misuse alcohol could not be established without affecting the choices available to the majority of the population who drink sensibly. Also, while the misuse of alcohol may cause

> serious health and social problems, the production of and trade in alcoholic drinks form an important part of our economy in terms of jobs, exports, investment, and as a source of revenue for the Government – all of which could be adversely affected by any measures designed to restrict consumption. (DHSS, 1981; 65)

The solution currently being posed is to define the problem primarily in terms of a troublesome minority who do not drink sensibly – 'alcohol may be misued by a minority but the consequences are far reaching and have to be borne by society as a whole' (*ibid*). Youth have often been regarded as such a minority, and are the only special group singled out in *Drinking Sensibly* (p.27), and in the press release accompanying its publication. This provided the framework for newspaper reprints based on the booklet.

> *Battle is on to save teeny tipplers*
> The battle against Britain's increasing teenage drink problem is being stepped up by the Government. Schools are being urged to start lessons on the use and misuse of alcohol in a new document issued by the DHSS . . .Further evidence that under-age drinking is on the increase comes from a survey by the Christian Economic and Social Research Foundation . . ." we have got to the point of no return". (Daily Mirror, 14th December 1981)

This study investigates the historical preconditions of this definition of 'the problem', and reports on a case study of the actual form of drinking in one teenage group.

The Sociology of Moral Panics

The moral panic which currently focusses upon youthful drinking is by no means the first focussing upon youth and social indiscipline. Such panics have attracted considerable sociological attention:

> Societies appear to be subject, every now and then, to periods of moral panic. A condition, episode, person or group of persons emerges to become defined as a threat to societal values and interests; its nature is presented in a stylized and stereotypical fashion by the mass media; the moral barricades are manned by editors, bishops, politicians and other right-thinking people; socially accredited experts pronounce their diagnoses and solutions;

> ways of coping are evolved or (more often) resorted to; the condition then disappears, submerges or deteriorates and becomes more visible. Sometimes the object of the panic is quite novel and at other times it is something which has been in existence long enough, but suddenly appears in the limelight. Sometimes the panic passes over and is forgotten, except in folklore and collective memory; at other times it has more serious and long-lasting repercussions and might produce such changes as those in legal and social policy or even in the way the society conceives itself.
>
> One of the most recurrent types of moral panic in Britain since the war has been associated with the emergence of various forms of youth culture (originally almost exclusively working class, but often recently middle class or student based) whose behaviour is deviant or delinquent. To a greater or lesser degree, these cultures have been associated with violence The Teddy Boys, the Mods and Rockers, the Hells Angels, the Skinheads and the Hippies have all been phenomena of this kind. There have been parallel reactions to the drug problem, student militancy, political demonstrations, football hooliganism, vandalism of various kinds and crime and violence in general. (Cohen, 1980;9)

The post-war sociology of deviancy and social problems has been much concerned with the processes underlying this recurrent moral panic. The initial impetus came from labelling theory, which advanced the bold claim that social control causes deviancy; that is the policing of moral and behavioural boundaries, and the social reaction against those who infringe them, that defines individuals and groups as deviant. Furthermore, the argument went, the apprehension, labelling, and treatment or punishment of those whose rule-infringement was minor and 'out of character' might have the unfortunate effect of forcing them into the role of habitué.[4] Most sociologists of labelling adopted a transactional perspective within which the social outcome was contingent upon processes of negotiation, rather than following in a predetermined manner upon the pronouncement of a label.[5] It was observed, however, that not all social actors enjoyed the same opportunities to promulgate and apply labels, and that particular social groups – e.g. working class youth – seem to be regular recipients of labels.[6] Such observations led to a series of questions being formulated about the social construction of labelling processes – in the juvenile justice system, in psychiatry, in schools, and in the media.[7] Following these early studies, the focus shifted from questions about the consequences of labelling for those who receive them; through questions about the consequences of moral panics for those not labelled; to questions about the relationship between moral panics and the political strategies of dominant or ascendant social class groups. Reviewing progress in this area following the publication, in 1972, of his study of the moral panic over mods and rockers, Stanley Cohen says:

> First, the intevening years have seen much interest in the major promoters of moral panics – the mass media – and in analysing the relationships between deviance and the media. This interest initially took the form of putting together various disparate contributions about how the mass media select and present news about deviance, what models of society are revealed in this presentation and what effects they might have, particularly in shaping the control culture. There have also been a number of empirical studies in Britain on media coverage of industrial conflict, on the 1972-73 'mugging' panic and on crime reporting – each of which has contributed to building up media theory. The mugging study is espcially important in locating the media's broader ideological role . . .The level for explaining labelling, societal reaction or moral panic is shifted from social control agencies or cultures – or vague allusions to the 'wider society' – to the specific operation of the state. This means relating the working of the moral panic – the mobilisation of public opinion, the orchestration by the media and public figures of an otherwise inchoate sense of unease – to overall political shifts. (Cohen, 1980; xxiii-xxiv)

This interest in relating the development of social problem imagery to 'overall political shifts' is one specific aspect of increasing sociological interest in *materialist* methods of social analysis. The historical origins and basic features of materialist theory, including classical Marxism, are outlined in the Annexe and the following paragraphs will do no more than draw out some implications for the study of drinking problems.[8] A basic feature of materialist approaches is that they analyse social problems in terms of relations between social groups. The most significant social groups are those that constitute classes. Classes are defined, primarily, as those groups whose members share the same relation to ownership or effective control in respect of the material conditions in which they must live.[9] Relations between the classes are played out in two spheres, that of the economy, and that of the state and its associated agencies (some of which, regulating the family and personal life, reach deeply into the working class). The development of relations between the classes in the sphere of production produces certain problems (destruction of the workforce, crisis of profitability, wage claims, etc) which require solutions which individual capitals are unable to provide, and this results in the growth of a particular type of state. The state intervenes directly in the operation of the economy, and also develops social policies – policies designed to regulate the life of the working class outside the sphere of production.[10] Additionally, whilst the dominant class may form a unified class, there may be several classes (e.g. landowners, merchants, industrialists) between which there is a shifting coalition; in such circumstances one of the dominant classes may emerge as the effective leader of the block, its definition of the economic and social problems becoming hegemonic and providing the backbone of policies towards the working class.

Work at the Centre for Contemporary Cultural Studies has demonstrated how Gramsci's concept of hegemony – the leadership by one dominant class of a block of others – may be used as the starting-point for analysis of social problems. Stuart Hall and his colleagues, whose work is referred to above by Cohen, locate the moral panic over mugging in the displacement of the relatively liberal consensus of the 1960s by the ascendancy of a 'new Right' in British politics (Hall et al., 1978). This political shift was closely bound up in a corresponding shift in social problem imagery. During the 1960s, the state had pursued a Keynesian policy of maintenance of consumption, which was considered adequte to stabilise production at a profitable level, to guarantee full employment, social justice and harmony. The post-war settlement between social classes (Middlemas, 1971) was reflected by the state's commitment to a society in which class divisions would become obscured by rising prosperity; social problems imagery concerned itself with explanations of why certain minorities failed to be fully integrated into the society (Young, 1973). During the late 1960s and the 1970s, however, liberalism was eroded by a more disciplinary politics, which displayed itself in a more straightforward notion of the need for firm policing of these social groups who were outside of or who contested the disciplines of the labour market in a 'free' market economy, and which advocated economic policies which caused the numbers and sizes of such groups to swell. Hall and his collaborators have discussed the emergence of a moral panic over 'mugging' in the 1970s, and have shown the relation of this panic to the broader politics of the times (Hall et al., 1978). Not only did the media–orchestrated panic over young blacks (increasingly expelled from the labour market) and the call for a 'firm' response to them legitimate the development of new and heavier policing procedures, it also legitimated the emergence of a 'soft law and order society' (Hall, 1980a) – a society whose economic and political crisis was to be solved by massive personal and collective sacrifices of all the social classes (with the exception of financial capital). This was part of a general move to the right in British (and subsequently, other countries) politics: the state attempted to solve the crisis by a combination of the discipline of the 'free' market for those involved in it, and the discipline of police for those outside of or unresponsive to the market (Taylor, 1980). Moral panics about social groups or situations which would be represented as 'naturally' violent played an important part in legitimating such a political solution: as Hall et al show, black people form a group which, thanks to imagery derived from Britain's imperial history, can quite easily be represented as uncivilised, dangerous and violent. This is also the context in which youthful drinking became 'recognised' as a social problem closely related to indisicipline.

The question then arises, can a materialist analysis be brought to bear on this problem? It would be easy, within an appreciation of a general shift towards a disciplinary politics, to ascribe the growing concern over youthful drinking to worries that children might be more likely to become undisiciplined, when intoxicated, than when sober. Such an easy conclusion, however appealing in its simplicity, overlooks two major problems which form the main foci for this study.

The first problem, which occupies the first three chapters of the study, concerns the *specificity* of the moral panic over youthful drinking. The fact that a certain moral panic arises in a particular political context does not mean that it can be reduced to an effect of context. Cohen suggests that 'the diffuse normative concern about delinquency is, I think, more diffuse and less political than is suggested. And the assumption of a monolothic drift to repression leaves little room for our understanding why some objects are repressed more severely than others. This, paradoxically, is the same criticism which applied to labelling theory' (Cohen, 1980; xxv). This critical remark of Cohen's requires some reformulation and extension. It is not only the case that 'some objects are repressed more severely than others' (black young people more than the majority of whites, for instance), but also that different social objects attract qualitatively different forms of social reaction. The moral panic about teenage drinking, for example, plays not only upon fears of violence and indiscipline, but also upon themes of moral scandal ('tipsy teenagers'), and of childsaving and disease ('the battle to save Britain's boozing kids'). The moral panic over youthful drinking is indeed a bricolage of such themes, in contrast to that over mugging, which is organised around the one core theme provided by racism. Furthermore, the panic over youthful drinking specifies not one particular stratum of youth, but all and any youth indulging in this particular social activity, and activity generally regarded as legitimate in adult life. Youthful drinking is problematised in much the same manner as is youthful sexuality: neither activity is wrong *per se*, but both are covered by situational norms defining acceptable times, places and participants. Youthful indulgence is proscribed in both cases, albeit with some softening of the proscription in specific circumstances (drinking within the family on special occasions; a degree of intimacy between members of the opposite sex who are 'serious' about each other). In both cases, privacy and the company of carefully selected others are pre-requisites of acceptability: collective and public indulgence is wholly unacceptable, an occasion for outrage and dismay. So although moral panics about youthful drinking seem reliant upon mobilisation of a disciplinary politics for their full development and expression, such panics *also* seem to tap a complex structure of social anxieties, about use of the body in public, that predate such mobilisation. This leads us away from detailed accounts of the *contemporary* crisis of capitalist society, and towards an *historical* investigation of the emergence of drink-related problems, which occupies the first three chapters of this study.

The Historical Question: Origins of 'alcohol problem' conceptions and policies

The main problem with the existing literature bearing on the question of the historical origins of the 'alcohol problem' is its tendency to analyse the issues as if they were purely moral, *or* political, *or* economic. Temperance accounts have, for example, been dominated by a focus upon the moral qualities of leading reformers, upon the details of their campaigns, and upon the magnitude of the evils they fought (Harrison, 1971; 406-9). The primary value of these writers lies in the clear accounts they give of their concerns in relation to working class people (e.g. Williams & Brake, 1980). The work of Harrison himself comes nearer to an overall political analysis of the vicissitudes of nineteenth century alcohol politics, his illumination of the complexity of relations between political parties, alcohol industry and temperance movements being especially useful in helping us to avoid any over-generalization about political alliances and pressure groups (Harrison, 1971). He does not, however, set events well in their economic context. Some quantitative economic studies of the alcohol industry have been conducted, sometimes with the co-operation of the industry (Hawkins & Pass, 1979), and these are useful for an understanding of the commercial problems facing the trade at particular times. More adequate from the point of view of understanding the relation of the industry to the social and economic structure of England as this developed over the years is the historical scholarship of Mathias, who relates the capitalisation of the industry to the family structures of its owners and to technical developments that facilitated mass manufacture (Mathias, 1959, 1979). But all of these remain rather partial analyses. Whilst Mathias' analysis integrates economic, political and family considerations, its scope is restricted to the development of capitalist forms of production within the alcohol industry, and has little to say about the broader conflicts in which the industry became embroiled. And whilst Harrison's work relates alcohol politics to the shifting play of political relations between classes, and between parties, he tends to abstract this politidcal analysis from the development of the whole economy. What is lacking is integrative work that locates these partial perspectives within a general discussion of class relations, the development of the economy, and the state's social and economic policies.

A secondary problem with the existing literature is its restricted historical scope. The literature focusses narowly upon the nineteenth and twentieth centuries. Yet, as reference to the records of English legislation shows, alcohol-related legislation was amongst the earliest to be passed by parliament: eighteenth, nineteenth and twentieth century legislation bearing upon alcohol is by no means a simple recapitulation of earlier legislation, but neither did the latter periods start with a 'blank slate' regarding conceptions and control policies.[11] This points to the need to take a longer-term historical view than is usually attempted in the alcohol problems literature.

The adoption of a historical perspective on the development of contemporary social problems is finding increasing favour in sociology, and has generated considerable debate around methodological issues. One approach, hinted at by the authors of 'Policing the Crisis', ties the development of social problems imagery in very closely to the development of colonial expansion and capitalist development.

> Race, for the black labour force, is a critical structure of the social order of contemporary capitalism.
>
> History plays a significant part in this story. The period of commercial colonial exploitation, followed by the period of military and economic imperialism, served an important function in securing Britain's past and present economic position. It also imprinted the inscription of racial supremacy across the surface of English social life, within and outside the sphere of production and the expropriation of the surplus. The debate as to whether the British working class as a whole, or, if not, then at least an 'aristocracy of labour', benefited economically out of 'high imperialism' continues. It is certainly the case the colonialism, as well as establishing internal relations of opposition and competition within the British working class (for example, between workers in the cotton industry as against other sectors), also set in motion relations of opposition between the British metropolitan working class as a whole and the colonial work-forces. Further, the imperial period provided the dominant classes with one of the most effective and penetrating ideologial weapons with which, in the divisive period of class conflict leading up tthe First World War, they sought to extend their hegemony over an increasingly strong, united and confident proletariat, especially through the ideologies of popular imperialism and race superiority. During the decline of the Empire and the rise of post-war national independence movements, these 'colonial relations' were internalised through the importation of immigrant labour.

> The differentiated structure of class interests between the British and the colonial working classes was then, in a complex manner, reproduced within the domestic economy by the use of imported immigrant labour, under conditions of full employment, often to fill jobs which the indigenous work force would no longer do. Capitalism has continued to reproduce labour in this internally divided form to this day. (Hall et al, 1978; 345-6)

One danger of historial analysis is the tendency to a deterministic, functionalist approach:

> First, it is assumed that *conditions are continuously met* and that the 'system' reproduces itself in the same old forms. 'Conditions', in other words, cease to be conditional: they become functional *necessities.* The sense that their relization depends on the outcome of struggles, which include but are not limited to forms of willed and conscious politics, may be altogether lost. Second, , there is too swift a move from simple description, theory, or abstraction to the full account of complex, concrete historical events and determinations. The relations described in a logical, simplified and schematic way are held to work, *just like that* in the historical sequences, uncomplicated by *further* relations and determinations, many not yet grasped theoretically. Theory is realized in history without additions to and transformations of the categories. This tendency, which we would call in a general way 'functionalist', involves a drastic simplification of history. It also tends to make historical social relations more or less self-reproducing, eternal and immune to collective human control. According to Marxist accounts, the system which is reproduced is fundamentally unfair and contradictory – whereas in structural-functionalist sociolgoy or pluaralist political science, the system is basically liberal, progressive and easily reformed. But as critics have pointed out, particular forms of functionalism are indeed common to both traditions, or to tendencies within them. (C.C.C.S., 1981; 20)

One of the main impetused for questioning functionalist approaches in sociology has been provided by historians who have insisted that the making of history is a process contingent, at every step, upon the consciousness of class actors, and upon the struggle between them (Thompson, 1980). One problem with this 'history from below' is that its vidid descriptions of working class insurgency tend to be obtained at the expense of understanding the backcloth of economic development, which is an integral part of the development of social relations between classes (Johnson, 1979, Merrit, 1980). The problem of how to combine, within one analysis, an appreciation of the relation between social consciousness and material conditions continues to constitute the central analytic problem within the social sciences (Hall, 1980b), and has given rise to a variety of solutions, resting upon psychoanalysis, political economy, and the structuralism of Foucault (ibid, pp. 70-71). None of these appear to have been brought to bear upon the historical development of discourses and legislation on alcohol, though a rather deterministic political economy has been brought to bear upon contemporary alcohol policy.[12] The approach taken within chapters 1 and 2 of the present study makes no claims to overcome fundamental problems of historical analysis, but it does attempt to be methodologically coherent and to avoid the worst excesses of functionalism and reductionism. The general point of departure is close to that described by the authors of 'Unpopular Education':

> One corrective to all this is to write and think more 'historically'. By historically, we do not merely mean in a way that is concerned with the past, though this longer historical reach is important. We refer to two main features of the best historical work; first, a concern with close and detailed description and analysis, firmly set in its time and place and, second, a preoccupation with continuity and especially with change, with crisis and with transformations . . .(C.C.C.S., 1981; 20)

The position taken in the present study is that the state's general social and economic policies can be analysed as an aspect of transformations in the relations between social classes, these transformations being brought about by classes' responses to the crises produced by the maturation of the contradictions latent in previous transformations (c.f. Wright, 1978). The development of alcohol-related policies is an integral part of the development of broader social and economic policies, and so subject to analysis the same manner. The historical span of the development of these policies covers several centuries, and this obliges us to pay rather more attention to the economic aspects of these crises and transformations than would be required in a study covering a shorter period (during which economic structures might not change fundamentally). This highlights the question of how to relate the social consciousness, concerns and policy objectives of dominant social classes to the major economic and structural circumstances confronting those classes. In chapters 1 and 2 of this study, this question is answered by way of an examination of the development of the economic and political philosophies of successively ascendant social classes: landowing, merchantalist, laissez-faire capitalist, etc. These philosophies may be regarded as formal statements of the classes' various conceptions of the problems confronting them – in relation to labour, land, trade, etc – and of their proposed solutions:

> As with other forms of ideology, the evolution of economic ideas depends directly upon the evolution of economic forms and the class struggle . . . Often they arise directly out of the stir and strife of social conflicts, upon the battleground between different social classes. In these cases, economists have acted as arms-bearers for these classes, forging the ideological weapons needed to defend the interests of particular social groups – often not concerning themselves any longer with developing their own work and giving it greater theorectical foundation. This was the lot that befell the economists of the merchantalist school, who devoted countless topical pamphelts to the ardent defence of the interests of merchant capital. Yet even if we look at the physiocrats and the economists of the classical school, whose works conform far more to the demands of theorectical clarity and logical coherence, we have little difficulty identifying the social and class forces behind the different currents of economic thought. (Rubin, 1979; 9)

In some cases, political economists have referred directly to alcohol-related problems in the midst of or as an example of their general arguments about production, trade and consumption. (An example of this is given by William Petty, when he argues that the glutony and drinking of labourers proves that wages are too high – see chapter 1). In these cases, the relation between the general social and economic preoccupations of the dominant classes, and their concerns about the production and consumption of drink, is directly spelt out for us. In other cases, this relation has to be deduced from an analysis of economic developments, economic and political philosophies and concomitant alcohol-related legislation.

These considerations led to the following procedures for carrying out the work described in the first part of this study. First, following an initial survey of alcohol-related legislation since the fourteenth century, rough notes on these statutes were compiled. Second, these notes were arranged according to historical periods corresponding to general economic developments (such as the break up of the local feudal economy, the rise of merchant capital, the rise of industrial capitalism, etc).[13] Third, the central concerns of alcohol-related legislation in each period were interpreted within the context of the ascendant economic and political philosophies. Lastly, the resulting picture of development of alcohol-related problems and legislation was elaborated in the light of the existing alcohol-problem literature. Chapter 1 offers an overview of the development of legislation from the fourteenth to the nineteenth centuries, showing how working class youth became a special object of concern. Chapter 2 goes into rather more detail about the development of the alcohol industry as an integral part of capitalist development, and about the development of temperance politics, and shows that these were by no means totally opposed interests. Chapter 3 brings the analysis almost up to date, situating disciplinary alcohol-related controls within the context of the relatively consensual politics of the early post-Second World War period. Alcohol education is described as the depository of historically generated ideas about drink-related problems, reworked within frameworks generated by health and educational institutions in the post-war period. This chapter also contains some empirical data which calls into question the efficacy of such education in changing alcohol-related behaviour.

Contemporary Youth Culture Research: Some Lacunae in the Literature

Part II of the study makes a contrast with part I. Where part I examines the historical processes that have given rise to the state's conceptions of drinking problems as a specific form of disciplinary problem amongst the working class generally, and working class youth specifically, part II examines the actual form of drinking practices amongst strata of working class youth today. These chapters focus upon an area case study of the general circumstances, culture and drinking practices of a group of school-leavers in inner London at the close of the 1970s.

Chapter 4 shows that existing social research into youthful drinking practices may be divided into the two broad categories: (a) the mainstream of social-psychological and sociological research that aims to attribute such behaviour to the moral beliefs of individuals, to 'peer pressure', and to the general structure of beliefs in society (loosely following Drukheim); (b) sociological work on lower working class male youth cultures that portrays youthful drinking as one element in a general pattern of masculine exploit, definace, or delinquency (loosely following Marx). Whereas the first type of research generally fails to relate moral beliefs, social practices and the cultures that support them to social class and to broader material circumstances, the second approach is marred by its inadequate treatment of sexual divisions in society, and by its neglect of youth other than lower working class males.

The absence of materialist research into the drinking practices of 'ordinary' (non-delinquent) boys and girls within the central and upper strata of the working class is a reflection of the more general weaknesses of materialist research into the youth cultures constructed by these social groups. These weaknesses can be seen to stem from a romantic attachment on the part of 'radical' researchers to the possibility of proletarian resistance, and an underestimation of the importance of sexual divisions. These two problems lead, if unchecked, to research that ignores the cultures and social practices of youth other than those exhibiting signs of social indiscipline; that appears to confirm that youthful drinking can (as suggested by the moral panic) be understood as a form of indiscipline; and that underestimates the ways in which social class and sexual divisions interact to provide the material preconditions for a wide range of working class youth cultures and drinking practices.

The problem of over-attachment to the possibility of proletarian resistance derives, in part, from the enthusiasm engendered by recent advances in the materialist study of history. The history of drink-related legislation offered in chapters 1-3 of the present study is very much a history 'from above', that is to say, a description of some problems facing dominant and ascendant classes and of the role played by the state in attempts to solve these. During the 1950s and 1960s, however, English historicans began to construct a 'history from below', concerned with the conditions, consciousness and struggles of the lower classes: Edward Thompson is the doyen of this school, his *Making of the English Working Class* (1980) being a major landmark in historical and social studies. This work has however been taken up somewhat inappropriately by some sociologists of youth culture who, assuming continuities in the conditions and consciousness of the working class, have tended to project onto present-day youth vestigial aspects of the politial struggles of their forebarears. Recent sociological work has, for esxample, described 'Paki-bashing' as somewhow related to nineteenth century machine-breaking, and football hooliganism as a recreation of the historical working class community.[14] The assumption of such historical continuities is, however, extremely hazardous, as Cohen and others have pointed out:

> Where we are really being directed is towards the 'profound line of historical continuity' between today's delinquents and their 'equivalents' in the past. And to find this line, we have to ask questions like 'How would "our" hooligans appear if they were afforded the same possibilities of rationality and intelligibility say as those of Edward Thompson?'
>
> To afford them these possibilities, what these theorists have to do is subscribe to what Ditton nicely calls the dinosaur theory of history. A recent zoological argument apparently proposes that dinosaurs did not after all die out: one group still lives on, known as – birds! Similarly, historical evidence is cited to prove that mass proletarian resistance to the imposition of bourgeois control did not after all die out. It lives on in certain forms of delinquency which – though more symbolic and individualistic than their progenitors – must still be read as rudimentary forms of political action, as versions of the same working class struggle which has occurred since the defeat of Chartism. What is going on in the streets and terraces is not only not what it appears to be, but moreover is really the same as what went on before. (Cohen, 1980; viii)

Not all youth culture research displays these features, but nearly all does share the focus upon delinquent and semi-delinquent males in the lowest strata of the working class. Researchers have primarily been concerned to construct an anthropological account of the everyday life of these boys, and to establish the nature of the process whereby most 'naughty' teenagers become quite conformist adults, parents and workers. These processes have been variously ascribed to the actions of social control agencies (Parker, 1973) and to features inherent in the working class culture (Willis, 1978) but, regardless of differences in the form of explanation, the focus upon delinquency and indiscipline has remained constant. This has severely curtailed the potential contribution of sociologists of youth culture to a *general* understanding of youth cultures.

To say that girls are not adequately researched by the sociology of youth culture is not to say that girls do not figure in the narrative of such studies: they do, but only as an object within male discourse, and not in their own right. It is now quite widely acknowledged within sociology that, whilst girls might be described as 'marginal' or as part of the scenery from the point of view of male youth cultures and investigators thereof, both this appearance of marginality and the conditions that produce it need to be explained. Sociologists of youth culture have, however, exhibited a tendency to shift out of a materialist analysis and into a Durkheimian perspective (focusing upon beliefs, ideology) when faced with the problem of sexual divisions:

> Women do not inhabit a separated and invisible part of the social formation, but are engaged in exactly the same institutional structures as men, but in different relations. It is the dominant *ideological* division between Home and Work which structures the invisibility of women, and not their real absence from the world of work. Their identification solely with the privatised world of the family has masked, firstly, the historical . . . removal of work from the home, and secondly, the continuing presence of working women. (It also masks the men's presence in the home). Men and women do not inhabit two empirically separated worlds, but pass through the same institutions in different relations and on different trajectories. (Powell and Clarke, 1975; 226, emphasis added)

In this early account, the emphasis is upon ideological divisions between the labour market and the home, and within each of these spheres. In drawing attention to the withdrawal of waged work from the home and in counterposing the home to 'the world of work' and to 'working women', the authors come close to describing the home as a sphere devoid of labour. This tendency continues in a different form in the work of Paul Willis, in which sexual divisions are conceptualised in terms of men's perception of housework as being other than 'real work', since it reproduces the conditions of domestic recouperation, rather than converting labour into permanent objects.[15] Such accounts may serve as descriptions of the content of masculinist ideology, but cannot be accepted as explanations of the dominance of that ideology.

The conceptualisation of sexual divisions attempted in this study begins by acknowledging that there is no good scientific reason for supposing that houswork is any less a form of labour for being unpaid, privatised, and denigrated. The work of the materialist feminist Christine Delphy (1980), in which the appropriation of married women's labour in housework occupies a central explanatory position, is taken up and used as a basis for understanding sexual divisions. This results in a perspective similar to that advanced by Lyn Perry in an important article on women's use of legal and illegal drugs:

> The position of most women in characterised by economic dependence. State restriction of abortion and childcare facilities, coupled with the traditional responsibility of women for upaid domestic work and childrearing in the home, places them at an inherent disadvantage in the job market, a disadvantage aggravated by recent cutbacks in the public service industries. Tax and social security systems based on family units rather than individuals reinforce this, and social systems divide 'personal' and 'work' life into separate spheres with women's 'proper place' still seen as in the former. This is the socioeconomic context within which women use drugs and through which the images of their drug use are returned to them and broadcast to society as a whole. (Perry, 1979; 1)

Such is the general structural position of adult women as a group in contemporary capitalist society. From this perspective, childhood and adolescence may be seen as a period of socialisation for and transition into the role of socioeconomic dependency, and girls' cultures and drinking practices seen in such a context. Sexual divisions are not, however, so cut and dried as this in practice. The development of the economy (in particular, the development of a large service sector), the experience of women's factory work in two world wars, and the historical struggle for women's rights has produced a situation in which some women are, for part of their lives, relatively free and independent economically – albeit within an ideological atmosphere conditioned by the continuing dependence of the majority of women – and this makes it questionable that the cultures and practices of all women and girls can be understood as instances of socio-economic dependence.

The second major omission from the sociology of youth culture, equalling that of girls, is that of upper and middle strata of the working class.[16] This study attempts to fill out this double lacuna – girls, upper and middle strata of the class – by focussing upon the circumstances, culture and drinking practices of a mixed group of boys and girls in the middle sections of the working class.

The Case Study

In this study, drinking practices are conceptualised not as the result of individual or collective belief systems, but as social practices that make sense within the context of the cultures that boys and girls collectively construct in response to their experience of social class and sexual divisions in society. Making selective use of youth culture research, and building upon recent advances in materialist feminism, chapter 4 develops a theoretical framework and outlines some basic principles for conducting an 'area case study' of the prospects, culture and leisure (including drinking styles) of specific groups of young people. These principles are taken up and applied, in chapter 5, in a study of one particular borough (called 'Servicetown' because of the relative importance of the service sector in the local economy), of the labour market facing young people therein, of the schools which discharge them into that market, and of one particular group of young people making that transition.

The group upon which I focussed was made up of boys and girls who were white, and who had recently obtained employment in the service sector, or who expected to do so after leaving school. Both in terms of their background (white, living in a variety of housing other than reputedly 'bad' housing estates), and in terms of their occupational status (or immediate prospects), they may broadly be described as belonging to middle strata of thee working class.[16] They are quite distinct, both in background and in social attitudes, from the 'naughty' or delinquent all-male groups so beloved of the post-war sociology of youth culture. In my ethnography, I describe them as sharing a culture, related to their present or anticipated occupations, which I call 'service sector youth culture'. This culture builds, upon the themes – independence, sociability, and a temporary sex-equality – that characterise the social relations of employment in the service sector. Relations between the sexes, and the ways in which these relations structure drinking occasions, constitute a major concern of chapter 5. The result is a description of mixed-sex round-buying, and an analysis of its meaning to participants, that differs substantially from those accounts that characterise 'teenage drinking' as a form of delinquency or social pathology. Rather, the typical drinking occcasion within this youth culture is analysed as an integral part of that culture – as a form of celebration of the social relations of the relatively privileged sector of the economy into which these boys and girls are making a transition. The case study concludes by drawing distinctions between the drinking styles adopted by this, and by other strata of youth, and by suggesting the limits within which it may be reasonable to generalise the main findings.

The Relationship between Parts I and II

It is useful, before mentioning the final sections of the study, to note some correspondences between parts I and II. At first sight, part I, focussing upon the historical development of alcohol-related policies, may seem to share little other than a common interest in alcohol with part II, which focusses upon contemporary drinking practices in particular strata of youth. But beneath this dichotomisation of the substance of study (history and policy on the one side, present-day working class drinking practices on the other), there is a close correspondence between the methodological principles underlying the two parts. In both cases, the point of departure is structural and economic conditions and the positioning of social classes in relation to these conditions. In part I we are concerned with the historical development of the economy and of class structure and with the ascendance of particular social classes; whilst in part II we are concerned with contemporary economic conditions and class structure in a limited geographical area, and with the position of strata of working class youth in relation to other strata. The next step, in both cases, is to identify the main concerns of social classes in relation to the material problems facing them; for the historically dominant social classes, these problems have often focussed upon the indisicipline of the lower, labouring classes; whilst for modern service sector youth, their present or future position in the labour market is of great concern. Finally, the consequences of such concerns for policies and practices relating to alcohol are discussed.

The third and final part of the study assesses some implications of the previous two parts. Chapter 6 draws upon the theoretical position developed in this study and applied in the area case study; presents a model outlining the relations between labour market, family, schools and youthful drinking practices; and suggests the outlines of an approach to health and social education that is sensitive to those relations. It would take a separate study of health education practice to develop these general principles into detailed curricula and teaching materials, but the emphasis upon the need for sensitivity to material conditions and collectively-constructed practices is, it is suggested, an advance upon currently dominant, individualistic approaches to health education.

The conclusion summarises the main aspects of the study – both in relation to the historical development of alcohol-related policies bearing upon the production and consumption of alcohol, and in relation to the case study of contemporary drinking practices – and offers some speculative suggestions about the prospects for alcohol-related policy and health education. A comparison of the substantive findings of parts I and II of the study suggests that there is a discontinuity between the conception of youthful drinking practices underlying alcohol-related policy and health education, and the actual form of those practices in at least some major strata of working class youth. Whereas the history of economic and political conflicts between social classes has given rise to state policies premised upon anxieties about the possibility that public and collective drinking (e.g. the round) amongst the working class may be an opportunity for disruption of or failure to take on economic and political disciplines, contemporary drinking practices amongst one important sector of working class youth are premised upon a close engagement with the disciplines of the labour market. Other strata of youth doubtless differ from service sector youth in their drinking practices, as in other practices, and this is a matter for investigation. Alcohol policy and health education should, it is suggested, take as their point of departure not the historical legacy of class struggles, but the material positions and forms of consciousness of contemporary working class men, women and children.

PART 1

HISTORICAL BACKGROUND TO ALCOHOL-RELATED POLICIES

1 DRINK AND DISCIPLINE: A SOCIAL CLASS HISTORY OF CONTROL OF PUBLIC DRINKING

This chapter is concerned with the historical development of the state's discourse on drinking, within which public drinking (and especially youthful public drinking) is closely identified with fears of breakdown in political stability and in the moral conduct necessary for work-discipline. Two main methods are employed. First, and on a purely descriptive level, it is shown that the emergence of restrictive alcohol-related legislation cannot be attributed to the evolution of the state's earliest concerns with alcohol *per se*, since those concerns were orientated towards the encouragement of a cheap and plentiful supply of alcohol beverages and other 'victuals'. Second, an analysis is made of early vagrancy legislation, within which restrictive regulation of public drinking places was first attempted, and of subsequent, legislation designed to suppress customary drinking and other social 'leisure' traditions in favour of enhancing work-discipline. The method of analysis is to relate the content of specific statutes to the material interests of dominant and ascendent social classes, within the general framework of changing demographic, social and economic conditions in English society.[1]

Early Encouragement of Trade in Alcohol

The earliest English legislation related to alcohol drink was concerned with the encouragement of a market in drinking through the restriction of prices. Acts of Edward III sought to ensure that 'greater Plenty may come, and greater Market may be of wines within the Realm' and 'Ships shall be freighted to bring wines to England above all other'.[2] A 1381 Act of Richard II set out the measures to be used for the sale of wine, and the 'several prices of several sorts of wines to be sold in Gross or by Retail'.[3] Acts with a similar purpose can be found up until the seventeenth century, but changing circumstances required some changes in the administration of the policy. In 1511, for example, an Act was passed to ensure that the prices of victuals, including wine and beer, were set locally by persons other than those who sell these goods.[4] A 1531

Act declared that Brewers, together with Bakers, Surgeons and Scriveners (writers) were not to be considered practitioners of Handicrafts subject to Guild control, thereby encouraging open competition in the brewing industry.[5] In the same year an Act was passed preventing the giving of short measure:

> Whereas the Ale-brewers and Beer-brewers of this Realm of England have used, and do use, for their own singular Lucre, Profit and gain, to make in their own House their Barrels, Kilderkins, and Firkins, of much less Quantity, Content, Rate and Assize than they ought to be, to the great Hurt, Predudice and Damage of the Kings liege People . . . all such Barrels . . . shall henceforth be made and marked accordingly as hereafter be expressed, by the Common Articles of Coopers exercised and practiced in the said occupation.[6]

The Act also provided that 'Brewers shall sell their Beer at such Prices per Barrel as shall be settled by Justices' – so it is unlikely that its sole purpose was to favour the Coopers. Also in 1531 an Act 'For the Maintenance of the Navy' declared that wines were henceforth to be imported only in English ships; this Act also set maximum prices for the retail sale of different types of wines.[7] The restriction of importation to English ships, however, had the effect of forcing up prices – 'whereas (the previous Act) was supposed to be made for the maintenance of the Navy of this Realm, and also to be Intent, and upon good Hope and Trust, to have had the same Wines and Woad at more easy Prices than before they had been, the Experience whereof have been to the contrary' – and the Act was repealed, allowing foreign competition in shipping-in wines.[8] In 1549 'An Act for the true making of malt' forbade the sale of poor quality malt from which 'no wholsom Drink for Man's Body can by any means be thereof made, which is not only to the Great Peril and Danger of the Nobility and other of the Kings Highness' Subjects within this Realm, but also to the utter Impoverishment of the Brewers'.[9] Now, whilst not all of these Acts may have been primarily designed to minimise the price and to increase the availability of alcoholic beverages, it is clear from the wording of the Acts that such consequences were by no means avoided by the State. The general policy of minimising prices continued into the period of the Revolution, with the passage of a 1657 Act 'for settling the prices of wines'. Such policies were by no means peculiar to the state's regulation of alcohol, but were part of its more general concern to regulate the prices of 'victuals': in 1533, for example, an Act of Henry VIII proclaimed that cheese, butter, capers, hens, chickens and other necessary victuals' must be sold at 'reasonable' prices.[10] This concern to reduce the rate of increase in the prices of victuals was, in turn, part of the state's overall attempt to restrain price- and wage-inflation, and to prevent cheapening of the coinage.[11]

Early alcohol-related legislation was, then, restrictive neither of the level of the circumstances of drinking. This is, indeed, a discontinuity between the earliest legislation, facilitating the supply of alcoholic beverages, and the emergence of legislation restrictive of drinking and drinkers – the latter having quite distinct historical roots, as demonstrated in the following paragraphs.

The Vagrancy Statutes

William Chambliss has analysed the development of the laws of vagrancy, in which he shows that these laws underwent a 'shift in focal concern' corresponding to dominant social classes' changing problems in managing the lower classes. His thesis is that, during the thirteenth, fourteenth and fifteenth centuries, the vagrancy laws were primarily concerned with the problem of minimising labour mobility and wage levels, whilst from the turn of the sixteenth century onwards, the statutes became more broadly concerned with the maintenance of public order. This analysis is of particular interest to us because the period of 'shift in focal concerns' identified by Chambliss is also the period in which mention of alcohol enters the vagrancy legislation.[12]

Chambliss' point of departure is the need to analyse 'the relationship between particular laws and the social setting in which these laws emerge, are interpreted, and take form' (Chambliss, 1971; 206). It is therefore useful to summarise the social and economic conditions in which the first vagrancy laws emerged:

> The economy of the later middle ages (the 12th to 15th centuries) can be characterised as a town of regional economy. Each town, together with its surrounding agricultural district, comprised a single economic region, within whose confines all exchange between town and countryside took place. A substantial portion of what the peasants produced went for their own consumption. A

> further part was given over as quickrent to the feudal lord, and what meagre surpluses were left were taken to the neighboring town for sale on market days. Any money received went to purchase goods fashioned by urban craftsmen (textiles, metal-wares, etc). The lord received a quickrent – established by custom – from the peasant serfs who lived on his estates. Over and above this, he also received the produce from his manor's own tillage, which was worked by these same peasants doing compulsory labour service (the barshchina or corvee). A large part of these products were for the lord's own consumption, or for that of his innumerable household servants and retainers. Anything left over was sold in the town, so that the receipts could be used to buy either articles made by local craftsmen or luxuries brought in by traders from far away countries, primarily from the East. What therefore distinguished rural feudal economy was its overwhelmingly natural character and the feeble development of money exchange. (Rubin, 1979; 19)

It was within this setting that 'vagrancy' became a problem for the state. As Chambliss points out, the waging of wars, including the crusades, obliged the landowners to sell some serfs their freedom, and others had run away to seek waged work in the relatively congenial setting of the larger towns, which were slowly becoming more industrialised. These changes made the working of the manorial system more dependent on use of waged labour. Then, in 1348, the Black Death reached England, killing over half of the population, and causing a severe labour shortage.

> The immediate result of these events was of course no surprise: wages for the 'Free' man rose considerably and this increased, on the one hand, the landowners' problems and, on the other hand, the plight of the unfree tenants. For although wages increased for the personally free laborers, it of course did not necessarily add to the standard of living of the serf, if anything it made his position worse because the landowner would be hard pressed to pay for the personally free labor which he needed and would thus find it more and more difficult to maintain the standard of living for the serf which he had heretofore supplied. Thus the serf had no alternative but flight if he chose to better his position. Furthermore, flight generally meant both freedom and better conditions since the possibility of work in the new

> weaving industry was great and the chance of being caught small.
>
> It was under these conditions that we find the first vagrancy statutes emerging. (Chambliss, 1971; 209)

The first vagrancy statute, passed in 1349, the year following the Black Death, observed that a

> great part of the people, and especially of workmen and servants, late died in pestilence; many seeing the necessity (i.e. predicament – N.D.) of masters, and great scarcity of servants, will not serve without excessive wages, and some rather willing to beg in idleness than by labour to get their living.[13]

The statute made it an offence to refuse any offer of employment; laid down a standard wage; and made it an offence to give alms to those fit for work (Chambliss, 1971; 207-8). In the following year the Statute of Labourers adopted a rather stronger tone, referring to

> the Malice of Servants, which were idle, and not willing to serve after the Pestilence, without taking excessive wages . . . (and) do withdraw themselves from serving the great men or other, unless they have Liveries and wages to the double or treble of what they were wont to take . . . to the great Damage of the great Men.[14]

This statute set out a scale of maximum wages for workers in a number of common occupations – including haymaking, mowing, reaping, threshing, tiling, plastering, carrying, tailoring, etc – and stated that all labour should be hired in a public place, where the terms of hire would be publicly observable. In 1351 a further statute was passed seeking to prevent labourers from moving to areas where wages might be higher. Chambliss says that 'there is little question but that these statutes were designed for one express purpose: to force labourers (whether free or unfree) to accept employment at a low wage in order to ensure the landowners an adequate supply of labour at a price he could afford to pay' (Chambliss, 1971; 209). An earlier sociologist summarises the origins of the vagrancy statutes in these terms: 'The anti-migratory policy behind vagrancy legislation began as an essential component of the wage stabilisation legislation which accompanied the break-up of feudalism and the depopulation caused by the Black Death' (Foot, 1956;615). As social and economic conditions changed, however, so did the vagrancy statutes.

Labour Surplus, Public Order Legislation and Licensing

'Wage stabilisation' remained the policy concern of the vagrancy legislation for one and a half centuries, although there was a tendency, reflecting a general tendency in English laws during this period, towards increased penalties (Chambliss, 1971; 210-11). But from the turn of the sixteenth century the vagrancy laws express a 'shift in focal concern', widening their focus from wage control, to crime control and to the maintenance of public order (ibid; 211-215). This shift in socal concerns may be understood as resulting from the changing economic and social conditions of the late fifteenth, sixteenth and seventeenth centuries:

> The English landowners of the end of the 15th and the beginning of the 16th centuries often cleared the small-scale peasant tenants off their land, or 'enclosed' the communal land which the peasants had previously used for grazing their cattle, since the areas thus made free could be put to better use raising sheep. As English or Flemish cloth manufacturers increased their demand for wool, so prices shot up and sheep breeding became a more profitable undertaking then cultivating the soil. 'Sheep swallow down the very men themselves', said Thomas More at the beginning of the 16th century. Another of his contemporaries wrote: 'Gentlemen do not consider it a crime to drive poor people of their property. On the contrary, they insist that the land belongs to them and throw the poor out from their shelter, like cows. In England at the moment, thousands of people, previously decent householders, now go begging, staggering from door to door'. (Rubin, 1979; 23)

The population had by this time recovered in numerical strength, following the passing of the Black Death, and this increase in population, together with the landowners shedding of labour, resulted in a reversal of labour market conditions. In contrast to the previous labour shortage – in response to which the early vagrancy and wage control legislation had been enacted – there arose a labour surplus, a corresponding weakening of the bargaining position of the 'free' working class, and a fall in the real value of wages (Rusche & Kirchheimer, 1968; 8-23, Rubin, 1979; 22). Evidently, if economic conditions themselves became more effective in imposing wage restraint upon the working class, then the need for the state to pass legislation on behalf of employers was considerably diminished. Equally, however, the creation of a surplus population of 'thousands of people, previously decent householders . . . begging, staggering from door to door' posed new social control problems for the state, which extended and refashioned the vagrancy statutes to meet this new situation. From the turn of the sixteenth century, the vagrancy statutes concern themselves not only with the punishment of the unemployed, but also with the regulation of the collective conduct of the working class, and with the monitoring and regulation of the public meeting-places in which such conduct may take place.

It is in these circumstances that regulation of the conditions of ale-selling became a concern of the vagrancy legislation. The 1495 Act Against Vagabonds and Beggars reads as follows:

> For moderating the provisions of (previous vagrancy Acts) it is enacted, that Vagabonds, idle and suspected Persons, shall be set in the Stock Three Days and Three Nights, and shall have none other Sustinance but Bread and Water, and shall be put out of the town . . .
>
> No Articier, Labourer or Servant, shall play at any Unlawful Game, but in Christmas. Two Justices of the Peace may reject common Ale-selling in any Place, and take security from Sellers of Ale for their good behaviour.[15]

The reference to 'unlawful games' recurs in subsequent vagrancy statutes, including that of 1530, which prescribed heavier penalties for those 'using divers, subtil and unlawful games and plays' than for those who were merely idle or begging. A 1571 statute refers to 'idle persons going about using subtil, crafty and unlawful games or plays; and some of them feigning themselves to have knowledge of absurd sciences . . . and all fences. bear-wards, common players in interludes, and minstrels, juglers, pedlars, tinkers . . .'. But this Act specifically excluded 'cookers, or harvest folles, that travel for harvest work, corn or hay' (Chambliss, 1971; 214). It seems clear that the Act was concerned to discourage those games, plays and entertainments that might provide a focus for public congregation of the working class, rather than to discourage travel in pursuit of work. This concern is also reflected, in firmer form, in other statutes, against unlawful assemblies and political agitation. An Act passed in 1495 (the year in which the vagrancy statutes first concerned themselves with ale-selling) provided that the leaders of unlawful assemblies should be sent to prison for a 'long time', and added that 'if the Riot be with Forty Persons or thought heinous, then the Justices of the peace shall certify the same, and send up the Record of Conviction to the King and Council, which may punish the Party'.[16] A similar Act passed in 1549 declared it to be high treason for twelve or more people to publicly agitate for any changes in the laws of of the land.[17]

The state was, then, acutely sensitive to the political dangers of public gatherings. Given that ale-houses provided a venue for congregation of the working class, it is unsurprising that the state's increasing concern with social and political control should lead it to attempt to regulate 'common' Alehouses (i.e. those frequented by the common, working class, people). The 1495 Act laid the basis for the first statute specifically and solely concerned with regulation of ale-houses – the 1552 'Act for Keepers of Alehouses to be bound be Recognisance'. This latter Act, conventionally regarded as providing the basis for modern licensing legislation (Williams & Brake, 1980; 1), concerned itself with how 'intolerable Hurts and Troubles to the Commonwealth of this Realm doth daily grow and increase through such Abuses and Disorders as are had and used in Common Ale-houses', and repated the provision of the 1495 Act for Justices to 'put away common selling of Ale and Beer in the said common Ale-houses'.[18]

We can now summarise the significance of the emergence of licensing legislation within the context of the historical development of English vagrancy legislation. The vagrancy statutes were, from their inception, concerned with the control of the poor and labouring classes. From the fourteenth to the fifteenth century, there was a labour shortage, and the vagrancy statutes served the interests of the landowners and other employers, outlawing labour mobility and attempting to force labour to accept low-wage employment. During this period, neither the vagrancy statutes nor any other legislation sought to restrict the level of circumstances of drinking; indeed state policy was much concerned with facilitating trade in, and minimising prices of, alcoholic and other 'victuals'. Not until the end of the fifteenth century, when a growing labour surplus and increasing political agitation provided new problems for the state, did the vagrancy legislation concern itself with suppression of social and recreational gatherings of the working class, and it was in that context that restrictive alcohol-related legislation arose. It is clear that the object of this early restrictive legislation was selective suppression of those gatherings of the poor at which political remedies to their problems were advocated, and that public houses became a focus of control not because they sold alcohol, but because they provided meeting places. In subsequent centuries, however, drinking itself was to become a focus of control.

The Rise of Merchant Capital and the Reconstruction of Leisure

During the seventeenth and eighteenth centuries the traditional regional economy, based upon the combination of rural feudal estates and urban guilds, continued to break up, trade accelerated, and there were considerable changes in the class structure.

> If in the countryside the feudal order was in a process of decomposition, in the towns the growth of merchant capital was causing a simultaneous decline in guild handicrafts. The petty craftsman could preserve his independence only so long as he was producing for the local market with exchange taking place between the town and its immediate environs. But side by side with the growth of international trade there was also the development of trade between the different regions and towns within a given country. Certain towns specialised in the manufacturing of particular items (e.g. textiles or armaments), which they produced in too large a quantity for their sale to be limited to the local surroundings; hence markets further afield had to be sought. This was particularly true of the cloth industry, which had started to flourish in the towns of Italy and Flanders (and later on, in England) even by the end of the middle ages. Even then the master weaver could no longer depend on the immediate consumption of the local market for sales, and so he sold his cloth to middlemen, who transported large consignments to areas where demand existed. The buyer up now occupied an intermediary position between consumer and producer, gradually asserting his domination over the latter. At first he puchased individual batches of commodities from the craftsman as the occasion arose; later he bought up everything the craftsman

> produced. With the passage of time he began to give the craftsman a money advance; and in the end he came to provide the raw materials at his own expense (e.g. thread or wool), farming them out to individual craftsmen (spinners, weavers, etc) who were then paid a remuneration for their labour. From this moment the independent craftsman was turned into a dependent handicraft worker, and the merchant into a buyer up – putter out. In this way the merchant capitalist, moving from the sphere of trade, worked his way into the production process, organised it and gained control over the labour of large numbers of handicraft workers working in their own homes. (Rubin, 1979; 23-24)

Whilst the 'process of separation of direct producers from the means of production' (ibid; 24-25) produced, for the first time, a large working class, it did not, however, guarantee the economic and social discipline of that class, as the work of historians such as Thompson (1980) makes clear. Whilst the merchant capitalist controlled his work-force insofar as he could withdraw the means of production, distribution and exchange, he did not (before the development of the factory system) supervise the actual production process in cottage industry, and hence found it difficult to force increases in the rate of production. Since a high rate of return required not only low wages, but also a high level of production (necessary for a good return on fixed costs), merchant capitalists were keen to increase the intensity and the direction of labour. A longer and more disciplined working week, however, required a dismantling of historically established leisure customs, of which drinking customs were an integral part. It was in these circumstances that the merchantalist literature begins to complain about hitherto accepted drinking customs. In his book *Political Arithmetic*, the economist William Petty said:

> It is observed by Clothiers, and others who employ great numbers of poor people, that where corn is extremely plentiful, the labour of the poor is proportionally dear: And scarce to be had at all (so licentious as they Who labour only to eat, or rather to drink). (Petty, 1963; 274)

The merchantalists advocated two linked remedies – one bearing upon wage levels, the other bearing upon the impediments inherent in existing leisure customs – for increasing the discipline and productivity of the working class. The more clearly 'economic' strategy was to advocate high corn prices. This was of most direct and obvious benefit to the landowners, rather than to the commercial bourgeoisie, but the latter supported the policy vigorously because high food prices reduced the real value of wages, hence obliging employees to work harder (or to starve). The more 'social' strategy took the form of an attack – largely mediated through religious and anti-papist ideology – on historical leisure customs. Since there was, during the seventeenth and eighteenth centuries, 'a close alliance between the state and the commercial bourgeoisie' (Rubin, 1979; 25-26), these sentiments found expression in law during that period; drinking, in common with other traditional leisure customs, became denigrated as undisciplined and immoral. Drink-related legislation, which had during the fifteenth and sixteenth centuries concerned itself with the selective suppression of those specific drinking-houses which became foci for expression of political discontent, broadened its focus to encompass the general regulation of leisure customs. An Act 'to restrain the inordinate Haunting and Tipling in Inns, Ale-houses and other Victuall houses', passed in 1603, forbade inkeepers to allow their premises to be used for the entertainment of non-residents, on the grounds that Inns were 'not meant for Entertainment and Harbouring of lewd and idel people to spend and consume their Money and their Time in Lewd and drunken manner'.[19] This was followed in 1606 by an Act 'for repressing the odious and loathsome Sin of Drunkenness' which blamed drinking for 'the overthrow of many good Arts and manual Trades, the disabling of divers workemen, and the general impoverishment of many good subjects'.[20] This Act made drunkenness an offence for the first time, and was followed in 1635 by a further statute 'for the better repressing of Drunkenness'.[21] A Cromwellian Ordinance of 1644 provided for the 'better observation of the Lords-Day' by outlawing Sunday 'shooting, bowling, Ringing of Bells for Pleasure of Pasttime, Masque, Wake, otherwise called Feasts, Church-Ale, Dancing, Games, Sport or Past-time whatsoever', and ordered that historic focus of revelry, the Maypole, to be taken down.[22] A 1647 Ordinance 'concerning days of Recreation allowed unto scholars, Apprenticies and other Servants' declared it illegal for such classes to remain in inns beyond eight o'clock in the evening.[23] And in 1650 'An Act for the better observation of the Lords-Days, Days of Thanksgiving and Humiliation' banned entry into 'any Tavern, Inn, Alehouse, Tobacco-house or shop or victually house' on such days.[24]

In these statutes, controls on drinking were advanced as part of a more general attempt to reform the recreational life of the working class. Collective activities such as feasts, drinking, dancing, games and sport were offensive to the rising commercial classes because both the time these activities took up, and the collective hedonism they generated, impeded the imposition of new industial disciplines. It is in this context that the drink-related legislation of the previous (fifteenth and sixteenth) centuries, which provided powers for the selective supervision of those specific meeting-places which became foci of political dissent, became joined in the seventeenth century by legislation concerned with the more general regulation of recreational life.

The Pub, Politics and Indiscipline: Unsuitable for Children

Alcohol-related legislation of the eighteenth and nineteenth centuries played variations upon the two historically-constructed themes of containment of political dissent and maintenance of leisure/labour discipline. The famous 'Gin Act' of 1736 paid particular attention to the disciplinary problem:

> Whereas the drinking of Spiritious Liquors or Strong Water is becoming very common, especially amongst the People of lower and inferior Rank, the constant and excessive use thereof tends greatly to the Destruction of their Healths, rendering them unfit for useful labour and Business, debauching their Morals, and inciting them to perpetrate all Manner of Vices . . .

This Act made it illegal to run a disorderly house, and prohibited the sale of spirits in quantities of less than gallons except from premises licensed at a cost of £50 per annum. In 1828 a consolidating licensing Act was passed and this provides the basis for contemporary licensing legislation (Williams & Brake, 1980; 5). The Act reiterated historical concerns with the suppression of political dissent and riot.

> And be it further enacted, That it shall be lawful for any two Justices acting for any Country or Place where any Riot or Tumult shall happen or be expected to take place, to order or direct that every Person licensed under this Act, and keeping any House situated within their respective Jurisdictions in or near the Place . . . shall close his House.

Set within the historical context of earlier statutes concerning vagrancy, political dissent, and social and economic discipline in the working class, eighteenth and nineteenth century alcohol-related legislation can be understood as a continuation of the state's general response to 'the problem of the workers'. The public house retained its historic role as providing a meeting place for the working class and, since any such congregation provided opportunities for expression of political dissatisfactions and for undisciplined and immoral revelry, the public house remained a focus for social control.

Given the character of the public house, it is not surprising to find that soon after the State had deffined children as a special class of people requiring protection from the excesses of adult life, it banned them from participation in pub life. Closely following Acts to limit hours of work of children and young persons in shops, an 1886 'Act for the Protection of Children' made it illegal for children under thirteen to be served alcoholic beverages for consumption on the premises of public houses. That this Act was designed to prevent children participating in pub life, rather than to stop them drinking per se, is shown by the fact that no restriction was placed upon children buying alcohol for consumption off the premises. Children did not, of course, have the financial resources to buy alcohol on their own account but, as Williams and Brake report 'It was common practice for children to be sent as messengers to buy liquor in open jugs and other containers for their parents and others, which led many to take a swig on the way home. Surveys of public houses showed that a high proportion of unaccompanied children engaged in this practice.' (Williams & Brake, 1980; 179). Faced with this situation temperance reformers remained highly active and argued for restrictions on children's drinking *per se* (Williams & Brake, 1980; 177-191). Given the historical association between the public house, with its attendant political and moral hazards, and drinking itself, the identification of drink as a moral hazard to children was difficult to refute in an age much concerned with the protection of children, and further legislation followed. The 1901 Intoxicating Liquor (Sale to Children) Act made it illegal to sell alcohol to children to take away except in sealed containers, and only children over fourteen were henceforth allowed to drink alcohol on the premises. A further Act in 1909 excluded children from the bar-rooms of licensed premises, though still allowing them in any room in which consumption of alcohol was not the chief feature (e.g. the 'jug and bottle' room, or off-license as we would call it today).

These Acts had a considerable effect on children's participation in pub life. By 1938, when Mass-Observation conducted its participant-observation study of pub life in a northern England town ('Worktown'), it was the case that:

> Children do not go into pubs. Selling drinks to persons under 18 is an offence, and so is permitting children within the pub . . . we have observed isolated instances of young people who were probably only 16 or 17 in pubs, but as all the other many thousands of pub-goers whom we have observed and counted have been above 18, we are justified in saying that pub-goers are over 18. (Mass-Observation, 1943; 135-136)

During the nineteenth century, as it progressively excluded children from the public house, the state constructed its educational system for children.[25] 'Temperance education', focussing upon the need for self-discipline of the individual, was an early feature of state education. In 1909 the first centrally-produced *Syllabus of Lessons on Temperance for scholars attending public elementary schools* was published by HMSO.[26] Alcohol was discussed as a food, and the 'evil consequences of intemperance to the individual, to the home and to the state' described. As Williams and Brake remark (pp.182-183):

> What seems to be a striking feature of the syllabus was the use made of the word 'temperance'. At that time it was manifestly an acceptable term, whereas later it seemed to lose its credibility. Certainly the Board of Education understood the classic meaning of the word and intended its meaning to be conveyed to children. The concluding sentence of the introduction still has relevance to those who wish to inculcate the 'temperance' sentiment – 'Instruction on the subject of Temperance should itself be temperate and should make a sober appeal to such reasoning capacity as the child possesses and to the ideas of decent, self-respecting and dutiful living . . .'

A decade later the syllabus was revised as *The hygiene of food and drink* (Board of Education, 1922). This syllabus was influenced by the publication, by the Central Control Board (Liquor Traffic), of the textbook *Alcohol: its action on the human organism* (Central Control Board, 1918). The Board had been set up by the Defence of the Realm (Amendment) Act of 1915, which extended earlier defence of the Realm Acts and aimed to improve 'national efficiency' by improving social discipline and industrial productivity in areas of manufacture and transport of the necessities of war.[27] Under the Act, the Central Control Board had powers to take over the production and sale of alcohol in those areas. Temperance reformers were at the time concerned that the state was turning itself into a purveyor of alcohol, instead of simply introducing national restrictions on, or prohibition of, its sale (Alliance News, August 1916; 123). A pro-temperance 'Strength of Britain Movement' was launched, which declared its concern in the following terms:

> We are convinced that the dangers confronting us arise from the sudden possession of abundant wages rather than from a lack of patriotic feeling: untrained in spending or in thrift, large numbers of our workers waste their resources on drink. The greatest good a Government can render to its people is to strengthen their right purposes and weaken the power of their temptations, and there lies upon us now the double duty of protecting our people from the temptation to drink away their earnings and of protecting the State from the intolerable folly of high wages turned to the advantage of our enemies. (Alliance News, February 1920; 25)

This movement received wide support from sections of the upper social classes: a meeting in London in 1917 was attended by 250 directors of munition factories, 200 other leaders of finance and industries, 100 admirals and generals, 100 MPs and Privy Councillors, 200 baronets and knights, 500 magistrates, over 400 headmasters and representatives of universities, and 450 doctors (Williams and Brake, 1980;58). The movement did not succeed in its aim of persuading the government to suspend all sales of alcoholic drinks for the duration of the war; but the influence upon health education was pervasive and longlasting. In a war situation in which the demand for labour was high, wages better than previously, and the working class increasingly confident, health education offered a channel for inculcation of habits of discipline and self-restraint. The 1922 Board of Education curriculum expressed its aim thus:

> It is hardly necessary to state that the one idea that should dominate any school teaching in hygiene is the paramout importance of self-discipline . . . The wise teacher will lose no oppor-

> tunity of impressing upon his scholars the vital importance of habits of self-control and it will be his constant aim to afford plain, simple, and satisfying reasons which the child will understand and appreciate. (Board of Education, 1922; 20)

Commenting on this approach, Williams and Brake say (p.184) that 'the contemporary educational concepts of motivation and decision-making had not then been developed, but those who drew up the syllabus were clearly moving towards them'. Board of Education suggestions about health education about alcohol developed over the next few decades, with a *Handbook of Suggestions on Health Education* being produced in 1933, and revised (under various titles) in 1933, 1939, 1956, 1968 and 1977.

The significance, for the purposes of our enquiry, of health education about drinking is the way in which it stands as a clearly crystallised form of 'knowledge' derived from the state's historical concerns about the public house and about working class participation in it. That it was 'hardly necessary' for the Board of Education to say that any such teaching must be dominated by the idea of self-discipline is comprehensible in the light of the state's ongoing concerns with engineering political acquiescence and work-discipline amongst the working class. The discourse of health education echoes that of alcohol-related legislation of previous centuries, and locates discussion of drinking practices within a broader discussion of the danger of breakdown in social and economic discipline.

Conclusion

The exclusion of children from the public house is, as this chapter has shown, a relatively recent phase in a much longer history of state regulation of public meeting places, designed to contain political dissent and to impose patterns of recreation compatible with industrial work-discipline. Legislation permitting the selective suppression of public houses arose at that point in transition, in the vagrancy laws, from a focal concern with wage control to a broader concern with the maintenance of public order and the suppression of political agitation and sedition. Then, during the seventeenth century, the state became concerned with methods of inducing the newly-created working class to take on the work-discipline required for profitable cottage production under merchant capital, and with the reform of social customs, including drinking and feasting customs, that impeded acceptance of these disciplines. Hence, by the eighteenth and nineteenth centuries, the public house and drinking therein were established, in the eyes of the state, as problematic because of the dangers of political agitation and of breakdown in the patterns of moral conduct required for work-discipline. Exclusion of children from the public drinking situation may, therefore, be described as a 'health' measure insofar as children's health is understood to include protection of them from the possibility of gaining a working class political education and from exposure to models of morally/economically undisciplined conduct.

Public drinking amongst working class youth thus becomes identified, by the state, as a symptom of failure of socialisation into the proper disciplines of adult life. That is to say, regardless of the *amount* of public-drinking amongst youth, its *form* is perceived by the state as a failure of social discipline. In periods of social and economic crisis, when particular sacrifices are demanded of the working class and of its youth, the concern with the maintenance of discipline becomes particularly acute, and it is hence at such times that social reaction against public drinking becomes especially strong. Indeed the alcohol-related legislation, reviewed in this chapter, reads like a roll-call of crisis-points in English history. There is, however, a distinction, clearly made by sociologists working in the period following the rise of 'labelling theory', between the social form attributed by social reaction to the practices it seeks to control, and the actual form taken by those practices as they occur within the working class. Whilst it would, presumably, be possible to identify some group or groups of youths who, in specific circumstances, use alcohol in ways which might be regarded as indicative of a specifically political resistance or a more general breakdown in social and economic discipline, it certainly cannot be taken for granted that all or most working class youth use alcohol in such ways.

2 DRINK AND POLITICAL ECONOMY: FROM FREE TRADE TO KEYNESIAN ALCOHOL POLICIES

By the end of the nineteenth century, temperance movements had succeeded in mobilising the ideological resources bequeathed by several centuries of state concern over the disciplining of the working class – concern produced by the transition from a feudal social order, through merchant capitalism, to industrial capitalism. The state's perception of working class drinking practices was, as described in the preceding chapter, mapped onto this general problem of maintaining social control and ensuring the economic and political subordination of that class. On these foundations twentieth century attitudes to working class drinking and health education were laid. Given the increasingly sharp struggle between the classes during the nineteenth century, the continuation of these historical concerns is not surprising. What does require some explanation, however, is the failure of the temperance sentiment to push through legislation bearing not only upon the conditions of consumption of alcohol, but also upon the level of production of this seemingly socially dangerous commodity. This question is of special interest because of current interest in the possibility of reducing 'alcohol problems' by reducing the level of alcohol production/consumption.[1]

In one sense, of course, the failure of the state to prevent increases in the production of alcohol is not a failure at all, since the historical concern has always focussed upon the public conditions and consequences of working class drinking, rather than upon the level of drinking *per se*. Nevertheless, there was a prohibition wing to the temperance movement and, given the (temporary) success of Prohibition in the United States, the question of the relative weakness of prohibition with the English temperance movement requires some explanation.[2] Furthermore, even within the sphere of consumption, temperance forces suffered considerable defeats throughout the nineteenth century – the most obvious (but by no means the most significant) being a loosening of licensing restrictions and considerable decontrol of working class drinking in the early part of the century (discussed below). This may seem paradoxical given that the period was marked by an increased awareness of class conflict. This chapter will address the question – what were the economic, social and political conditions that blunted the application of temperance concerns, leaving them to dominate only those areas, like education, which lay outside the market?

Family and Capital in Brewing

> In 1970 there were 996 Common Brewers in England and Wales, and 48,421 Brewing Victuallers – that is, almost 1,000 people who brewed only for sale to publicans and private customers away from their breweries, and over 48,000 who, like Peter Stubbs of Warrington, brewed mainly for their own Inn, but also for sending out to customers. In London alone, where production had been dominated since the seventeenth century by Common Brewers there were 165 of them, who together produced about one-quarter of the entre national output for sale. The differing roles of the entrepreneur in such an industry have, therefore, to be related to the several diversities contained within this national aggregate of firms. Only then will the common features, as well as the differences, become historically significant. Most entrepreneurs in the eighteenth century were opportunists – even if opportunists with vision to see opportunities not apparent to others equally anxious to get ahead and with determination to organise things in such a way that potential opportunities became actual ones. Effectively controlling the relevant factors of production, for example, could enable them for the first time to gain effective control over the product and so design it for a particular market. (Mathias, 1979; 231-232)

The development of the alcoholic drinks industries is, as Mathias and other economic historians have demonstrated, a complex and integral aspect of the development of capitalist industry in England.[3] As such, it is closely tied up with the development of sexual and social class divisions. Mathias' research pinpoints the importance not only of technical innovations, entrepreneurial ambitions and the development of mass markets, but also of the structure of family ownership and partnerships, and the ways in which family relationships were integrated with economic links between the brewing industry, the producers of agricultural raw materials, and banking (Mathias, 1979; 209-251, and 1959; 231-264). His detailed histories of the development of firms make it clear that it was men who controlled them. This industry, perhaps more than others, afforded males some opportunity of changing their station in life: managers could become partners, and partners could become 'recognised as belonging to the same club as the landed gentry, whose rents he was directly supporting and whose ranks he was rapidly joining' (Mathias, 1979; 248). The other side of this coin was the destruction of small-scale, household production, with particular consequences for women; the expulsion of women from the alcohol production process paralleled their expulsion from other areas of craft and skilled work.

> Although apprenticeships were generally reserved for males there were certain women's trades in which the women were protected against male competition. These were often trades which related directly to the work of women in the household because at this stage industrial and domestic life were not clearly separate. Women thus carried on food, drink and clothing production. Descriptions of these jobs have since become archaic or changed their meaning. 'Brewster' meant a female brewer, and a spinster was not an old maid but a woman who supported herself by spinning. But as the division of labour became more complex, and the workshops became bigger, informal customary arrangements were broken down and competition among the men intensified. Gradually women were forced out of the more profitable trades. Women's work became associated with low pay.
>
> This was not a single, once and for all process, but went on throughout the eighteenth and early nineteenth centuries. However, from the seventeenth century women were on the defensive and for a variety of reasons found themselves at a disadvantage in the new organisation of industry which developed with early capitalism. They resisted changes as they encountered them piecemeal and fought to protect themselves against the consequences of the new class and sexual division of labour which capital brought into existence. Sometimes it was the separation of the workplace from home which reduced women's productivity because it was harder to work and have the children around and work could not so easily be combined with housework. Sometimes it was the introduction of a new and heavier machine which secured the barring of women workers.

> In other cases the superior craft organisation of the men drove the women out. (Rowbottom, 1973; 1-2)

The emergence of capitalist forms of production was, then, closely tied up with changes in family structure. The emergence of the male entrepreneur, relying upon other male members of an extended family structure for financial and political co-operation, was accompanied by the dissolution of household production. With the decline of household production, the opportunties for women to combine childcare and profitable work also declined, and since men did not generally take on child-care responsiblity, women became increasingly tied to the home. The development of the alcohol industry, as one of the first major factory industries, was a prime mover in the creation of modern social class and sexual divisions.

The initial capitalization of the industry depended upon three circumstances: access to capital, either from profitable operation of small-scale plants, and/or by means of borrowing, often within the family; technical innovations that might be applied in mass manufacture; and access to a market capable of absorbing the product. These circumstances coincided in London in the eighteenth century, and elsewhere thereafter. Capital was available from investment in agriculture, foreign trade, national merchandising, coal, iron and cotton, as well as from within the trade itself (Mathias, 1979; 231). The growth of London offered an accessible market:

> Large breweries could develop only in the geographically confined, intensive market of the city, where many customers and publicans live within range of the drays from a single unit of production. And London was pre-eminently such a market, with one-tenth of the nation's rising numbers pressed within its boundaries . . . despite foreign markets in the Baltic, Ireland or elsewhere, and a considerable 'country trade', the metropolitan maket was the real development of their size and success. (Mathias, 1959; xxii-xxiii)

It was in this context of big capital and mass market that technical innovations permitting mass production were taken up:

> Both public taste and opportunities of lowering prices rest in part upon technical foundations; the salesman, the accountant, even the production engineer were dependent in the end upon the

> master brewer. We may claim therefore, that the unique expansion of porter breweries in the eighteenth century, with the commerical consequences following therefrom, almost certainly had a technical foundation . . . The appearance of the new beer should be seen, therefore, as an event of the first importance, or as an invention exactly equivalent in its own industry to coke-smelted iron, mule-spun muslin in textiles, or pressed-ware in pottery. (ibid; 13)

Porter was a dark beer produced by using differently-prepared raw materials; its advantage was that it could be made more easily in large quantities, using bigger brewery equipment but with no increase in labour, and hence more cheaply produced for a large local market. As Hawkins and Pass summarise the consequences for the London trade, 'the rise of porter brewing led to a remarkable concentration of output in the hands of about a dozen large commercial breweries . . . These brewers derived substantial cost and quality advantages from the scale of their operations (Hawkings and Pass, 1979; 19). Outside the metropolitan areas, however, household production took some time to die out: 'Single industries which were virtually nationwide, like textiles or brewing (or even, in a different way, farming), possessed within themselves, at the same point in time, a complete spectrum of industrial organisation from household production through cottage industry to powered factory' (Mathias, 1979; 231). With the advent of national transport systems capable of moving bulk goods eonomically, small country producers faced increasing competition from urban mass production units. First the canals, and then the railways provided a system of transportation that permitted competition between producers in different towns, and the breakdown of hitherto isolated rural markets. Another consequence was that Breweries no longer needed to be based in large towns at all, but could be located at the place most advantageous for raw materials and labour.

> Burton (upon Trent) is the only real example in England (except possibly Tadcaster) of a town whose growth and prosperity has been determined completely by the brewing industry. Its fate has been settled by brewing in exactly the same way as has Rochdale's by cotton or Sheffield's by steel, and for similar reasons. The great advantages of Burton brewers lay not in the size of the immediately local market. This was negligible until the brewing

> industry itself produced the expansion of the town in the nineteenth century, and remained negligible in relation to total production. They throve upon the very special nature of the local water, plentiful and excellent local barley and a long tradition of skills. (The Times, 1960; 81)

The development of large capital-intensive units serving a national market was both a consequence of the development of transport systems serving other industries, and a spur to its further development. The same may be said in relation to overseas trade. Beer was exported from London and other ports to the Baltic, Ireland and India, the main impediment to the trade being the low value, bulk and decomposable characteristics of beer. Burton's fortunes were given a further push when it was found that the gypsum in the local water stabilised the beer in conditions of heat and constant agitation: 'Burton's India Pale Ale had the remarkable virtue of arriving pale, clear and sparkling in Calcutta' (Mathias, 1959; 192). This gave it an improved economic base for its operations in the home market, and Burton brewing expanded to rival that of London.

The concentration of capital was rapid throughout the eighteenth and early nineteenth centuries, with the top twelve London brewers sharing 42% of that market in 1787 and 85% in 1830 (Mathias, 1959; 26). This concentration was mainly due to the cost advantages possessed by the larger production units but it was accelerated by other factors. From 1672 onwards, in order to ease the collection of excise duty and to reduce the chances of evasion, the excise adopted procedures that discriminated positively in favour of larger brewers, and this 'must have given a steady advantage to them above and beyond the economic advantages of large scale production' (Mathias, 1979; 216). The fact that brewing was, as a trade, highly variable in its profitablility (even though the average profit level was high), also encouraged concentration. The Trade's reliance upon agricultural produce meant that it suffered from cashflow problems in 'bad' years, when the cost of agricultural raw materials would rise, causing an increase in brewers' costs and also reducing workers' expendable income after paying more for food. Yet in good years, excellent profits would be made (over £20,000 from a large brewery – Mathias, 179; 226). The business thus alternated between years when loans were essential and years when a surplus was available for investment, and the most sucessful businesses were those that were able to invest consistently in the face of such incalculable variations in short term fortunes. It was the larger brewing concerns that had family links with other, less erratic industries and, especially, with banking, that were best able to do this. These circumstances encouraged concentration, and facilitated an unusually close relationship between this section of manufacturing industry and banking (eg the Barclay, Bevan, Hoarse and Hanbury families), which was well represented in Parliament (Mathias, 1979; 227).

The political influence wielded by the industry can not, however, be understood purely in terms of special pleading on behalf of the sectional interests of the industry, since its owners were simultaneously members of a class with much wider interests – as indeed were many of the industry's critics. It is in the development of this class as a whole, and in the development of its ideologies – its theories of political economy and moral order – that arguments about alcohol production and consumption can be understood.

Free trade and brewing

An understanding of the security enjoyed by the alcohol industry in the nineteenth century requires an understanding of changes taking place in the class structure and of concomitant changes in the dominant theories of political economy.

> Modern political economy came into being and developed in parallel with the emergence and growth of capitalist economy, its object of study. In its evolution it reflected the evolution of capitalist economy and that economy's ruling class, the bourgeoisie. Mercantilist literature for example clearly expressed the concerns and requirements of merchant capital and the commercial bourgeoisie. From the middle of the 18th century however, when strict state regulation and the monopolies of the trading companies had begun to put a brake on the growth of industrial capitalism, there was widespread opposition to mercantilist ideas . . .
>
> It fell to the English Classical school, which expressed in the first instance the interests of the industrial bourgeoisie, to make the major practical and theoretical advances. In Smith's doctrine the task of waging a struggle against the antiquated restrictions

> fettering the growth of capitalist economy managed to push into the background the conflicting interests of the different classes that make up bourgeois society. Ricardo's doctrine provided the theoretical foundation for the bourgeoisie in its clash of interests with the landowning class, a clash that revealed itself with bitter intensity in England at the beginning of the 19th century. (Rubin, 1979; 365)

Being closely related with agriculture, yet also being part of the new entrepreneurial class, the alcohol industry found itself confused and divided by this conflict, the consequences of which affected it in several ways. One of the pivots of the conflict was over corn.

> The defenders of the landowning class, including Malthus, were demanding high import duties on corn so as to keep corn prices from falling . . . Malthus labelled as 'extravagant' schemes to turn England into an industrial state feeding on imported corn. Ricardo foresaw that it would be necessary to import cheap foreign corn and that English capital would have to move out of agriculture and into industry. The prospect that 'the corn of Poland, and the raw cotton of Carolina, will be exchanged for the wares of Birmingham, and the muslins of Glasgow' not only failed to frighten him – he hailed it . . . cheaper corn would lead, he thought, to a rise in profits and a tremendous flowing of the country's industrial life. (ibid; 240)

Although related to agriculture, the alcohol industry had no specific interest in the price of corn; their entrepreneurial attitudes led many of them to lean towards the free trades (Harrison, 1971; 280). Free traders were firmly set against all forms of entrenched privilege and identified magistrates' control of the licensing system as part of that privilege. 'Liberal distrust of irresponsible power-wielders made their party always suspicious of monopolies: hence their continued dissatisfaction with the nineteenth century licensing system' (ibid; 291). For many of the larger brewers, the prospect of competition from a large number of unlicensed producers was no threat, for as the brewer Barclay said 'we are power loom brewers, if I may so speak' (ibid; 77); for them, if not for some of the smaller or less confident brewers, there was no conflict between sectional interest and political principle. The hatred of privilege also had a much more radical side, drawing upon the historical heritage of Jacobinism, inflamed by the example of the French Revolution, and commanding large sections of the swelling urban skilled and artisan working class. This radicalism was stirred up by middle-class reformers, who played the rather hazardous game of stirring up the artisan class against the old privileged classes (Thompson, 1980; 887-894). The lowest strata of the working class however, remained without political leadership or organisation, to the relief of their betters. 'The danger, from the point of view of authority (whether Whig or Tory), lay in a possible conjunction between the artisan socialists and the "Criminal classes". But the unskilled masses in London inhabited another world from that of the artisans – a world of extreme hardship, illiteracy, very wide-spread demoralisation and disease' (ibid; 895). Such a conjunction was prevented by a bifurcation of controls, in which the major alcohol legisaltion of the first half of the century was embedded. On issues affecting middle and artisan class interests, the old Tory order was forced to compromise, making a number of concessions that reduced the exclusive privileges of the upper class and its appointees in a number of areas. The franchise was marginally widened, after careful enquiries into the level of property qualification that would enfranchise only the 'respectable' (Thompson, 1980; 889-900). Several administrative functions – control of the Poor Law administration, of the prisons, and of law enforcement – were taken out of the hands of Justices of the Peace (Tobias, 1979, Corrigan & Corrigan, 1979).

After an intense struggle, the Corn Laws were abolished in 1846, opening up agriculture to free trade and fulfilling the ambitions of the industrial middle classes and of the economists who, like Ricardo, had theorised these particular class interests into a set of universal principles. The period saw the flowering of a social philosophy that corresponded to this political economy; the Benthamite, utilitarian assertion that the well-being of society had no other meaning than the greatest good of the greatest number, which could be achieved by 'the maximum freedom of the individual and the limitation of the state's function to the purely negative task of keeping its citizens from doing damage to each other' (Rubin, 1979; 237).

It was in this context that the 1830 Beerhouse Act was passed. This removed the monopoly right of magistrates to license public houses and introduced free trade within the beer industry, allowing any householder to sell beer from his own house on payment of a small fee to the excise. When viewed in the context of relations between the upper and middle classes, the free licensing campaign and the passage of the Beerhouse Act can be seen as 'a strategic retreat by the upper classes before the general contemporary attack on the hated patronage system – one aspect of the general attack on the JP's autonomy (Harrison, 971; 65). The Beerhouse Act also has to be understood within the context of the relations between on the one hand, the emerging political 'block' of upper, middle and artisan classes (within which the political economy of the middle class became hegemonic) and, on the other hand, the lower working class – to whom the newly liberalised state presented a decidedly less conciliatory face.[5] Conditions facing the lower strata were poor, and economic developments and state policy changes during the first half of the nineteenth century made them worse (Engels, 1969). Wages were low, food prices high (a condition exacerbated by the repeal of the Corn Laws), working hours were long and factory legislation absent, and the amendment of the Poor Laws worsened the provision of poor relief for the able bodied (Fraser, 1973; 45-50). The ascendant economic and social philosophy emphasised that, given the freedom to dispose of one's property or labour without legal hindrance, each individual was responsible for his or her own success or failure to prosper (Gouldner, 1971; 62, and 1976; 195-206). The victim-blaming views of the origins of poverty ascribed a moral inferiority to the able-bodied poor, and this helped to legitimise punitive social reaction – although utlitarian theory recognised the problems of those who were not able-bodied, and therefore could not be blamed for their plight:

> The 'solution' in social contract theory to the problem of inequality – in the final analysis – is an evasion, and it is best seen in Locke. He makes a distinction between those members of the poor who have chosen depravity and those who, because of their unfortunate circumstances, were unable to live a 'rational' life. Thus crime is either an irrational choice (a product of the passions) or it may be the result of factors militating against the free exercise of rational choice. In neither respect can it be fully rational action in the sense that conforming action is invariable seen to be. (Taylor et all, 1973; 6-7)

As the more 'respectable' artisan strata of the labouring classes became co-opted into political institutions, together with the middle classes, thus averting revolutionary change (Thompson,

1980; 781-887), so the lower strata came to be treated more and more as the 'dangerous' or 'criminal' classes, with the old order's paternalistic welfare provisions being restricted to the evidently infirm and incapable of labour. Historical concerns over the maintenance of social and economic discipline, exacerbated by fear aroused by the French Revolution and by an apparently near-insurrectionary atmosphere at home, were not defused by the construction of a new class alliance to underpin the liberal but that alliance and state did act as a lens, focussing those concerns upon *one section* of the class structure. During the early nineteenth century, the able-bodied poor were more intensively policed, with the result of an increase in crime conviction figures, giving the appearance of a 'crime wave' which, put alongside an increase in the consumption of gin, reactivated historical concerns over drink and disorder:

> Between 1811 and 1827, criminal convictions in the London area quadrupled, but few were shrewd enough to attribute this increase to improved police efficiency. Several important enquiries into police and crime were held between 1815 and 1828, though no causal connection between gin and crime figures was or could ever be proved, the two were linked in the public mind... (Harrison, 1971; 69)

Out of these enquiries came the 1829 Metropolitcan Police Act and the Beerhouse Act. That an enhancement of fears about drink and indiscipline could result in legislation, such as the Beerhouse Act, that increased the number of drinking places, may at first appear paradoxical. But when placed within the context of a primary commitment to free trade, and alongside the development of a full-time and professional police force to deal with those who did not seem willing to better themselves, the Beerhouse Act can be seen as part of a new, free trade approach to social control. The Act met concern about working class use of gin not by banning it, but by increasing the duty, and sought to encourage a swing away from gin, and towards the milder beer, by freeing the beer trade. So as to further encourage the swing to beer, and to avoid the need to collect duty from the increased number of beerhouses, beer duty was abolished and replaced by a lower duty on malt (Harrison, 1971; 70-74). In line with liberal philosophy, control shifted from regulation of the circumstances of drinking, to a reliance on the working of the relation between the individual and the market, the assumption being that freedom from arbitrary restrictions (eg licensing restrictions) would facilitate rational choice and behaviour. As Mill put it, the moral faculties, like the body, became developed only through use.[4] Such development, however, depended upon the market for its nourishment; hence any opportunity to consume alcohol outside the framework of the market continued to be morally suspect. Fairs and festivals, which were organized by the working class rather than by the new middle classes, continued to provoke consternation amongst the middle classes:

> Methodists had long been attacking the seasonal wake, to which their camp meetings were largely designed as a counter-attraction. Evangelists detested popular sports and papist festivals; industrialists found them inconvenient. Several fairs were discontinued during the eighteenth centuries but the attack on London fairs reached a peak in the 1820s . . .
>
> Temperance reformers argued that the expansion in retail trades, from which many of them drew their livelihood, had superceded the commercial role of the fair: the occasions were now 'not for the transactions of business of any kind, but merely for what is called *pleasure*, alias *drinking* . . . gambling and fighting'; they were feudal relics, or 'fossil memorials of obsolete degeneracy'. (Harrison, 1971; 328, emphasis in original sources)

It was then, only as a 'transaction of business' that the state liberalised drinking controls. In drinking at fairs and festivals, which were not part of the new bourgeois economy, the state sensed only trouble; whilst in householders, it recognised an opportunity to extend the market economy in a well-ordered manner.

In summary we can agree with Harrison (1971; 70) that 'the sentiments that lay behind the introduction of the metropolitan police act . . . also lay behind the Beer Act'. Harrison means this in terms of the relations between the upper and middle classes; both pieces of legislation are examples of the success of the middle class in breaking up old monopolies and privileges, and in reforming economic and coercive institutions. But the two pieces of legislation also form a couple of a quite different type that can be understood as the middle class, free trade answer to the centuries-old question of how to discipline the lower classes. The other side of political economy's coin of 'free trade' in the market was a punitive reaction against those who 'took advantage' of their newly won freedom and conducted themselves in a disorderly manner. This bifurcation of controls – the market for those who showed themselves worthy, and the police for those who did not – turned out to be a none-too-stable arrangement, and one whose philosophical rationale it was difficult to articulate (Taylor et al, 1973; 4-6). But if sufficed, during the second quarter of nineteenth century, to underpin many economic and political innovations, of which free trade in beer was one.

The consequences of the freeing of the drink trade, and of reliance upon policing methods to deter drunkenness and disorderliness, were an increase in consumption of drink, and an increase in convictions for drunkenness. The increase in consumption was accelerated, after the middle of the century, by an increase in wages:

> Rapid urbanisation was accompanied, at least after 1850, by a significant increase in working class spending power. Average real wages rose by 37% between 1850 and 1876 as money wages rose ahead of prices. At this time habits of consumption in most urban working class communities were determined by a combination of traditional social habits and limited choices. Alcoholic drink, especially beer, was a well-established part of this narrow and traditional pattern of consumption and up to the mid-1870s, at least, increased spending power tended to go in this direction. (Hawkins and Pass 1979; 16)

An increasing number of working class men and women were processed through the criminal justice system, and charges of 'drunkenness' provided one means of conviction. During the years 1860 to 1876, proceedings against persons charged with drunkenness more than doubled – and the numbers sent to prison went up sixfold (Harrison, 1971; 398). It was, as Harrison shows, the lower and poorer strata of the class who received this treatment – previous offences including such as stealing potatoes, want of sureties, misbehaviour at a workhouse, vagrancy, assault, neglect of family, stealing turnip tops (ibid, frontsheet and p.337).

The Decay of Free Trade, and the Rise of State Intervention in the Sphere of Distribution

During the second half of the nineteenth century, there was a retreat from and dilution of free trade policies. We now examine the way in which this retreat from the principles of classical political economy provided the setting within which continued anxiety about class discipline combined with changes in the structure of the brewing industry to effect a return to restrictive licensing.

Summarising the period up until the middle of the nineteenth century, we can say that the brewing industry developed as an integral and active part of English capitalism, and played a full part in the transformation of the class structure. It contributed to the destruction of the opportunities for male and female, adult and young, family members to co-operate as an independent petty production unit in the household, owning the means of production and selling the product on the market. Instead, both males and females were proletarianised: effectively stripped of the means of production (a small tun cannot compete effectively with a large brewery, and therefore ceases to be means of production for the market), they were forced to offer their labour for a wage. The very success of the middle class in expanding the capitalist economy, and in breaking through the privileges, monopolies and guilds of the old agricultural and trading classes, created a large working class, concentrated in urban centres of industry, and unrestrained by the economic, political or cultural controls of the old order. 'With the successful conclusion, in the 1930s, of its struggle against the landlords, the bourgeoisie began to feel itself increasingly threatened by the working class' (Rubin, 1979; 365). The middle class responded to this threat on several levels. Most fundamentally, it attempted to expand itself by encouraging the growth of small-scale business amongst the upper sections of the working class; that is to say it attempted to bourgeoisify the workers. The freeing of the beer trade is one example of this strategy. As an ideological collary of the attempt to expand itself numerically, it persisted in its attempts to universalise itself in its economic and political theory, in which its interests were presented as the interests of all classes. Two problems arose in this connection.

First, the liberal political economy of Smith, developed by Richardo, pivoted around a theory of value that, whilst it had been useful in uniting the middle class with the working class against the landowners, also legitimised a revolt by the working class against the middle. Central to the works of political economists such as Smith and Ricardo had been the identification of *labour* as the source of value in the economy: this theoretical advance over previous notions that land and nature were the source of value considerably weakened the position of the landowners, and strengthened the claims of industrialists who put labour to work in large quantities. Socialist writers as John Bray, John Gray and William Thompson took up this liberal political economy and reworked it so as to turn its moral implications against the middle classes:

> Here the novel and special meaning that socialists give the law of labour value shows itself brilliantly. They accept this law completely, just as Ricardo had formulated it. The socialists persistently repeat after Ricardo, 'labour is the sole source of value', without making any improvement whatsoever on Ricardo's formulation . . . Although they took over *in toto* Ricardo's labour value formula, the socialists imported a different methodological sense to it. Ricardo had seen in this formula a law *which actually functions* (albeit with deviations) within capitalist economy. The socialists assumed that in a capitalist economy this law is *violated and does not assert itself.* The socialists took what for Ricardo was *a theorectical law of the real phenomena* of capitalist economy and turned it into *a moral postulate* whose realisation awaited the future socialist society. They substituted the doctrine of *'the workers' right to the full product of labour* for the *labour theory of value*. 'Every man', wrote Bray, 'has an undoubted right to all that his honest labour can procure him'. (Rubin, 1979; 247-248, emphasis in original)

The middle class' second problem with liberal political economy was that it provided no justification for ameliorative welfare policies, and it became increasingly plain as the nineteenth century progressed that, since the working class was too strong to tolerate a purely repressive policy, a more integrationist policy, involving interventionist and welfare measures, was required.[6]

This is the context within which a new generation of 'revisionist' political economists and social theorists rose to popularity. John Stewart Mill drew upon many of these and presented the best-known theoretical justification for social intervention in his *Principles of Political Economy with some of their Applications to Social*

Philosophy, first published in 1848 (Mill, 1921). In this he moved away from the labour theory of value, and made a distinction between production and distribution, thus reconciling the continuation of free trade principles in the sphere of production with the increasing level of social intervention in the sphere of distribution (e.g. alcohol licensing). The technicalities in his argument are beyond the scope of this study (see Mill, 1921 and Rubin, 1979; 351-361). Suffice it therefore to say that, whilst continuing to acknowledge that labour makes a contribution to the production of value of the product upon which it is expanded, he also attributed value to the capitalist's expenditure of money on the cost of production (which Mill equates to wage costs, ignoring the costs of machinery etc), and to the capitalist's sacrifice in investing his money – his 'abstinence' from the short-live satisfaction of immediate consumption.

> In our analysis . . . of the requisites of production, we found that there is another necessary element in it besides labour. There is also capital; and this being the result of abstinence (on behalf of the capitalist – N.D.), the produce, or its value, must be sufficient to remunerate not only the labour required, but the abstinence of all the persons by whom the reumeration of the different classes of labourers was advanced. The return for abstinence is Profit. (Mill, 1921. Book III; 461-462)

This undercut socialist arguments, based upon the labour theory of value, that profit results purely from the labour of the working class, and is unfairly expropriated from them: both capital and labour contribute to, and are necessary for, the production of wealth. Mill, however, in common with most of his middle class contemporaries (and with the remainder of the older classes), recognised that the market could not by itself, provide social justice, and agitated for radical and socialistic measures *within the sphere of distribution*. This necessitated a hiving-off of 'social' from 'economic' issues:

> Instead of subordinating both production and distribution to the operation of laws that, while *necessary*, are nevertheless at the same time *historically alterable,* Mill subordinates production to the operation of *eternal* laws, but sees distribution as an arbitary realm within which the different economic forces display no

> necessary law-determined regularity. For all its mistakeness, Mill was compelled to divide up economic laws in this way if he was to leave the door open for social reforms and at the same time preserve the system of natural economic laws of production as established by the classicial school. (Rubin, 1979; 355)

This hiving-of 'social' (and moral) from 'economic' issues provided the basis for mid and late nineteenth century social welfare policy (Halevy, 1928). It has given its practical political form by men like MaCaulay: 'It is not desirable that the state should interfere with the contracts of persons of ripe age and sound mind touching matters purely commercial... (but) the principle of non-interference is one that cannot be applied without real restrictions where the public health or morality is concerned'.[7] Social welfare measures were introduced through 'municipal socialism' – especially in public health and housing reforms (Pearson, 1975; 54-176) – and also vigorously pursued through charitable and philanthropic effort. The middle of the nineteenth century witnessed a proliferation and vigorous growth of temperance organisations, closely associated with a variety of other movements for the moral improvement of the working clases, and these organisations exerted increasing influence within the ascendant Liberal Party, with consequences for alcohol legislation. As Harrison puts it, 'Liberal distrust of irresponsible power-wielders made their party always suspicious of monopolies: hence their continued dissatisfaction with the (early) nineteenth century licensing system... (but) by the 1860s this policy seemed to be conflicting with the liberal objective of moral improvement; under inspiration from several directions, the party's enthusiasm shifted towards popular control of the drink trade' (Harrison, 1971; 291-292). This shift – from the classical 'laissez-faire' stance to a more interventionist policy – was part of the general political shift occasioned by the development of relations between upper, middle and working classes during the middle of the nineteenth century.

Simultaneously – as we shall now demonstrate – the circumstances of the brewing industry developed in ways that left it considerably over-extended at the retail end of the industry, and by no means entirely hostile to suggestions of increased state controls on distribution, as long as these were imposed in particular ways.

The Brewers' Acquiescence to Controls

The initial concentration of brewing capital rested, as we have seen, upon urbanisation, technical innovation, transport, availability of capital from family relations and associates, and careful re-investment of profits. Small improvements in the production process, such as better preparation of raw materials, control of the industrial process, or productivity of labour, might give an appreciable return on a large turnover (Mathias, 1979;245). This improved the firm's ability to cover its costs, generate profits, attract outside loans for further investment and improvement, and maintain the family/economic/political relationships that kept temperance interests at bay. In Marxian terms, we can say that the conditions were favourable for the production of surplus value, and the rate of accumulation (rate of increase in stock of means of production) was high.[8] From the 1880s, however, whilst conditions remained favourable for the *production* of surplus value, conditions for its *realisation* (by sale in the market) took a turn for the worse. This was partly due to the general development of the economy, and partly due to the brewers' response to the changing conditions.

The most general aspect of the development of the economy in the late eighteenth and early nineteenth century was the rapid expansion of capitals in all branches of industry throughout Europe and the Americas, and the intensification of international competition. The expansion of the means of production, the increased productivity of labour, and the extent of competition led to a cheapening of commodities, with consequences for disposal of income:

> Up to 1880 a rise in real wages had tended to produce a more than disproportionate increase in the consumption of beer. During the 1880s, by contrast, while real wages rose sharply, beer output virtually stagnated and per capita consumption actually fell . . . The reaons for this decline in per capita output were both economic and social. A substantial fall in food prices and the availability of an increasing range of cheap mass-produced consumer goods brought about a reduction in the proportion of working class budgets spent on beer . . . social and recreational horizons widened, and the public house, although remaining the focal point of working class leisure pursuits, found itself increasingly in competition from the music hall, football matches, and even day railway excursions. (Hawkins & Pass, 1979; 27-28)

Brewing capital thus faced the problem of increasing large production units competing with each other for a market that was no longer expanding. This problem could not be solved by an expansion of overseas trade, since beer is so bulky in relation to its value that transport costs make it uncompetitive in export markets; and the colonies had developed their own alcohol industries by this time (Hawkins & Pass, 1979; 70). The brewers thus confronted the problem of being unable to realise, in the market, all the surplus value that they could produce. The situation deteriorate further from 1900 onwards, when real wages fell, leaving an increasing number of goods and services chasing less working class disposable income, and per capita consumption declined further (Hawkins & Pass, 1979; 27-28). There are two possible solutions to the problem of over-capaicity in an industry – expansion of demand for the product, or destruction of excess capacity. Unable to expand demand, the brewers had no alternative but to reduce total capacity by merger and amalgamation, closing down the least profitable plants. From 1890-1900 there was a sharp rise in the number of brewery mergers, as small units were bought up and shut down (Hawkins & Pass, 1979; 41-42). The rate of mergers, was, however, also partly due to each brewery's need to maximise its market share by establishing a strong presence at the retailing end of the business. Big brewers had become big by concentrating upon production, and selling to independent publican retailers. This independence began to be eroded after the 1860s, when escalating concern about widespread and disorderly working class drinking led to legislation restricting the numbers of retail licences that Justices could grant. Hawkins and Pass suggest (p.27) that 'By curbing the growth of public houses, thereby giving licensed property a higher scarcity value, the legislature in effect compelled the brewers to buy retail outlets in order to safeguard their trade'. Once the demand for alcohol stabilised and began to decline, this compulsion became stronger, since the realisation of profit depended crucially upon whether or not brewers controlled sufficient retail outlets to take the output of their plants working at full capacity. The costs involved in acquisition of public houses were considerable, and prices were pushed up to 'preposterous figures' by each brewer's attempts to prevent them falling into the hands of competitors.[9] Even an agreed merger between breweries could be expensive, if the purpose was to rationalise joint production capacity, leaving the most efficient plant to supply both breweries' public houses: capital invested in the smaller and less efficient plant had to be 'written off'. Given the scale of investment needed, and the uncertainty of a good return, there were problems of raising the necessary capital entirely from private sources. Increasingly, the breweries took advantage of the Limited Liability Acts of the 1850s, and became public companies whose shares could be bought and traded. Between 1886 and 1892 85 concerns, and between 1892 and 1900 145 breweries 'went public', raising £185 million in the process (Hawkins & Pass, 1979; 34).

The costs of this mass operation were not, it transpired, justified in strict commercial terms. The scramble for public houses and the expenditure of large amounts of capital in their acquisition was primarily a defensive and pre-emptive move by each brewery against others, rather than a positive entrepreneurial response to new opportunities. The industry was unable to raise productivity or output sufficiently to recoup the new capital invested in the retail end of the business (which had never been as profitable as production), and profitability fell. This was reflected in share prices, which fell by up to 92% (varying with company) in the short period 1989-1905.[10] Conditions remained unfavourable to the industry for the next fifty years. The depressed state of the national economy, poor wages and unemployment kept demand down, whilst retail capacity, exceeding requirements, tied up valuable capital, causing profit crises in the period up to the First World War (Vaizey, 1958; 405).

The contradiction faced by the industry was that whilst total capacity was too great, each firm's share of the market depended upon hanging on to its retail outlets: an orderly reduction of retail outlets was in the interests of the industry.

It was in these circumstances that the Unionist Government introduced a Bill to amend the Licencing Acts of 1828 to 1902 in respect of 'the extinction of licences and the granting of new licences'. This Bill, which was passed in 1904, set up a scheme whereby brewers and licencees who lost a licence were compensated out of a fund derived from a levy on all brewers and licencees in the licencing area (Williams & Brake, 1980; 24). However, this fund was administered in such a way that, when a public house was closed down, the main body of compensation went to the brewery owning it, and relatively little to the licencee of the public house (ibid;37). The extinction of surplus licences meant that costs were reduced and, since consumption (which remained quite static during this period) was transferred to the remaining public houses, 'the trade had simply got rid of worthless licences without great sacrifice' (ibid; 124). In other words, the industry was able to take advantage of temperance pressure, coming to a compromise – to reduce the number of pubs – that was in reality totally in its interests. The compensation scheme offered a means by which the good offices of the state could be used to selectively suspend those competitive pressures that had the industry into over-investment in retail outlets; and for each brewer to co-operate with its competitors, to rationalise and restructure the holdings of each (Vaizey, 1958;405).

We can now summarise the consequences of temperance attacks on the brewing industry at a time of retrenchment of the latter and in the broader context of the shift from state policies of laissez-faire to those of intervention in the sphere of distribution and consumption (but not in production). This shift had been sufficient to undermine belief in the efficacy of the market economy (assisted, in the face of a seemingly irrational minority unresponsive to the market, by the police) as a panacea for social problems. This did not however signal a return to eighteenth century restrictions on economic activity, since these would have been wholly inconsistent with the operation of a fully developed capitalist economy, upon which the state depended not merely for its tax income but also as the underpinnings of the social order. Rather, it led (a) to the development of policies that, whilst leaving the means of production in the hands of their owners, made a number of interventions into and adjustments to the manner of distribution of the products (e.g. municipal socialism, public health and housing reforms, etc) and, (b) to 'revisionist' economic and social theory, such as that of J.S. Mill, that legitimated these policies. Within the atmosphere of greater tolerance of social welfare interventions into the sphere of distribution, specific legislation regulating the distribution of alcohol became more acceptable, and the conjunction of temperance campaigning and alcohol industry retail over-capacity provided the impetus required to reintroduce restrictive licencing legislation and a phased reduction of retail outlets.

Temperance interests were far from satisfied with this conclusion, and attempted to introduce firmer legislation involving an abolition of compensation; the prohibitionist wings of the movement went further and called for production itself to cease. The House of Lords, in which family networks spanning the alcohol industry, agriculture and banking interests were still strong, blocked temperance legislation in 1906. But, even after the Lord's veto had been removed by the 1911 Parliament Act, no legislation touching upon the production of alcohol, nor upon more vigorous curtailment of its distribution was introduced by the government – in spite of the strength of temperance sentiment in the Liberal Party from 1880 onwards (Harrison, 1979; 284) and in spite of resounding election pledges given by that party (Williams & Brake, 1980; 25-43). The balance of legislation, steering clear of the sphere of production, and making a limited intervention into the sphere of distribution (and one not inconsistent with the interests of the industry), can be seen as an instance of the policies and political philosophies adopted in response to the changes in the balance of class forces during the nineteenth century. It was to take a major emergency to modify these policies.

War Nationalisation

Whilst the state has generally concerned itself with the conditions of distribution and consumption of alcohol, it is only in the exceptional conditions of war-mobilisation of the economy that it has intervened directly into the sphere of production. The declaration of war with Germany was followed, in 1914, by the passage of the Defence of the Realm Act. This gave the state wider power to direct capital in the interests of the war effort – but the consequences for the alcohol industry were relatively few, since the industry's means of production were not of such forms as could be employed in the production of munitions and other accoutrements of war. The Act also raised taxation on drinks over a certain strength, this being justified on grounds of reducing drinking amongst those engaged in war industries. This last concern was pursued in a more selective manner in a Defence of the Realm Consolidation Act later in the same year, which set up the Central Control Board with powers to take breweries and public houses in the areas of munitions manufacture, war transport and armed forces encampment into public ownership. These powers were implemented on a small scale in the area surrounding the Royal Small Arms Factory at Enfield, the naval dockyard at Cromarty Firth, and the relatively large area of Carlisle, in which a large explosives factory was built (Williams & Brake, 1980; 106-107). A total of 368 licenced premises, including four breweries, various stores and over one hundred public houses were taken into public ownership in Carlisle; some were closed and the rest improved, restaurant facilities and games rooms being provided (ibid).

The effects of the Carlisle 'experiment' in publis ownership were that expenditure per head on drink went down and there was a decrease in insobriety and arrests for drunkenness.[11] A Royal Commission on Licensing, surveying these advantages, suggested an extension of the experiment to other areas of the country, to see if they could be achieved elsewhere.[12] The scheme was, after initial resistance, also well received by the local labour movement. A Conference of delegates representing 15,000 trades unionists passed the following resolution:

> That this Conference of Trade Union Organisers in the Carlisle area, convened by the Carlisle Trades Council and Labour Party, affirms its belief in the Public Ownership of the Liquor Trade, and urges all local Labour Parties and Trades Councils to press for the extension of the principle of State Ownership and Control to the whole country, subject to such modifications in the administration as experience may have shown to be necessary (quoted in Greenwood, 1920; 186-187).

Labour was, of course, predisposed towards policies involving public ownership of the means of production and, additionally, believed that insobriety was one of the specific impediments to mobilisation of the working class.

> The evils associated with the drink traffic are serious enough to warrant the most drastic treatment. The social, moral and economic effects of insobriety are, it may be said without exaggeration, of the gravest kind, intensifying the acute problems of the time. The conversion of the nation to strictly temperance habits, or even to total abstinence, would not solve the major problems of society, for these arise out of defects in the structure of society itself. But such a change in national habits would undoubtedly remove a powerful corrupting influence and an important disturbing and complicating factor. (Greenwood, 1920; 85)

Had Labour, once in power, adopted a general policy of socialisation of the means of production, then the Carlisle experiment might have been extended to other areas of the country, as suggeted by the Royal Commission, or generalised to the rest of the country as a whole. However, the crisis of 1931, the formation of a National Government, and the political demoralisation of the 1930s (Milliband, 1972) did not provide conditions conducive to such an extension.

Keynesian Policies, Service Sector and Alcohol Production

Economic policy during the post-Second World War period has been marked by the adoption of, and subsequent retreat from Keynesian economic policies of expansion of demand (Stewart, 1967). These policies were for two decades fairly successful in stabilizing the previously chaotic conditions in which business operated, in increasing profitability, and in providing 'full' employment (i.e. within 2% of the pool of those available for wage work where this excludes approximately half the number of married women). Also, partly because of the generally favourable position of male labour in this situation of 'full' employment, and partly because it was not difficult for capitalists to pass on increased costs to consumers, wages were good in relation to the pre-war years – though at the cost of increasing inflation (Glyn & Harrison, 1980; 16-17). The combination of high employment and high wages increased the level of expendible income, and expenditure on non-durables – including alcohol – increased (Brewers Society, 1980; 45). The increase in demand stimulated new investment and innovation in the production and distribution ends of the alcohol industry. There were a series of brewery mergers, especially in 1959-61, leading to rationalisation of production, the bringing into service of very large production units, and a subsequent reduction in labour costs of production. 'The fall in the index of Unit labour costs reflects increases in productivity as fewer employees operate larger blocks of capital equipment' (Hawkins & Pass, 1979; 100). Brewing is today one of the most capital-intensive industries in Britain (ibid; 104). The development of keg beers, together with a new emphasis on promotion of bottles and cans, met the criteria of mass production, easy distribution, long shelf life, and retail by unskilled labour, and it is these products that have been most heavily advertised and which now dominate the market (Protz, 1978). In this connection it may be mentioned that, whether or not advertising contributes to expansion of total sales, it is essential to an industry whose profit rests upon the adoption by the public of those types of products most suitable for mass production and distribution.

The *pattern* of demand is, however, conditioned not only by the needs of the industry but also by social, demographic and cultural changes in the population, and these have been shaped by more general changes in the economy. The main change in the structure of capital during this century has been the relative stagnation of industrial capital and the growth of the service sector of the economy. This trend, which has been most marked in the south of England, has had consequences for inner city working class areas: de-industrialisation, mobility of labour, and post-war rehousing policies have combined to dislocate the pattern of community based upon local work and extended families and associated cultural traditions (Cohen, 1972). Population has been decanted to the New Towns, and more generally, to the suburbs, where social life has focussed upon the nuclear family, and the home is increasingly regarded as a place of leisure, recreation and consumption. It is in this context that off-licence sales have become more important. The 1961 Licensing Act relaxed restrictions on the opening of off-licences, and the 1964 Licensing Act facilitated supermarket sales. By the late 1970s, most beer was still sold in public houses, but one third of all wine and half of spirits were consumed at home (Thurman, 1981; 4).

The development of the drinks industry in the post-war period has meant that it has regained its place as a leading section of UK capital. The Brewers Society estimates that the industry provides over £2200 million in farmers' income; uses about half the total number of bottles produced in the country; employs three-quarters of a million people in production, distribution and retail; contributes almost £500 million to the balance of trade; and the government receives over 5% of its total income from excise duty and value-added tax on drinks (Thurman, 1981; 9-14). Clearly, 'the drinks industry is an integral part of U.K. Manufacturing Industry' (ibid). It is against this economic background that the state's policies bearing on the production of the alcohol – as distinct from its policies bearing upon the consumer, and his or her health and orderliness – are drawn up.

In 1978 the then Labour Government commissioned its Central Policy Review Staff to review state alcohol policy. This body acts as a 'Think Tank', supposedly independent of Government departments and of particular professions and interest groups, and is supposed to transcend all partial interests and to analyse social and economic problems in terms of the interests of the State as a whole. The Report was prepared on the basis of soundings conducted with the 'large number of different public interests involved' including no less than sixteen central departments of the state, regional and local, law enforcement and health agencies and commercial interests. These soundings were done 'without indications that it is a review' (i.e. a review by the Central Policy Review Staff). In other words, the review was compiled covertly; it was never intended to become public property; and it remains unpublished. The unique value of the review is the evidence it gives of the difference between an alcohol policy that is concerned solely with alcohol, and an alcohol policy that places the question of alcohol into the broader context of the balance of social and economic forces as these are manifested at the level of the state. As the review states:

> We do not think that it is realistic to propose a policy that takes no notice of these influences. For this reason we cannot advocate the early adoption of the proposal of the Royal College of Psychiatrists. But we are convinced that, *from the point of view of alcohol policies alone,* it is a proper objective. (C.P.R.S., 1979; 17, emphasis added)

The Royal College of Psychiatrists had recommended that 'steps should be taken so as to ensure that per capita alcohol consumption does not increase beyond the present level, and is by stages brought back to an agreed lower level' (1979; 139). The Royal College made this recommendation on the basis of evidence that the amount of alcohol-related harm in a society is related to the total consumption of alcohol in that society. This is generally referred to as the 'distribution of consumption' model of alcohol problems: it predicts that, in a social system, alcohol-related harm is causally related to the number of heavy drinkers, and the number of heavy drinkers is causally related to the total (and hence average) consumption.[13] The Central Policy Review Staff themselves adhered to this model of 'the issue':

> The fundamental issue is whether there is an association between increasing consumption of alcohol and increasing numbers of alcohol-related disabilities; and, if so, what aspects of Govern-

ment policy should be reviewed . . . the evidence we have gathered in the course of the year shows, in our view quite conclusively, that there is a correlation between increasing per capita consumption and increases in the number of disabilities. (C.P.R.S., 1979; 5)

Basing itself in this view, the C.P.R.S. went on to consider two alternative policy options: to hold consumption at its present level, *or* to reduce the rate of increase of consumption (p.6). They did not put forward the objective favoured by the Royal College – reduction in consumption – as a serious policy option. Of the two options which they did consider, they favoured the first:

level consumption . . . This provides a benchmark against which the various policies can be assessed, and is a clear and comprehensive objective. It should be associated with a secondary objective of also holding at their present level the indicators of alcohol-relating disability. (C.P.R.S., 1979; 6)

Viewed 'from the point of alcohol policies alone' and compared with the more radical Royal College recommendations of actual reductions in consumption, the objective of the C.P.R.S. may appear timid. But central government policy-making is made in a broader context than 'alcohol policies alone', as the Review illustrates. The state's interests are quite diverse:

The government is directly or indirectly involved in nearly every aspect of the production and consumption of alcohol. It has an interest in the well-being of the alcohol industry, in the trade in alcohol and in the employment generated; it receives a large amount of tax revenue from the sale of alcohol; it imposes certain restrictions on consumption; and it bears the cost of many of the consequences of alcohol misuse. There are thus a great number of alcohol policies. (C.P.R.S., 1979; 4)

Any alcohol policy has to be concerned not simply with drinking and its consequences but also 'with Britain's economic interests in terms of wealth creation, employment and exports'. There are several aspects to this. First, there is the obvious sectional interest of the alcohol industry, which is not too shy to draw attention to its importance to the economy. The Review refers to a report of the

Distilling Sector Working Party of the National Economic and Development Organisation: 'Any reduction in consumption or change in the future growth rate (of alcohol production) may affect the prosperity of the industry and so its ability to employ and generate wealth. Moreover, as the Distilling Working Party has pointed out, sudden large changes in duty may be particularly disruptive' (C.P.R.S., 1979; 14). Secondly, there is the Government's own interest in maintaining or increasing tax revenue from the duty imposed on alcohol. Were the duty to be raised to a considerable extent in an attempt to reduce consumption, then sales might fall to such an extent that total revenue would be decreased: this would be 'counter-productive from a taxation point of view', as would any measure 'which in the long term weakens the attraction to drink in such a way which might inhibit its ability to be a source of future revenue' (ibid; 13). Thirdly, 'the ethic associated with drinking is an important influence. It is arguable that a given increase in alcohol duty is more unpopular than a similar change in other taxes and expenditure – perhaps because its effect is particularly apparent on many wage-earners' personal spending power' (p.14). Finally, each of these considerations was posed within the framework of acceptance of the state's role in facilitating the operation of the economy as a whole:

> We have considered how far an approach on the lines indicated above would be compatible with Britain's economic interests in terms of wealth creation, exports and employment. This is not easy to qualify. In particular, different elements of our proposals are likely to lead to different results. And it is not possible to balance precisely, say, the advantages to industry generally from reducing the costs of misuse with the possible results of restricted growth in the alcohol industry. (C.P.R.S., 1979;8)

It would therefore be much too simplistic to suggest a conspiracy theory of alcohol policies in which the policy makers are said to be in the pockets of one section of private capital. The state also has fiscal and electoral considerations, and fields these considerations within the general framework of commitment to 'industry generally' – capitalism as a system – as distinct from any particular section of capital.

What is left out of this supposedly comprehensive approach to policy-making is any consideration of the collective interests of working class men, women or children as separate from that of capital. One major consequence of the adoption of any analytic framework within which working class men, women and children cannot be clearly conceptualised is that the review can make no clear suggestions relating to those major population groups. The review is broadly in favour of public debate and health education, and makes a reference to existing health education activities and trends:

> There is a good deal of activity in health education in schools. A number of themes emerge as far as alcohol is concerned. There is a growing and convincing belief in the need not to teach about alcohol(ism) problems but about the attitudes and pressures associated with drinking in contemporary society, and the nature of the decisions associated with its consumption. (ibid; 67)

This is however a gloss upon existing opinion in the field of health education, rather than an interrogation and evaluation of that opinion. The review is in fact sceptical of the value of health education, in spite of its advocacy of it; 'a clearer assessment is required than at the moment seems to exist of the potential contribution of health education on alcohol to a strategy on alcohol-related problems' (p.63). One of the factors obstructing such assessment is, however, the class perspective adopted in the review, and in state policy-making more generally. The following chapters attempt a more adequate assessment.

Conclusion

The overview, presented in this chapter, of the process of capitalisation, decline and revigoration of the alcohol industry shows this process to be an integral part of the uneven development of the broader economy, and illustrates how state policy towards production of this commodity is conditioned by this historical fact. The lesson to be drawn is that whatever political muscle may be put behind arguments about what the state 'ought' to do to restrict production and total consumption, the state's policies on alcohol production are *actually* conditioned by its broader concerns with private production, profitability, and electoral and fiscal considerations. Whilst historically, the state has consistentlypursued policies *within the spheres of distribution and consumption* that aim to minimise the extent and reform the nature of working class drinking, translation of this restrictive intent *into the sphere of production* has been impeded by an equal commitment to freedom of private investment. The balance between liberal and restrictive alcohol control policies has shifted one way and then the other, but always between these parameters.

Whilst these shifts took place within the context of (at times quite acute) class struggle during the nineteenth century, it is not possible to assign any particular 'alcohol politics' to whole social classes, since there were quite characteristically splits within the classes, and cross-class alliances grew up around specific issues. Within the land-owning classes (which were in the process of becoming integrated with the newer business classes), the historically generated concern about drinking, vagabondage and labour indiscipline was offset by interest in supplying the raw materials required by alcohol production. Within the rising industrial middle classes, the 'protestant ethnic' and its temperance correlates found itself at odds with the commitment to free trade. Within the working class, concern about the dehabilitating consequences of over-indulgence sat side-by-side with a continuing attachment to public and often boisterous drinking occasions – reminders of previously-enjoyed leisure rites and customs, and resources in the fight to assert a collective identity within urban environments. Women's organisations were frequently involved closely in temperance politics (Sebestyen, 1980). It is by no means surprising, therefore, that complex alliances sprang up, and that the political parties were often split on 'the drink question'. The consequence of this is that, although alcohol politics in previous centuries can be quite closely equated with class politics, by the nineteenth century this was no longer the case.

3 DRINK AND HEALTH EDUCATION

Introduction

In the two preceding chapters the historical genesis of state concern over drinking has been outlined. Public drinking situations became a focus of legislative contol within the context of the often quite acute class struggle that accompanied the development of capitalist social and economic relations. The early vagrancy laws, primarily concerned with the suppression of labour mobility and political agitation, provided the first legislation to touch upon the public house. During the seventeenth century, traditional feasting, drinking and associated leisure customs were seen by the ascendant class of merchant capital to be incompatible with work-discipline, and hence became objects of state legislation. The eighteenth and nineteenth centuries were marked by the formation of a large urban working class and considerable political agitation, often focussing upon the traditional meeting-place of the public house, and licensing legislation concerned itself primarily with the maintenance of 'public order' where this was defined in terms of an absence of political meetings. It was in this historical context that pressures were successfully brought to bear to exclude children from the public house. During the late nineteenth and early twentieth centuries, the state's policies in relation to alcohol seemed set in a disciplinary mould; the discourse of alcohol education, stressing the need for social discipline in relation to work, leisure and political life, was broadly synonymous with temperance education.

Historically-constructed theories and policies about alcohol, education and social discipline do not, however, project themselves directly upon modern times, but we are mediated by the economic and social policies, institutions and class cultures that characterise the post-war period. This chapter locates contemporary approaches to health education about alcohol within the cotext of the development of health and educational policies in the post-Second World War period, and goes on to discuss the efficacy of such health education.

Origins of Health Services

Historically, the social welfare, health and educational services that make up the contemporary welfare state evolved out of developments in nineteenth century Poor Law Legislation and administration (Fraser, 1975, Thane, 1978, Foucault, 1977). The National Health Service originated in the nationalisation of municipal and private hospitals, which themselves originated from the Poor Law workhouse medical wards and from the voluntary hospitals of the eighteenth century. The abolition of outdoor relief (in the 1834 Poor Law Amendment Act) 'pushed more people into the Poor Law infirmaries and so reinforced their character as public state hospitals' (Fraser, 1975; 87). During the nineteenth century the Poor Law administrators increasingly came to subscribe to the voluntary hospitals and to send paupers there for treatment. This practice, strictly illegal (since by providing free medical care for paupers it made them 'more eligible' than those working), was legalised in 1851, and in 1952 the Central Poor Law Board authorised local authorities to give free medical treatment to poor families even when the head of the family was in work. This dissolved the anomaly that made paupers 'more eligible', and recognised that those on low wages could no more pay for medical care than could paupers. Thus the poor law authorities increasingly became involved in providing services to a wider section of the population. The 1840 legislation providing for free vaccination demand also fuelled this tendency, since the Poor Law medical officers, attached to the local authorities, were the only channels for free treatment open to the state. Increasingly, as poor law authorities came to see poverty as a cuase of ill-health rather than as a moral matter, the sick wards of workhouses were expanded, so that by 1861, over 80% of the hospital beds in England and Wales were in workhouses rather than in voluntary institutions (ibid).[1]

Women were especially reliant upon Poor Law relief, including the medical services, and the ways in which these developed was strongly influenced by conceptions of women as dependent upon the male wage-earner (Thane, 1978). Conceptions of women as responsible for childcare and for maintaining family life also imbued the early twentieth century preventive health policies stimulated by concern over the poor health of army recruits:

Although the rhetoric of prevention extends across the spectrum

> of health and social policy, it is in the field of maternal and child health that it has been most fully articulated. Its articulation in this area is again not without historical precedent. In fact the major way in which women and children gained access to medical care was under the rubric of preventive health. Thus, it was in the name of prevention that health measures were introduced in the aftermath of the Boer War in an attempt to improve the physical condition of the nation's stock. The Report of the Inter-departmental Committee on Physical Deterioration (1904), for example, recommended the provision of school meals as a means of improving the country's health 'provided it could be done quietly and without impairing parental responsibility'. The first conference on infant mortality, held two years later, extended the principles of preventive health to cover mothers as well, with the plea 'concentrate on the mothers, for what the mother is, the chidren are'. (Graham, 1979; 166)

Such considerations continued to mould the form of health service provision, as Graham and a number of other writers have shown: the form of provision reflects the outcome of struggles, alliances and compromises between social classes, men and women and particular professional groups.[2]

The relative prosperity of the post-war period provided the conditions in which compromises were more easily struck then hitherto, and the primary strategy of the state has been government by consent: although backed by coercive powers (e.g. by law enforcement, anti-truancy officers, provision for compulsory psychiatric treatment, etc), welfare, health and educational services present a consensual, even participatory public face.[3] These services form an integral part of the post-war settlement between social classes, based upon the adoption of Keynesian social and economic policies.[4] It is within this framework that pre-war and wartime social welfare provisions were expanded to produce the contemporary Welfare State, of which the health and educational parts are of special interest for an understanding of health education about alcohol. Two primary assumptions underpin the functioning of the National Health Service. The first assumption is that of control of the form of service by the medical profession: Navarro suggests that social class relations were reproduced within the N.H.S. in the form of control by the medical profession in general and by the Consultants in particular (Navarro, 1978). This has resulted in an

N.H.S. orientated primarily to curative medicine, and has contributed to the tendency for preventive medicine to focus upon the individual who may become ill rather than upon the conditions which may make him or her ill.

The second assumption underlying the Welfare State generally, and the National Health Service in particular, was that ill-health due to poverty and adverse material conditions would be sharply reduced as the mixed economy expanded. It was assumed that, whilst demand for free health services might expand rapidly in the early years, this demand, and the requirement for state expenditure, would eventually be limited by a general increase in the health of the population.[5] In the event, however, the demand upon the health service has continued to increase, and the costs of pharmaceutical and other medical services have also increased, contributing to the fiscal problems experienced by the state throughout the post-war period.[6]

Additionally the state's commitment to consensus management of social and economic life has led it to interpret those social practices that it considers problematic as symptoms of individual or family pathology, instead of dealing with them in more straightforward disciplinary ways.[7] This tendency – sometimes referred to as the medicalisation of social problems – extended to cover drinking problems in the early 1960s, when the Ministry of Health issued a circular recommending that each Regional Health Authority set up a specialised alcoholism treatment unit: alcoholism was thereby designated as a treatable disease (Royal College of Psychiatrists, 1979; 13). Public and medical acceptance of this new disease category was accelerated by a 'fruitful partnership' between psychiatric hospitals and the first modern self-help organisation, Alcohlics Anonymous, which now has over 1,000 branches. In 1971 a Home Office Committee recommended that vagrant alcoholics should be treated in a programme of detoxification, counselling and rehabilitation, rather than being processed through the penal system (ibid; 15). Since it was within the context of the suppression of vagrancy and labour mobility that the state had first become concerned about drinking, the switch from a penal to a treatment response may be regarded as evidence of the state's commitment to consensus management of social life. At the same time, however, it has to be recognised that the extension of health services to cover problems of social discipline, such as vagrancy, has implications for the development of those services, as the social control function of medicine becomes more clearly visible. During the 1960s and 1970s there arose a considerable body of literature critical of the state's increasing reliance on methods of social control – in psychiatric, social work, intermediate treatment and delinquency programmes – legitimised by medical and quasi-medical theories and authorities.[8] State strategies for maintaining social discipline were not only partially displaced by Keynesian health and welfare provisions – they were also incorporated into the latter. It is within the contest of such incorporation that 'prevention' has developed in particular forms.

Prevention and Health

The state's interest in prevention springs from three problems inherent in the Keynesian solution to the economic and social problems of capitalism. The first of these is the failure of the mixed economy to eliminate poverty and other material causes of ill-health in the population. The second is the failure to generate sufficient income for the state to be able to finance the level of service that would be required to treat all ill-health. The third is the attractiveness of health rhetoric, with its emphasis upon individual responsibility, discipline and self-help, in a period state retreat from the Keynesian solution. Let us take each of these in turn.

The most extensive study of the material causation of ill-health in contemporary British society is contained in the recently published report *Inequalities in Health* (Working Party on Inequalities in Health, DHSS, 1980). The working party collated a large body of data on the difference between the health (as measured by a variety of indicators) of different social class groups, and examined the ability of various theoretical approaches to explain the observed differences. They concluded:

> We do not believe there to be any single and simple explanation of the complex data we have assembled. Whilst there are a number of quite distinct theoretical approaches to explanation we wish to stress the importance of difference in material conditions of life. In our view much of the evidence on social inequalities in health can be understood in terms of specific features of the socio-economic environment . . . (Working Party on Inequalities in Health, 1980; 357)

The Working Party concluded that a structuralist or materialist explanation[9] of the differences between the health or the social classes best fitted the available data. They refer to Marxian approaches:

> Crudely expressed in its original form, the argument was as follows. Capitalism is in essence a system of economic organisation which depends on the exploitation of human labour. The accumulation of profit, the guiding principle not only of the economic system, but of the whole of form of capitalist social organisation, is the storing up in tangible form of the human effort and resources expended by individual workers over and above what they either require or have been allowed, to maintain their bodies in a fit and healthy condition . . . In the process of immiseration the worker experiences economic deprivation on an ever increasing scale until finally he is left with insufficient resources to maintain bodily health. (Working Party, 1980; 157-158)

The Working Party suggested that this analysis still has value, in spite of increased living standards, because it remains the case that those at the bottom of the class strata remain relatively disadvantaged, leading to relatively poor health. This has direct implications for the social production of ill-health: 'In the collective effort of social production, some workers literally give of themselves more than others and hence their bodies wear out first. But inequalities . . . also emanate from the distribution of rewards associated with the social division of labour' (Working Party, 1980; 193). That is to say, inequalities of income cause inequalities of access to the prerequisites of health, such as good housing, warmth, food, etc. Furthermore, the Working Party suggests that material inequalities lead to inequalities in health-related knowledge: 'People with low incomes are less able to gain access to the facilities and knowledge commanded by those with high incomes (p.160). 'It can certainly be argued that what is often taken for cultural variation in cognition and behaviour is merely a superficial overlay for differing group capabilities of self-control or mastery, which are themselves a reflection of material security or mastery' (p.169). Thus, they suggest, the social division of labour, the income differentials associated with that division, and the resulting differentials in access to health-related facilities and knowledge, all contibute to the observed class inequalities in health. Their recommendations are directed towards state policies that might loosen the links between the social division of labour, income differentials and access to facilities and knowledge (rather than those that might dissolve the social division of labour *per se*). They suggest increased public expenditure to compensate for social class inequalities. In relation to prevention and health education, they suggest that individual responsibility alone is an insufficient basis for action, and that various changes in the social and economic environment are required to facilitate such responsibility:

> Effective prevention requires not only individual initiative but also a real commitment by the DHSS and other government departments. Our analysis has shown the many ways in which people's behaviour is constrained by structural and environmental factors over which they have no control. Physical recreation, for example, is hardly possible in inner city areas unless steps are taken to ensure that facilities are provided. Similarly, government initiatives are required in relation to diet and to the consumption of alcohol. (Working Party, 1980; 364)

The government was less than enthusiastic about the Working Party's report, since it had committed itself to a prevention policy that rested upon the assumption that material conditions were now adequate for a healthy life for all. The Government's paper *Prevention and Health* had said:

> In the past, improvements in the health of the population derived largely from advances in environmental conditions and measures to control infectious disease. (Whereas) today, the greatest scope would seem to lie in seeking to modify attitudes and behaviour in relation to health. (DHSS et al., 1977; 10)

The responsible Minister, Patrick Jenkin, writing a foreword to the Working Party's report, virtually dismissed it, referring to its progress in analysing the data as 'disappointing'. He continued:

> It will be seen that the Group has reached the view that the causes of ill-health are so deep rooted that only a major and wide-ranging programme of public expenditure is capable of altering the pattern. I must make it clear that additional expendi-

ture on the scale which could result from the report's recommendations – the amount involved could be upwards of £2 billion a year – is quite unrealistic in present or forseeable economic circumstances, quite apart from any judgement that may be formed of the effectiveness of such expenditure in dealing with the problems identified. I cannot, therefore, endorse the group's recommendations. I am making the report available for discussion, but without any commitment by the Government to its proposals.

The manner of making the report available reflected the government's 'disappointment' with its contents: a small number were made available through the DHSS, in contrast to the usual practice of HMSO publications of a printed report. It seems clear that the Working Party's conclusions were rejected for political reasons. In the first place, the use of a neo-Marxian perspective must have seemed quite inappropriate to the incoming Conservative administration, committed as it was to methods for resuscitating the free market economy. This aspect of the Working Party's report appears to have been too unpalatable to merit mention in the Minister's forward. Secondly, there is the objection raised by the Minister – increases in state expenditure are incomparable with a retreat from Keynesian solutions to social and economic problems. Such retreat was by no means unique to the Conservative administration, but was also quite marked under Labour administrations. The 1976 consultative document on *Priorities for Health and Personal Social Services in England* took as its point of departure not the health needs of the population, but two problems outlined in the *Expenditure Paper* of the same year:

> The first has been with us for many years. Popular expectations for improved public services and welfare programmes have not been matched by the growth in output – or by willingness to forgo improvements in private living standards in favour of these programmes. The oil crisis intensified this gap between expectations and available resources. The second problem is that of cost inflation, which has become acute in the last few years, and has added an extra dimension of difficulty. (White Paper on Public Expenditure, 1976; 1)

As the House of Commons Expenditure Committee – set up to scrutinise public expenditure budgets and to devise means of making savings – said in their first report, *Preventive Medicine:* 'This enquiry was undertaken in response to concern at the high and increasing cost of the National Health Service, which absorbed 5.65% of the Gross Domestic Product in 1975, as opposed to 3.71% in 1959' (House of Commons Expnditure Committee, 1977; xv). Such considerations underlie the state's increasing interest in prevention as an alternative to public expenditure on curative services. An emphasis upon individuals' responsibility for maintaining their own health is compatible with the ideology of individualism that underpins commitment to the market economy and, within that context, legitimates curbs on health and welfare expenditure. As the foreword to the DHSS consultative document *Prevention and Health* put it:

> During the present period of economic restraint it is all the more essential that available resources are used to best effect, bearing in mind that not all preventive measures necessarily require additional, or massive resources. Much could be done by more effective deployment of existing staff and facilities; and much will depend on encouraging members of the public to make better use of the preventive services already available. We as a society are becoming increasingly aware of how much depends on the attitude and actions of the individuals about his health. (DHSS, 1976; 7)

It is within this context of attempts to reduce public expenditure and to 'encourage individual members of the public to accept a greater responsibility for their own health and that of their families' (DHSS et al, 1977; 3), that prevention has emerged as an important aspect of government policy. This political impetus provides the general conditions within which aforementioned developments within the health and welfare services – namely, their extension to deal with problems previously viewed as moral or disciplinary problems, such as intemperate drinking and juvenile naughtiness – come to the fore and help to shape the ideological form of prevention rhetoric. The more 'health' discourse is stretched to cover social practices, such as drinking, which carry historically-derived connotations of immoraltiy and indiscipline, the more it becomes infused with such connotations, and the more 'prevention' becomes a moral and disciplinary issue as well as a medical matter. This concept of prevention is well in tune with the ideology of individual responsibility and self-help that is deployed to legitimise curbs on health and welfare expenditure.

The process of emergence of prevention policy is summarised very schematically in diagram 3.1. Keynesian management of the mixed economy involved an expansion of health and welfare provision, which resulted in escalating public expenditure. Such management did not, however, abolish the material causes of ill health, nor did it dissolve the need for social control. In an attempt to cope with these problems, health and welfare services were further extended, and broadened to deal with a number of problems previously construed in terms of morality and social discipline, causing a requirement for more public expenditure. This then clashed with the state's retreat from Keynesian policies and its adoption of monetarist and self-help policies in response to falling capitalist profitability, the oil crisis, and the beginnings of recession. The consequence, within the arena of health and welfare policies, was an increasing emphasis upon prevention of ill-health by means of individual responsibility and self-restraint. In the following paragraphs, we look at how this emphasis became appropriated within health education.

Health Education about Alcoholism

Health education is the public presentation of prevention policy:

> It can contribute significantly to the public's understanding of ill-health and its prevention and of the value of adopting healthy living habits. (DHSS et al, 1977; 7)

Health education is undertaken within the National Health Service, in public propaganda and campaigns, and in the school systems, and the form it takes is influenced by the institutional and ideological conditions within these three arenas. For the health departments, 'Health education is one of the most important aspects of preventive medicine' (DHSS et al, 1977; 7), and this concept of health education is dominant in the NHS and in public propaganda. In 1964 a health services report recommended the setting up of a specialist profession of health educators within the NHS, and the strengthening of public propaganda about health, and these recom-

Diagram 3.1: Origins of 'Prevention' in Post-War Britain

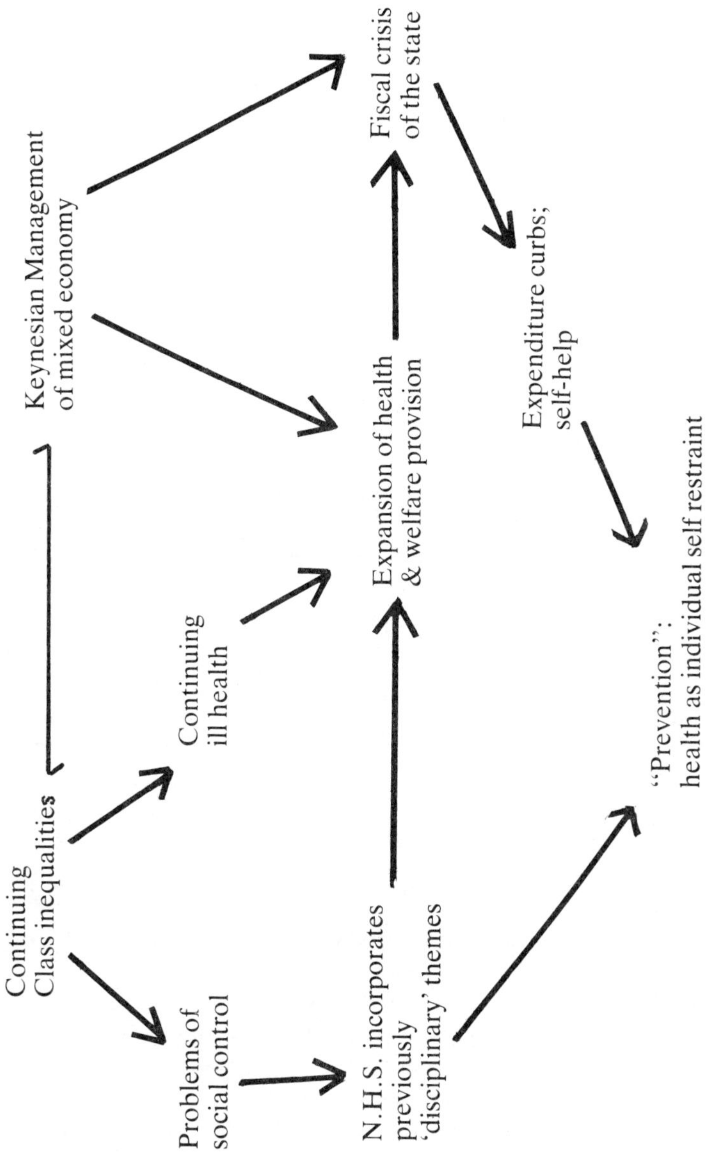

mendations were later taken up in the context of the state's growing commitment to prevention, resulting in the creation of a profession of Health Education Officers and in the Health Education Council and its Scottish counterpart.[10] The sort of health education activity favoured by these bodies is the public campaign, using cinema advertisements and regional television and press. Alcohol education campaigns, run in the north-east England and in Central Scotland, have revolved around the health services' concept of alcoholism. Evaluations of these campaigns suggest that they are not very successful.[11]

Much of alcohol eduation in schools is of a similar nature. As outlined in chapter 1 of this study, the historical origins of alcohol education in schools lie in nineteenth century appropriations of older themes concerned with the moral, political and wage discipline of the working class. Handbooks of health education, periodically issued by the Ministry of Education, concerned themselves principally with the moral and health dangers of insufficient self-discipline in relation to over-indulgence in food and drink, and with the necessity for restraint. Such education continued in a largely ad-hoc manner in secondary schools during the post-war period, receiving a boost from 1960's and 1970's moral panics about illegal drugs;[12] and being encouraged by temperance education organisations.[13] Temperance-inspired health education about alcohol and drugs did not, however, become a standard feature of the curriculum in most schools, nor of teacher training courses, and continued to be given or not according to the interests of individual teachers and headteachers. This is the context within which new ideas about alcoholism as a disease, generated within the health system, first began to be deployed, with consequences for the development of alcohol education. During the 1960s, Department of Education and Science Handbooks of Health Education, which had hitherto discussed youthful drinking mainly within the context of disciplinary and moral problems, also began to refer to the disease concept of alcoholism (D.E.S., 1968; 139). There was a considerable increase in the number of alcohol (and drug) education films, booklets, and other materials, designed for use in schools, but produced by health professionals and portraying drinking as an object within the discourse of preventive medicine.[14] Such health education about alcohol and alcoholism – sometimes referred to as the 'factual' approach (because it focusses upon medically-guaranteed knowledge) – continues to be given in schools. The past two decades have also, however, seen the ascendance of a rather different approach.

Affective Approaches in Health Education: the new orthodoxy

> Most teachers are by now aware of the tension between the 'preventive medicine' and 'personal development' models of health education. This is what a teacher said to me recently when I asked him what sort of health education he thought his pupils needed: 'Specifically in terms of relationships to start with (all-boy schools sometimes play down relationships) rather than the obvious areas such as smoking and personal hygiene'. These comments are typical of a general rejection of overtly 'medical' health education in favour of a more 'educational' model. It is often not realised that these two models share a common orientation – they both ask the same question 'What is wrong with you,' though (they differ in) attributing the pathology to faulty bodies or faulty socialisation respectively. (Jenks, 1979; 9)

The ways in which health education has developed over the latter part of the post-war period reflects broader political shifts in society, mediated through the institutions and ideologies of the health and education sections of the welfare state. The authors of *Unpopular Education* suggest that the 1960s were characterised by the ascendancy of a primarily social democratic political consensus, manifested in the educational sphere as alliance between the Labour Party, certain groups of intellectuals (including sociologists and economists of education), and the organised teaching profession (C.C.C.S., 1981; 63-99). Educational and welfare reports of the period were concerned with increasing educational opportunities for the working class, and with the control of those who, for whatever reasons, failed to take full advantage of these opportunities, or who persisted in behaviour which, although part of the lower working class culture and traditions, were 'socially unacceptable'. The reports were ambivalent over whether the labour market would in future demand new and specific work skills, less skills, or simply all-round intelligence, but

> Either way the reports foresaw that jobs might be boring and worried that 'responsibility might fall into irresponsible hands'

> where in large unskilled groups 'difficult problems of human relations' arose. This anxiety was linked to others about youth crime, youth spending and youth sexuality as part of the registration in the reports of a crisis of authority. They led onward to the demand that there should be a conscious effort, through education, to prepare both sexes for the family, if the family were to remain 'secure . . . and we can be content with nothing else' (Crowther Report). From here it was a matter of stages to Plowden's view that education involved 'the whole family'. In a savage passage Crowther complained that, for those not doing homework, and even despite some paid work for boys and some home help for girls, the gap between work and school hours was excessive. Many had 'too little to do' and their 'lack of ability and purpose' suggested that directed activities would be required outside school hours and terms. (C.C.C.S., 1981; 117)

It was in this context of concern to reconcile the objective of work and sex-role socialisation of working class children with social democratic commitment to increasing social equality and justice, that the concepts of child-centred teaching and social pathology came to the fore (Sharp & Green, 1975; 44-46). As the Birmingham workers put it,

> The main themes were youth and work, youth and school, but also youth and the family and youth and social services. By the time of the Plowden Report (1967) and the 1968 Seebolm Report on local authority services, the need was argued for co-ordination across all the social services, while attention broadened outwards to areas and to 'communities'. Where comprehensives had been pragmatically commended by Crowther for areas where they could 'act as a socially unifying force', Plowden proposed criteria for 'deprived areas' as such, in which schools needed extra support and where 'community schools' should first be tried out. Earlier, the reports had advised the state to take greater responsibility through schools for appropriate work training and for the sensitive handling of transitions from school to work and from youth to parenthood. Now whole districts were solicited by Seebolm as state clients. (C.C.C.S., 1981; 117)

These reports placed emphasis upon the reduction of deprivation and inequality by means of social work and educational methods stressing the reform of individual morality and of the 'whole cultural outlook' of the family. Plowden specifically dismissed socio-economic classes as 'heterogenous and artificial' (see C.C.C.S., 1981; 119). In contrast to the didactic tradition of education (as the means of teaching 'facts'), it laid stress upon the need to instill appropriate values and attitudes (Plowden report, para. 505, cited in Sharp & Green 1975; 45):

> A school is not merely a teaching shop, it must transmit values and attitudes. It is a community in which children learn and live first and foremost as children and not as future adults. In family life children learn to live with people of all ages. The school sets out deliberately to derive the right environment for children, to allow them to be themselves and to develop in the way and at the pace appropriate to them. It tries to equalise opportunities and compensate for handicaps. It lays special stress upon individual discovery, in first hand experience, and on opportunities for creative work. It insists that knowledge does not fall into neatly separate compartments and that work and play are not opposite but complementary.

The methods of child-centred education revolve around the concepts of 'readiness', 'choice', 'needs', 'play', and 'discovery' (Sharp & Green, 1975; 42). 'Briefly, it is believed that given an innovatory setting, when the child is 'ready', he will 'choose' what it is that he 'needs'. This selection is believed to be facilitated through 'play', which gets in train the 'discovery', or 'learning processes' (ibid). Such methods have been most taken up in the primary school system,[15] but have also had some influence in 'non-academic' parts of the secondary school curriculum, such as moral and health education.

> The idea providing the focus for these new directions in curriculum development is that of the 'individual' characteristics of child-centred, integrated curriculum. 'Myself', the central core of the Schools Council Health Education Project 5-13 (1977) illustrates how the self-image of the child is seen to be vital to the development of good health behaviour. John Wilson and the Farmington Trust's work (1967) on moral education makes a clear link between the 'healthy' and the 'moral' (1972) which is taken up by McPhail (1972) in the handbook to the Schools Council Moral Education Project, Living Well (1977). 'Lifeline'

> aims to develop the pupil's concept of a 'person' and modify the pupil's 'role supporting feelings' in situations of moral choice. The common basis of health and moral education re-affirms the nature of health education as a moral enterprise, emphasising, in the traditional manner, the qualities of 'responsible behaviour' and 'self-control'. (Jenks, 1978; 107-108)

These curriculum developments provide the circumstances in which the historical concerns of the state in relation to alcohol – concerns focussed around the possibility of breakdown in discipline of the working class in collective drinking situations – once again become articulated within health and social education. The rise of child-centred teaching dampened the enthusiasm of teachers and curriculum planners to present health education 'facts' that might not be directly relevant to pupils' existing experience and interests. This weakened the legitimacy, within the school system, of approaches to health education derived from the health services and from prevention policy, with the result that education about alcohol and alcoholism increasingly became described as educationally inadequate.[16] The individualistic framework of child-centred education was, however, quite compatible with the older, anti-collectivist concerns of temperance education. It is generally accepted, both by those working in the alcohol field and by those working in the school system, that there has been a recent shift away from 'factual' education about alcohol and alcoholism, towards a more overtly moral basis for eduation about alcohol (Williams & Brake, 1980, Jenks, 1978): 'alcohol education' *per se* has been joined by, and particularly displaced by, an emphasis upon the psychological characteristics and the emotions of the individual child. 'Affective education', as it is sometimes called, is concerned to help children to clarify their values, develop self-reliance, and hence come to mature decisions about their personal behaviour. This approach was advocated in the 1968 edition of the D.E.S. *Handbook of Health Education* which said that 'Health education should attempt to inform young people about the risks of misuse of both tobacco and alcohol and, *even more important,* should try to impart attitudes which allow young people to make *independent* decision and to *free them* from the necessity of always following their social groups' (DES, 1968; 138 emphasis added). The underlying concept is of the individual as a free agent; free and independent decisions are assumed to be the ones that lead to health; collective decision-making traditions (e.g. of the working class) must be replaced by education about individual choice. The rise of the effective approach to health education has resulted in the production of educational curricula in which the former warnings about alcohol abuse and its dangers are displaced by warnings of 'peer pressure' and the dangers of acceding to it. *The shift is from anti-drink, to anti-collective sentiments.*

The new approach underlies a number of recent curricula, in which information about drinking (and about other health-related social practices, such as sexual behaviour) is de-emphasised and is integrated into wider social, oral or health education courses that aim to develop individual decision-making. The model of the individual underlying child-centred health education is one that locates him or her not in relation to material conditions or to social classes or sexual divisions, but in relation to his or her own biography. Affective methods have introduced into health education a *developmental* dimension, and this dimension can be found in prevention programmes for maternal and child health before school age, as well as in the school:

> Prevention is interpreted not simply as a means of maintaining and improving the physical standards of child health at a time of economic stringency, but of protecting and fostering the child's future physical and emotional development. It is this orientation to development, particularly to social and emotional aspects of development, which gives preventive policies for children their distinctiveness – and their political potency. The developmental dimension is captured in recent writings in the concept of *child need.* This concept draws attention to those relationships and experiences which are seen as critical for the child's emergence as a socially competent adult. For example, Mia Pringle argues that children need relationships which are loving and secure, which give the child recognition and responsibility, and the opportunity for new experiences. Bound into her conception of children's needs (for love and security, recognition, responsibility and new experiences) is thus the identification of a set of relationships through which such needs are met. And this set of relationshups is provided by and through the family. Mia Pringle outlines the child's needs for love and security as follows . . .the centrality of the family comes across again when we move from a consideration

> of the aims of prevention to examine the strategies of prevention currently being proposed in the field of maternal and child health. For example, the proposals outlined in the Court Report for a child-centred service orientated to the 'special needs of children' hinge around a recognition of the significance – and ubiquity – of the family. (Graham, 1979;167-168)

Health education is, then, not simply concerned with teaching facts about alcohol and other 'topics' that might have reference to health. Its concern with socialisation and personal development of the individual in the context of family life provides a developmental dimension to health education that is lacking in alcohol education (whether of the temperance or the preventive medicine inclination). Recent developments in health education, and in particular the development of integrated health education curricula into which both alcohol and sex education are integrated, draw heavily upon the developmental framework fostered within child-centred education. Typical is the Schools Council Health Education Council Project, which deploys its emphasis upon individual responsibility and self-discipline in the context of the child's development within the family and other small groups. The project talks of 'health careers' as produced by decisions that pupils make in response to two sets of influence: their own 'image' of their internal 'essence' of self, and pressures which other people bring to bear upon them. The aim is to help the individual to develop the self to its full potential, so that it is strong enough to override the outside influences. This, the project considers, is something that has to be begun early in the child's life, before attitudes and self-image 'harden up' in patterns that leave the teenager dependent upon peers and/or upon alcohol for his/her sense of self. The project put it this way in the teachers' guide *Think Well:*

> The rationale of the project is based upon a belief that the health behaviour of individuals – be it related to eating, cigarette smoking or any other behaviour likely to influence one's health – is likely to have a history of development. Shakespeare's *Seven Ages of Man* should not be viewed as separate periods of time isolated from their predecessors but rather, as interconnected labyrinths of knowledge, values, beliefs, attitudes, expectations and experiences. Each age exerts a compelling influence upon its successor by the development and shaping of attitudes and

> knowledge. Thus, long before individuals become, for example, habitual smokers, there is a period during which attitudes, knowledge and values related to smoking are being formed. Research in several areas of health behaviour confirms that attitudes, values and knowledge *which help determine the way in which we behave* are forming at fairly early points in childhood and that attitudes in particular *begin to harden* in adolescence. It seems *reasonable,* then, to want to help children work out what choices are open to them – in terms of health-related behaviour – when their attitudes are beginning to form rather than *when they are hardening or have already hardened.* (SCHEP 5-13, 1977, *Introduction and Planning Booklet,* p.2, emphasis added)

The project refers repeatedly to the 'hardening' of attitudes during adolescence:

> In many instances, children's attitudes to the use of tobacco and alcohol are already beginning to *harden* during their middle school years. *It seems reasonable* to assume, then, that this is the best time to help children look at what they know and feel about these matters. (SCHEP 5-13 *Deadly Decisions* Booklet, p.1.)

How 'reasonable' the project's affective approach is depends upon the extent to which the project's view of the relation of the development of individuals to the broader society is an accurate one. The project relates the development of children to other parts of society in the following way:

> The attitudes which children develop are fostered by the social influences upon them. These come through families (sometimes unwittingly), through peer groups, advertising and by identification with their chosen idols in the world of sport or entertainment.

This view of child development and social behaviour as a matter of the attitudes of individuals and of the 'social influences' upon them is also the view that has underpinned most research into youthful drinking (as we show in chapter 4). The unspoken assumption is that society is held together by, and social behaviour and health determined by, the shared values and moralities of individuals; improvements in health therefore hinge on improvement in individual morals. Material conditions such as environmental, economic and working conditions are outside the frame of the picture of the social world held up by health education, as are collective responses to those conditions. In the following section some empirical evidence of the inadequacy of such approaches to health education is presented.

Evaluating Health Education About Drinking

The term evaluation is used in many ways in social and educational research. Dennis Lawton has suggested that the various approaches to evaluation of eduational curricula of programmes can be categorised under five headings (Lawton, 1980; 111). These are (a) the classical experimental design model, using experimental and control groups of pupils, and focussing upon the 'average' response of the pupils; (b) the research and development model, similar to the classical approach, but laying more emphasis upon the clarification of goals before the education begins; (c) illuminative evaluation, in which the evaluator seeks to use qualitative methods to explore the ways in which the education is produced within the school and selectively appropriated by the pupils; (d) democratic evaluation, which is concerned to provide non-technical feedback on the balance of power in education to all those involved in it; (e) evaluation based on the teacher's perspective on the teaching he or she gave; and (f) eclectic evaluation, which uses a mix of methods to produce a rounded case study of education. Additionally, attention has recently been drawn to the ways in which small groups such as families and friends may play an important part in the process whereby individuals form or change beliefs (McCron & Budd, 1979; 207). Lastly, there is the broader task of contextualising educational curricula and programmes within the historical, structural and institutional conditions in which they arise, and characterising the theoretical assumptions that underpin those approaches that become dominant – as has been attempted in the present study (in chapter 1 and above). The relations between these various types of evaluation methodology have not yet been established in the social sciences.

Within the arena of health education research, it is the experimental design approach that generally has been regarded as most appropriate (Gatherer et al, 1979). This is probably partly due to the individualistic and empiricist nature of post-war Anglo-American social science, and partly to the fact that this approach is consonant with health education methods that conceptualise teaching as having effects that crystallize at the level of individuals. As McCron says in a Health Education Council evaluation working group document, 'the dominant strand in health education in Britain has developed as a specialisation with an individualistic orientation – a prime assumption being that whatever its methodology, its focus is in informing, persuading, propagandizing, individual people' (McCron, 1980;2), the expectation being that this will result in changes in social behaviour. Evaluation researchers working in the field of health education related to drinking have generally accepted this orientation, and have regarded a comparison of those normative and/or behavioural statements made by pupils polled as individuals before teaching, with those made afterwards, as providing an appropriate methodology for assessment or comparison of health education strategies. In answer to the question 'does the teaching work', evaluators have sought evidence of a decrease in the frequency of drinking occasions or in the number of drinks consumed or, failing that, attitudinal changes consistent with such a decrease. Such evidence would be taken as an indication that, whatever theoretical difficulties might surround the education, these were not so great as to impair its practical value. If, on the other hand, it can be shown that, despite a considerable number of evaluation studies, evidence of the expected outcomes is lacking, then this would call into doubt not only this or that specific curriculum or programme, but the underlying strategy and theoretical assumptions shared by apparently disparate approaches, and would strengthen the case for a fundamental re-orientation of health education. It is from this perspective that the following paragraphs consider the findings of evaluation studies of health education related to drinking.

Studies which aim to evaluate the effects of health education on the alcohol-related behaviour of individuals have been most common in the United States, though there have also been a small number of such studies in other countries. In the United States, the relatively restrictive controls on youthful drinking (compared with the UK) and the relatively widespread use of marijuana and other illegal drugs creates a situation in which many youthful users of alcohol are also users of other drugs. This being the case, alcohol is quite often conceptualised as a drug, and no distinction made between health education relevant to drinking and that relevant to drug use. This is reflected in evaluation studies of health education, which frequently aim to assess the efficacy of teaching in terms of its effects on individuals' self-reported sentiments about and use of alcohol and other drugs. A recent and extensive review of such evaluation studies has recently been published by Schaps and his collaborators. Their review is based upon work done under contract to the Department of Health, Eduation and Welfare (Schaps et al, 1978), and revised for publication in 1981 (Schaps et al, 1981). The range of health education programmes included in the review was wide, including the 'traditional' approach of providing information about effects of legal and illegal intoxicants and/or trying to persuade children not to use them; through 'mixed' approaches which united information and persuasion with the 'new' strategies of affective education (and sometimes counselling), approximating quite closely to some UK approaches such as that of the Schools Council Health Education Project (noted above); to purely affective and/or counselling approaches without any specific information or persuasion about intoxicants and their effects. Table 3.1 below (taken from table 13 of Schaps et al) indicates the numbers of each type of educational programme included in the review and it can be seen that just under half the programmes evaluated were of the 'traditional' type, whilst just over half were 'new' in that they either combined affective and similar strategies with information/persuasion, or used affective or similar approaches without making explicit reference to 'facts' about alcohol and other intoxicants. The methodology of the evaluations varied widely, rarely approaching the criteria required in true experimental-design research. Only 40 per cent of the studies employed a control or comparison group of acceptable composition (Schaps et al, 1981;30), and many studies suffered from other methodological faults, leaving only 20 per cent having what the reviewers described as 'strong research designs' (ibid;20). Additionally, only half the studies utilised questions about drug or alcohol use, as opposed to pupils' reported attitudes towards or intentions to use alcohol and/or other drugs: this is a significant research weakness since changes in reported knowledge, attitudes or intentions cannot be taken as predictive of changes in behaviour. Furthermore, half of the education programmes studies were weak in 'programme intensity', where this is defined in terms of length of time over which the education continued and in terms of the scope of issues addressed in the programme: just under a quarter of the programmes involved education of high intensity. Generally speaking, it was those programmes that were of brief duration and limited scope that were evaluated in a more rigorous manner, it

Table 3.1: Health Educational Strategies Evaluated by Schaps et al.

Types of Strategies	Number of Programmes
1. 'Traditional': information and/or persuasion	56
2. 'Mixed'	
Information/persuasion and affective	15
Information/persuasion, affective and counselling	7
3. Without explicit information/persuasion component	
Affective only	24
Counselling only	4
Affective and counselling	9
4. Other combinations	12
Total number of programmes reviewed	127

Table 3.2: Apparent Outcomes of 127 Health Education Programmes, regardless of variations in programme intensity and research vigour

Types of educational strategy	Preventive indication	No Change	Counter-preventive	Number of Programmes
1. 'Traditional': information and/or persuasion	25	25	9	56
2.1 'Mixed' strategies including information/ persuasion and affective/counselling	12	10	0	22
3. Affective/ counselling *without* information/persuasion component	16	19	0	37
4. Other	4	7	1	12

Table 3.3: Behavioural outcomes of those 10 programmes of high intensity which were rigorously evaluated

	Alcohol/drug use:-			
	Decrease	No Change	Increase	not measured
1. 'Traditional'	–	–	–	1
2. 'Mixed'	–	1	–	2
3. Affective & other programmes without information	2	1	–	3

being easier to achieve methodological purity in studies of brief educational interventions that approximate to laboratory-type experiments than in larger and more complicated field research situations. This means that the more rigorously evaluated programmes included in the review are not necessarily a good guide to the potential of extended health education programmes in schools – as Schaps et al put it (p.31), 'Much of the better research was focussed upon many of the less deserving programmes'. The review would have to be restricted to that relatively small number of programmes of long duration and wide scope that were rigorously evaluated for its conclusions to be of practical interest. Lastly there is the possibility, given the level of fiscal and political investment in health education about alcohol and drugs, that evidence of 'negative' outcomes may not have been published. There may have been cases of 'suppression of evaluation reports which show highly adverse outcomes, such that these reports are simply not available; (and) selective reporting or programme outcomes in available reports, such that negative findings are suppressed whilst positive findings are given prominence' (Schaps et al, 1981;33). If all of these problems are ignored, and if the findings of all the studies are aggregated together regardless of methodological rigour and programme intensity, then their conclusions are quite encouraging for those who wish to advance some variety of health education for individual change: relatively few of the programmes studied had counter-productive effects, and about half had 'preventive' effects (see table 3.2). If, however, the review is restricted to those studies in which both evaluation methodology and programme intensity were reasonably high, then the picture is distinctly less encouraging:

> Of the 127 evaluations, only 10 met both of these criteria. Eight of the ten studies produced positive drug-specific outcome ratings. One showed no effect, and one showed a negative effect on attitudes toward drug use. This pattern of findings is encouraging, especially in light of the fact that the only program showing a negative drug-specific impact was the single information type in the group. The remaining nine programs were comprised of Affective or Peer strategies alone or in combination with other strategies, and eight of these nine produced positive drug-specific effects. It should be noted, however, that six of these studies only showed positive impact on attitudes toward drugs, and that attitude change does not necessarily result in behaviour change. Only four of the ten studies employed measures of drug use behaviors, and only two of these showed positive impact upon such behaviors. (Schaps et al, 1981;39)

It is not possible, on the basis of two evaluation studies, to make unequivocal statements about the success or otherwise of current health education approaches. The two programmes that may have resulted in a decrease in alcohol or drug use were both of the purely affective type without any alcohol/drug information – i.e. were not the same as the 'mixed' approaches to health education most common in the British school system (e.g. Schools Council Health Education Project). It would however be hazardous to generalise from two American studies to other affective health education curricula. Whilst it is true that there is no available evidence that such approaches have the effect of increasing alcohol and/or drug use, the absence of measures of such outcomes in the case of six out of ten of the evaluations means that such outcomes cannot be ruled out (see table 3.3). The total of two studies in which some reduction in alcohol and/or drug use might reasonably be claimed shrinks further in significance when the possibility of suppression of less encouraging evaluation studies is considered. One certainly could not claim, on the basis of this evidence, that any of the various forms of individualistic health education evaluated in the studies reviewed can be regarded as proven – and Schaps et al do not attempt to do so. The findings of the relatively small number of European evaluation studies are consistent with the American data. Those studies which have employed rigorous experimental-design methodologies to determine the outcome of a variety of health education strategies have failed to generate evidence of any reduction in youthful alcohol consumption (De Haes & Schurrman, 1975, Dorn et al, 1977). The conclusion is supported by a recent New Zealand study that attempted to improve on European approaches (Caswell, personal communication). These studies promote the general conclusion that, despite considerable effort, health education in its various current forms has failed to demonstrate evidence that it can affect youthful drinking in the manner intended by its designers.

The failure of evaluation research to generate a consistent body of evidence that health education, as currently conceptualised and practiced, produces the expected changes in individuals' drinking behaviour, is not very surprising when viewed against the background of post-war developments in communications theory. As Budd and McCron have pointed out, the individualist 'effects' model of communication has largely been abandoned in other fields:

> It came to be realised soon after the second world war that the simple 'effects' model, in which simple exposure to a message resulted in compliant behaviour . . . could not be replicated in the real world . . . This simple persuasive campaign model has now been replaced by a more socially orientated approach in which the mass media are viewed as one of many potential sources of information in society which cannot be discussed in isolation from personal information sources – families, friends and so on – which may support or may contradict the media messages. The audience are now regarded as active participants in the communication exchange process, who bring their own sets of beliefs and attitudes, previous experiences and knowledge to the scene of transaction, choosing which information they wish to receive and how they wish to interpret it. (Budd & McCron, 1981;35-6)

These authors note that, despite the general abandonment of the individualistic effects model of communication, 'its abandonment by health educators does not, unfortunately, appear to have been so rapid or so complete' (ibid). In one sense this judgement may be regarded as too sweeping, since many of the affective health education programmes – e.g. the School Council Projects – do clearly conceptualise the individual pupil as a member of primary social groups such as peer-groups and the family. It is also the case, however, that currently dominated health education approaches do retain a conception of the individual as the primary social unit – as indeed do Budd and McCron – and that material conditions and social class and sexual divisions, and the ways in which social groups are located within and respond to those conditions, are simply ignored within health education.

Conclusion

Historically, health education about alcohol developed as a means of inculcating self-discipline in the individual. During the post-war period, alcoholism became defined as a disease, and drinking problems became redefined in medical as well as moral terms. The retreat from Keynesian policies involved an increasing emphasis on self-help and individual responsibility for health, this being manifested in an ideology of 'prevention'. Within the educational system, the impact of prevention policies was mediated by the post-war advances of child-centred, developmental teaching methods, particularly in the areas of health and personal relationships education, resulting in affective education about development of the individual, within which the historical concerns of temperance education find a place. A review of the empirical evidence bearing upon the efficacy of such education suggests that convincing evidence of its ability to reduce levels of youthful drinking is so far lacking.

It is striking that these existing alcohol education programmes and their evaluators do not address the issue of the qualitative *forms* taken by drinking practices. This lacuna may be explained by the historically-derived and now pervasive assumption that *all* youthful drinking takes *one and the same* form – a breakdown of social controls and personal discipline – and that this is so 'obvious' that quantification on the basis of amount drunk presents no problems. The failure to raise the question of the forms taken by youthful drinking practices may also be related to a reluctance, on the part of social welfare institutions such as health and educational agencies, to recognise that the forms of such practices may vary from group to group, reflecting more general social, cultural and even economic divisions: post-war social welfare policy has rested upon the assumption of a consensus of interests and a lack of such divisions.

Part I of this study, now concluded, has concerned itself with the historical process of construction of the 'common-sense' conception of youthful drinking – as a form of breakdown in personal and social disciplines – that underlies mainstream health and social education touching upon alcohol, and that also underlies the current 'moral panic' about youthful drinking (see Introduction). Part II will concern itself with the question of the forms that youthful drinking practices actually take in contemporary English society. This investigation begins with a review of existing research into youthful drinking (most of which conceptualises drinking purely quantitatively, and fails to problematise its social form), and with a discussion of the potential contribution of research conducted from the perspective of the sociologies of delinquency and youth culture. This sets the parameters for an 'area case study' which examines the labour market confronting school-leavers in an inner London borough, the management of school-leavers by the school, and the social form taken by the drinking practices of one group of youth in transition from school to labour market. There is a discontinuity between parts I and II insofar as Part I deals with history and social reaction, whilst part II deals with contemporary school behaviour of working class youth. There is also a continuity between the two parts insofar as the historical development of the economy, of social classes and of state institutions and policies, discussed in part I, provides the background to contemporary conditions facing youth.

PART II

YOUTHFUL DRINKING PRACTICES – THEORY AND ETHNOGRAPHY

4 DRINK AND SOCIAL RESEARCH: REVIEW OF THE ALCOHOL PROBLEMS LITERATURE, AND DEVELOPMENT OF AN ALTERNATIVE METHODOLOGY

The purpose of this chapter is to review the social science literature on youthful drinking, to identify some of its problems, and to construct a methodology for conducting a study that is free from such problems. The main problem in the mainstream of the alcohol literature is a tendency to focus upon the moral beliefs and predispositions of individuals; shared cultures, when considered, are generally conceptualised in terms of collective mores unrelated to social class and sexual divisions. Some of the sociological studies of youth culture overcome these problems, and recent studies have touched upon drinking practices as one aspect of a wider investigation of youth cultures. These studies have however focussed almost exclusively upon the cultures of 'delinquent' working class boys, discussing drinking within this context; and their conceptualisation of the relation between sexual divisions and youth cultures is generally unsatisfactory. The present chapter discusses the advances and continuing problems represented in these studies, and tried to develop a more adequate 'area case study' methodology that relates youth cultures and drinking therein to sexual divisions as well as to social class. The next chapter then applies this methodology in an empirical study of the circumstances, culture and drinking of boys and girls from the central strata of the working class.

The Social Production of Alcohol Problems Research

It is beyond the scope of this study to review the whole social science literature on alcohol problems. The literature is vast in terms of its quantity: there are approximately 20,000 abstracts of published articled in the Classified Abstracts Archive of Alcohol Literature (CAAAL), which was maintained by the Centre of Alcohol Studies at Rutgers University up to 1978.[1] The Centre's current Alcohol Information Retrieval System, which Rutgers run in association with Control Data Corporation, has a monthly input of 200 abstracts and 400 other publications from the world literature: the literature is, therefore, being added to at the rate of over 7,000 items per annum. Many of these are, of course, slightly differing reports on the same work; and most reported studies are similar in general scope, methods and perspectives to work previously reported by the same authors, or by others. More important than an exhaustive compilation of the findings of this literature, therefore, is an attempt to report is main characteristics systematically and according to the theoretical and methodological assumptions underlying it.

Social research is carried out in society rather than in a social vacuum, and an understanding of any field of social research therefore requires an appreciation of the social conditions in which it was produced, and of the ways in which those conditions tend to structure the resulting knowledge.[2] In the longer-term historical sense, the social conditions that lead up to contemporary alcohol-related research are the same as those that produced the state's policies on public drinking, discussed in the preceding chapters. This history has facilitated the development of social and economic sciences in which a distinction is made between the spheres of production and consumption (see discussion of Mill in chapter 2), and 'social problems' are conceptualised as arising in the latter sphere. The work of Emile Durkheim has been especially influential in the sociological study of 'social problems' generally, and of 'alcohol problems' in particular.

> The distinguishing characteristics of the Durkheimian system can best be discerned by a comparison between it and the corresponding Marxian work on historical materialism. Durkheim and Marx had certain important traits in common. They shared a materialistic, scientific orientation. The discourse of each started from liberal economics and from the conflicts and crises of a capitalist society confronted with the 'Question of the Workers'. (Therborn, 1976;250-1)

Both Durkheim and Marx were concerned with the ways in which the 'individual person' arises out of definitive historical and social circumstances, rather than being a universal and trans-historical type; with the ways in which social life is underpinned by structures that often escape observation and consciousness; and with the ways in which shared consciousness and cultures (or ideology) derive not simply from manipulation by elites, but from the objective nature of society. These concerns, shared by Durkheim and Marx, were however answered by them in different ways corresponding to the ways in which they sought to answer 'the conflicts and crises of a capitalist society confronted with the "Question of the Workers"'. For Marx the answer was that the material basis of capitalist society, its mode of production and the distribution of the means of production, necessarily produce immiseration and injustices that no amount of social reforming could correct. For Durkheim, on the other hand, and for the broad tradition of western sociology, society is underpinned not by the economy, but by social forms (beliefs, custom, ideologies, etc) which act as the container or framework within which the economy works; believing that the mainstpring of social action was social (non-economic), Durkheim believed that social problems could (and indeed must) be defined and solved in purely social terms. He was critical, not of the capitalist economy as such, but of the notion, inherent in liberal economics, that capitalist society could be held together by an ethic of egoistic individualism in which each individual preserved his or her own self-interest. A moral community – or, as Therborn calls it, an ideological community – was necessary to guarantee social order and to complement (or mitigate the effects of) the economy (Therborn, 1976, chapter 5) and 'social problems' tackled on the level of moral rather than economic reform.[3] Sociology has indeed been closely tied up, throughout the nineteenth and twentieth centuries, with ideologies and practices of moral and religious reform movements, generally focussing upon the working classes. The question has been, what *is* the moral or ideologial community that guarantees the social (and here also the economic) order; in what ways are working class men, women and/or children not fully bound up in this community; and how can the situation be rectified by state and/or voluntary intervention? This, broadly, is the historical origin of the social research into alcohol problems and youthful drinking reviewed in the first half of this chapter.

Having described the general theoretical tendency of the alcohol problems literature in terms of its historical origins, it is important to periodise this literature within the broader history. The period in which the bulk of social science research on youthful drinking was published was not coterminous with any period of moral panic over youth, drink and indiscipline. The bulk of the existing literature on youthful drinking was produced in the decades following the second world war, that is to say, *after* the nineteenth and early twentieth century periods in which young people were excluded from the public house on the grounds that it was a sphere of social and moral indiscipline, but *before* the disciplinary moral panics of the 1970s. Most published research on youthful drinking practices, then, does not concern itself particularly with the *explicitly* disciplinary concerns voiced in the current moral panic, but applies itself to the task of explaining drinking practices as the result of individuals taking on, or failing to take on, consensual beliefs about self, alcohol and/or society. This chapter reviews some landmark studies in the development of such research in the USA and in Britain.

It should be recognised, in anticipation of the latter part of the chapter, that exclusively 'moral' approaches to the analysis of social problems generally, and alcohol problems specifically, have not gone competely unchallenged. Changing social and economic conditions in the post-war period have, as noted in the Introduction, provided a spur to the development of materialist approaches in the social sciences. These take as their point of departure not the presumed existence or need for a moral consensus, but material (e.g. environmental, biological, economic) conditions, and the social differences and divisions which these stimulate. The historical origins and the main characteristics of these approaches are discussed in the Annexe. In this, two types of materialist approach are distinguished. First, according to mechanistic types of materialism, material conditions directly determine social thoughts and action. Such approaches can be found in the alcohol field in the form of the distribution of consumption model of alcohol problems, according to which material factors such as cost and availability of alcohol impinge in the same manner upon all persons regardless of their social positions and their culture. In the social sciences, however, such crude and mechanistic accounts of social behaviour have been largely displaced by more sophisticated materialist approaches which acknowledge the importance of moral sentiments as a mediating link between material conditions and social action. According to these approaches moral sentiments are neither independent of material conditions nor determined by them. Rather, sentiments are actively constructed by social groups within the context of, and as a collective response to, the material conditions (biological, economic, etc) in which they find themselves, giving rise to shared cultures, which provide the framework for and social meaning of drinking. The specification of the relevant material conditions can hardly be restricted to the question of the availability of alcohol, nor to any other 'factor'; it is essential to consider the structure of social class and sexual division as these provide the general framework within which cultures, sentiments, and practices are constructed. We now move, by way of a discussion of the contributions of the mainstream of social science research on alcohol problems, to an exposition and application of this materialist approach to understanding drinking practices in teenage cultures.

Teenage Drinking as Learnt Behaviour

A US National Institute of Alcohol Abuse and Alcoholism review of the literature on alcohol and youth remarks of the currently dominant theories of youthful drinking:

> In terms of substance, all these theories view drinking (1) as a learnt behaviour, (2) with parents as the major source for learning, (3) which provides, among other things, a means for coping with frustration, stress or conflict. In addition, (4) all theories appear as incomplete explanations of drinking, (5) none is supported by a cumulative body of reasonably consistent findings, and (6) none is supported or refuted by the results of fairly well-controlled experiments. (Blane & Hewitt, 1977, XI; 40-41)

Within this general framework of explanation of youthful drinking, some theorists have viewed learning to drink as a normal part of socialisation into adult society, whilst others have conceptualised youthful drinking as the result of problems arising in that process of socialisation. An advocate of the former approach is the American researcher G. Madox:

> The teenage drinker . . . does not invent the idea of drinking; he learns it. He learns it from both parents and peers, and in the typical case, in that order . . . teenage drinking appears to be most adequately understood as a social act, as a mechanism of identification by which most teenagers' attempts to relate themselves, however, prematurely, to the adult world. (Maddox, 1962; 234)

This social learning approach (sometimes referred to as the 'anticipatory socialisation' approach) presumes a culture in which drinking is the adult norm. This approach, whilst it offers a welcome corrective to the notion that youthful drinking is necessarily a result of social indiscipline, does not take us very far in understanding the social basis of drinking in any given society. Why should any particular drinking norm arise in a society? David Pittman has suggested four categories of norm or attitude towards drinking, arising in abstinent, ambivalent, permissive and over-permissive cultures, respectively (Pittman, 1967;3, O'Connor, 1978;5-6). Such a categorisation does not take us much further, however, in understanding the social origins of such norms. The idea of the 'ambivalent' culture has been applied, particularly to the United Stages (Ullman, 1958;50), and to the Irish in England (O'Connor, 1978). As Robin Room, however, has pointed out, an adoption of the idea of cultural ambivalence over drinking norms leads us in the direction of adoption of a conflict model of society (Room, 1976), and this disrupts the assumptions of social homogeneity that researchers such as Maddox make. The same problem arises in relation to the cross-cultural studies of drinking in 'primitive' societies. David Stull (1975) has reviewed the literature on the types of social norm that have been linked with heavy drinking: the original hypothesis that levels of anxiety in a culture correlate with levels of drunkenness (Horton, 1943); Klausner's (1964) contrary argument that anxiety is linked with sobriety; Bacon, Barry and Child's (1965) suggestion that drunkenness is linked with failure to indulge childhood dependency needs; Davis' (1964) suggestion of a link between psychic conflict over dependency needs, and drunkenness; McClelland et al's (1972) explanation of male drinking in terms of the need for a sense of power; Schaefer's (1973) suggestion of a link between supernatural beliefs about fearsome spirits and drunkenness. All of these studies rest, as Stull (1975;5) has pointed out, upon the assumption that 'primitive' societies are homogeneous (i.e. that they have one unified belief system that confronts all members); this assumption is in line with Durkheim's assumption that 'primitive' societies have an undeveloped division of labour. Whatever the merits of an assumption of economic, cultural and moral homogeneity in primitive societies,[4] however, such an assumption is not warranted in relation to contemporary capitalist societies, and so any explanation of teenage drinking that seeks to explain it in terms of socialisation into an undifferentiated adult culture or morality must be rejected.

Other researchers have attempted to conceptualise youthful

drinking within the context of a differentiated economic and social structure. In the work of Jessor, for example, three linked social systems are described – society, family, and personality – and teenage drinking is explained as resulting from strains within each of these systems (Jessor & Jessor, 1977, Jessor et al., 1968). His theory draws upon Durkheim, insofar as it suggests that the lack of a strong normative order leads to 'anomie' and to deviant behaviour, and upon Merton, whose theory of deviancy rests on the assumption that deviancy occurs when the available social strcuture does not provide sufficient opportunities for satisfaction of the wants and needs that it encourages (i.e. there are inadequate means to desired mends).[5] Jessor and his co-workers describe three linked 'systems': the sociocultural system ('society'), the personality system (the individual), and the socialisation system (roughly equivalent to the family).[6] Each system consists of an opportunity or reward/punishment system, a normative system of social or personal beliefs, and a control system. When several factors coincide (e.g. when the sociocultural opportunity system is blocked, when the personality normative system is weak and underdeveloped, when social control is low) then social deviancy becomes more likely. Jessor found, from his research, that sociocultural and personality factors together predict social deviancy better than only one factor does; and that these variables are more strongly linked to a composite measure of deviancy than to any single behaviour, such as drinking. In his later research, he renamed the socialiation system the 'perceived environment system', laying stress on the child's perception of parental and peer attitudes to drinking.

With its stress on blocked opportunity structures, lack of strong normative structures, and breakdown in social and personal controls on drinking behaviour, the work of Jessor and his collaborators is evidently designed to describe the appearance of youthful drinking as a form of social deviance – as something resulting from things going wrong. This approach is not entirely comparable with the approach of those who, like Maddox, suggest that youthful drinking is an aspect of integration into the haven of adult society – i.e. as resulting from things going well. As Blane and Hewitt say of the work of Jessor and his co-workers: 'Although the view that such behaviour as alcohol consumption, marijunana use (in the USA), and sexual intercourse serve to define important changes in the transition between childhood and adulthood is seen as valid, the authors are interested in explaining the differential appearance of such behaviour in socio-psychological terms' (Blane & Hewitt, 1977; XI, 8). Such concerns seem explicable in terms of the view that, whilst childhood and adulthood are 'normal' states governed by established and stable systems of norms, transitions from one to the other is necessarily problematic since the systems of norms differ: adolescence is thus necessarily a form of deviancy, to be described in terms of theories of deviancy (lack of norms, blocked opportunities, inadequate constraints, etc).[7]

In a recent study of parents and teenagers from three social groups – English in England, Irish in Ireland and Irish in England – O'Connor has attempted to combine a study of drinking in different cultures with a study of development of adolescent drinking norms and practices. Her study is somewhat light on theory, and heavy on statistics, but a close reading of it suggests that it is more in the tradition of Maddox than Jessor, since she conceptualises teenage drinking as part of the taking-on of norms and practices prevalent in adult culture, but does not characerise this taking-on as a deviant process. Following a literature review, the theoretical basis of the study is indicated thus:

> To study the relative influences (on youthful drinking) the research design provided for a detailed description of drinking behaviour and attitudes and a comparative study of (1) parents and children and (2) young people differing in country of origin and parental ethnic background.
>
> Three groups of young people – aged 18-21 years, were chosen to be studied. This age group is of particular relevance in understanding the emergence of patterns of drinking, because it is at this age, the transition stage, that the roles of childhood are replaced with those of adulthood. The precise definition of this transition stage is neither possible nor relevant. (O'Connor, 1978; 21)

O'Connor adopts a model wherein social behaviour results from 'influences' upon individuals, disregarding any question about how teenagers may be conceptualised in relation to social structure. Four types of influence are posited – ethnic and cultural, parental, peer, social and personal – and answers to interview questions in each of these areas are fed into a statistical analysis to see which of these 'variables' best predicts reported drinking behaviour. Her main findings are summarised thus (p.159):

> The four most powerful variables to emerge from the detailed analysis undertaken in the chapter were sex status, peer group support for drinking, (children's perception of) father's attitude to mixing drinks and drinking three or more drinks on one occasion, and ethnic status. This analysis illustrated how culture, parents and peers interact in influencing a young person's drinking behaviour.

The results of this investigation clearly bring out the inadequacy of its theoretical framework. O'Connor found that gender was the biggest influence on drinking, males being more liekoy to be heavier drinkers. Next most important 'influence' was peer group support for drinking, as reported by the respondent. This finding does not, however, demonstrate that it is peer norms that cause drinking behaviour – the opposite possibility (that heavier drinking groups or individuals are more likely to generate or report social support for their practice) is just as likely. The fact that it was children's perceptions of their father's attitudes, rather than the father's attitudes as reported by them that was most closely related to the drinking behaviour of children (O'Connor, 1978;160) also calls into question the model of normative influences on the individual. Ethnic status, O'Connor reports, influences fathers' attitude, rather than having a direct effect on youthful drinking – 'Though influential, (it) has not sufficient effect to be counted on its own as an explanatory variable in the study of drinking behaviour' (p.161). Thus, out of all the variables – ethnic and cultural, parental, peer, social and personal – thrown into the statistical analysis, only one variable is strongly associated in a way that is clearly causal. Only in the case of gender do we have a factor that is strongly correlated with drinking and yet cannot be a consequence of that social behaviour. Yet, being male or female is a material fact that cannot be reduced to the status of a 'normative influence'. Since O'Connor's study stands upon a theory that does not relate material circumstances (such as biological) sex to social norms (such as those arising around sexual divisions in society), her study fails to make sense of its main empirical findings.

The work of Jessor, O'Connor and others shows how the use, within a broadly Durkheimian theoretical framework, of methods of investigation that organise 'data' in the form of individuals' statements about attitudes, norms and behaviour, leads away from a consideration of cultural norms as such, and towards a social psychology of influences upon the individual. This approach can be found in a very explicit form in the well known Scottish work of Davies and Stacey. Their research leads them to suggest (1972; xvi) that:

> Whilst an informational approach can be beneficial in providing young people with knowledge about the possible benefits and dangers of alcohol use, the results from the present study suggest that group pressures have a major part to play in the instruction of adolescent drinking. An approach which is purely informational, and which does not attempt to deal with group dynamics, probably neglects a very important area.

In this statement about health education, two possibilities are offered – a purely informational approach, or one that also attends to social factors. The latter, however, are defined primarily in terms of personal beliefs about self, and openness to peer pressure. In particular, Davies and Stacey suggest – on the basis of comparisons of young people's statements about their perceptions (a) of self, (b) of ideal-self, (c) of people who drink heavily and (d) not at all – that young people drink in order to feel that they correspond to their ideal-self. On the basis of this interpretation of their data, they then deduce that 'peer pressure' (i.e. what *other* young people might think or say about the person) is a 'very strong influence':

> Compared with the 'ideal self', the heavy drinking teenager seems to be *too* tough, and insufficiently sociable. The non-drinking teenager, on the other hand, *fails to score highly enough* on both the toughness and sociability factors. Since the majority of young people drink, it follows that although both the heavy-drinking and non-drinking teenager are inadequate models, the heavy-drinking teenager is the more attractive of the two.
>
> It seems reasonable to conclude that for most teenagers, drinking behaviour is, initially, an attempt to satisfy certain personality aspirations in terms of toughness and sociability, and to avoid the stigmatising implications of the categories which they themselves apply to others. The effects of peer group pressure, and the parallel need for peer group standing or esteem, appear to be very strong influences upon adolescent drinking. (Davies and Stacey, 1972; xiii)

There are two large 'jumps' in this argument. In the first place, it is by no means evident that normative statements delivered in one sort of social circumstance (e.g. answers to a questionnaire) cause motivation and behaviour in another social situation (e.g. of potential drinking).[8] In the second place, it is by no means self-evident that motivation to correspond to a self-image stems from peer group pressure or need for peer group standing and esteem. 'Motivations' to show a particular social self (sociability, toughness or whatever) can be understood, within a materialist framework, as the result of collective engagements, by youth, with aspects of the labour market, relations between the sexes, and social class and other traditions, as these confront youth in a locality (see later sections of this chapter). In a purely 'moral' analysis, however, youth culture is cut away from material circumstances, leaving it no other origin than 'other people's minds'. Given an orientation to the level of the individual and the small group, and given the fact that teenagers were the only group included in Davies and Stacey's study, it is the peer group that becomes identified as the origin of norms and motivations. This 'finding' of 'peer pressure', therefore follows from the choices of theoretical basis and of methodology of the study. 'Peer pressure' continues to guide the mainstreamof government-funded social research into youth drinking (Jahoda, personal communication).

To question the pride of place so often allocated to peer pressure in explanation of youthful drinking is not to deny that individuals seek to influence each other. This, however, is not a phenomenon restricted to youth. Nor is it possible to attribute a specific social practice, such as a particular style of engagement with alochol within a youth culture, to a general social cause such as mutual influence. Why is it that particular social groups are open to particular ideas and practices about drink? To pose this question is to draw attention to the fact that social groups differ in their orientations to drinking. This has, of course, been well recognised in the anthropological literature – but the solution to the question of differences between group practices has generally been sought through investigations of the normative structure of each culture. Adoption of the Durkheimian model of society held together by a consensual moral community has led to a glossing over of the possibility that moral and ideological conflicts and divisions exist within any given society. Theories of the nature of such divisions, their relation (if any) to the economy, and their expression in alcohol-related moralities and practices, provide the substance for the remainder of this chapter.

Pluralist Approaches

The Durkheimian model of contemporary society (underlying the bulk of existing research into the social use of alcohol) is of diverse occupational groups, based on an increasing division of labour, being held together by a shared morality: society is constituted as a homogeneous ideological community. Some pluralist theorists, however, put forward a model of a heterogeneous society constituted of diverse groups with differing and shifting moralities. Jack Douglas, whose *American Social Order* provides a useful and readable review of this general position, suggests that whilst there has been concentration of capital in America (and, by extension, in other western societies), there have also been two trends towards decentralisation: the division of labour, as noted by Durkheim, continues to multiply occupational groupings; and increasing choice in relation to consumption, lifestyle and leisure patterns also increases social diversity (Douglas, 1971; chapter 7). So whilst some beliefs are widely shared (e.g. in democracy, free enterprise, America), there is no general agreement on a set of rules adequate for deciding what to do in many everyday situations. In such situations – e.g. in bars – the actors have to construct their own meanings, moralities and rules for behaviour (e.g. drinking).[9] The state is portrayed as an institution which, on behalf of and with the agreement of the majority, exercises legitimate power to uphold those procedural norms – e.g. relating to democracy – that are required as a framework within which the everyday and problematic job of establishing meaning goes on. But even the agents of the state themselves have to make up 'reasonable' or 'passable' definitions and procedures for the conduct of their duties, and these definitions and procedures necessarily make better sense to those who have constructed them than they do to those to whom they are applied (welfare recipients, persons apprehended by the criminal justice system, etc). Hence, many persons who are engaging in behaviour which to them appears reasonable and right, find themselves attended to and 'labelled' as 'deviant' by state agencies following their routine procedures. Douglas insists that neither the 'deviant' nor those who label him so can be regarded as irrational, since both parties are acting in ways that make sense of the circumstances in which they find themselves. His work is probably the most comprehensive available justification for investigative social research approaches, such as observer-participation, which aim to discover how social rules (and labels) are socially constructed, rather than being taken pre-formed and applied within situations:

> When we see that members of our society experience real problems in determining the specific implications of abstract morals for their actions in any concrete situation . . . then we can see that, even if individuals in our society shared all of the same morals, there would still be an indeterminancy in the relations between these abstract morals and the actions of individuals.
>
> Each individual would be forced to take into consideration factors other than the morals themselves in deciding what he should do in a given situation. We shall find then that in our highly complex and morally pluralist society there can never be any simple determinant relation between a given set of morals and the real actions of individuals. (Douglas, 1971;31-32)

Those following this perspective have generally used participant-observation or interview methods to explore how social meanings are established in particular situations. The main practial problem with this sort of research is that the theoretical framework gives no clear model of the relationship of the situation under study to the broader social and economic structure: this is a problem because the persons engaged in constructing meaning in any situation (e.g. a bar) are also persons involved in the broader social structure, and it is hard to see how the former could be explicated without reference to the latter. The literature partially evades this problem by focussing upon *deviance* and upon situations that appear so unconnected with the mainstream of life that the question of the relation between the situation and the broader society recedes. Deviance from societal norms becomes, in this approach, completely discontinuous from and unrelated to the social and economic structure of society.[10] Working within this perspective, Sherri Cavan has conducted a study of bar-room settings and behaviour (*Liquor License,* Cavan, 1966), in which she describes bars as areas in which people have 'time out' from their conventional activities, commitments and moralities. There is a 'discontinity' between leisure settings, such as the bar, and more conventional settings:

> . . .there are times and places within the course of the daily round when the consequentiality of everyday life may be conventionally suspended and the ensuing activity granted a special status of 'not really counting'. Such times and places are designated as 'unserious occasions', and the term 'unserious' connotating an anticipated discontinuity between the immediate present and the foreseeable future. (Cavan, 1966; 235)

Partly because of the historical circumstances surrounding drinking and drinking places (Cavan refers to the English study by Mass Observation, 1943), the public drinking place is, Cavan suggests, 'if not beyond the realm of respectability . . . at least on its fringes' (p.45). Whilst Cavan recognises that actions taking place in 'time out' may in fact have consequences that reach into other sectors of one's life, she still adopts the assumption of discontinuity between work and leisure, analysing bar behaviour as taking place within a framework of norms unrelated to other settings within the social order. The validity of such an analysis rests, in part, upon the validity of the model of the social order upon which it rests. (Later in this study, we shall employ an approach which analyses 'leisure' behaviour not as 'time out' from the social relations of work, but as intimately connected with those relations).

As we have already noted, pluralist theory concerns itself not only with the ways in which social groups construct meaning in social situations, but also with the ways in which state agencies and the professions 'label' some of the behaviour that results. David Robinson has published a study of how drinkers acquire the label of 'alcoholic' in the process of medical referral: a doctor's reference to the patient's drinking in the early case notes is remarked upon by another doctor, who asks about the possibility of a 'drinking problem'; the patient is then further referred as a 'possible alcoholic'; and this label/diagnosis confirmed by a specialist (Robinson, 1976). Robinson and Henry (1977) have also studied Alcoholics Anonymous, a non-drinking group whose members have been through the labelling/diagnosis process, have accepted their new status, and are collectively seeking to make sense of it. Such studies have no direct implications for recreational drinking in social groups who lack experience of diagnosis; but they do raise the question of the social of pro- and anti-alcohol social movements, and of state policy on alcohol. Pluralist theory has little to say about this question which has, however, been addressed by researchers working from Weberian perspectives.

Weber: Morality as a source of conflict

The work of Weber has informed work on alcohol-related social movements. Weber conceptualises society, not as one homogenous consensus, nor as a moral pluralism, but as a system of domination. He shares with Durkheim an interest in morality. But where Durkheim had stressed the function of an over-arching and shared morality in helping to hold together disparate social groups having differing locations in the social division of labour in society, and hence in guaranteeing a consensual and stable social order, Weber was concerned to illuminate the ways in which systems of ideas, moralities and religions, motivate social and economic change:

> Durkheim stressed the inhibiting and restraining function of moral values: he saw them as limiting men's appetites and thus as preventing anomic instability. Weber, however, tended to accept the energising, motivational signifiance of moral values: he saw them as stimuli to human striving. For Weber, values express and ignite passions rather than restrain appetites . . . (Gouldner, 1971; 122)

Weber was particularly concerned to describe the way in which particular systems of authority gain legitimacy at particular times, and provide conditions in which a particular form of economy can flourish. Most of his work focussed upon the role of the 'protestant ethic' in supporting ideas of rational calculation that underpinned the emergence of the capitalist economy.

> Weber, as a student of capitalism, concentrated on its ideological preconditions, on the rise of its 'spirit'. There are, indeed, observations in *Economy and Society* about other aspects of it; for example, a 'rational' bureaucratic state apparatus, including a 'rational' legal system, to a modern capitalist economy and their mutual interrelation. But given that *Economy and Society* was written as the first part of an encylopaedia of economics, limited attention is, in fact, paid to this sort of relation. Weber's major empirical studies of the rise of capitalism concerned rather the

> relationship of religion and economic ideology. He even said of his study of the Protestant ethic: 'The following study may, thus, perhaps in a modest way, form a contribution to the understanding of the manner in which ideas become effective forces in history'. Weber was, however, careful to deny that he intended 'to substitute for a one-sided materialistic an equally one-sided spiritualistic causal interpretation of culture and of history'. (Therborn, 1976; 309)

Weber's sociology has laid the groundwork for studies of how particular social issues, such as drinking habits and temperance, have played a part in social conflicts and in the attempts of social groups to gain domination over each other, where that domination is expressed in moral, ideological or 'status' terms (rather than in purely economic relations). Joseph Gusfield has coined the terms 'status politics' and 'symbolic crusade' to describe aspects of conflicts around temperance and prohibition in the USA. In his analysis, economic conflicts play a minor role:

> Our social system has not experienced the sharp class organisation and class conflict which have been so salient in European history ... In its bland attitude towards class issues, political controversy in the United States has given only a limited role to strong economic antagonists. Controversies of personality, cultural difference and nuances of style and modality have occupied part of the poltical stage. Consensus about fundamentals of governmental form, free enterprise economy and church power has left a politial vacuum which moral issues have partially filled. (Gusfield, 1966; 1-2)

Gusfield distinguishes between class movements, which are orientated towards attainment of the economic interests of the class, and status movements, which are concerned with the enhancement of prestige of status groups. Status movements are 'expressive' rather than 'instrumental', and seek symbolic evidence of social deference. Since different norms are applicable to drinking in different social groups, cultures or status groups, the possibility exists for one status group to seek dominance over and deference from another(s) by seeking to universalise its own drinking morms. Gusfield's study examines American Temperance Movements from this perspective.

> The political role of Temperance emerged in the 1840's in its use as a symbol of native and immigrant, Protestant and Catholic tensions. The 'disinterested reformer' of the 1840's was likely to see the curtailment of alcohol sales as a way of solving the problems presented by an immigrant, urban, poor whose culture clashed with American Protestantism. He sensed the rising power of these strange, alien people and used Temperance legislation as one means of impressing upon the immigrant the central power and dominance of native Amerian Protestant morality. (Gusfield, 1966; 6)

The main problem with this analysis is that, whereas Weber's work was concerned to show how particular moral or ideological philosphies advance the interests of particular class in respect of *economic* issues as well as 'expressive' issues of 'status', Gusfield defines the former as outside the scope of his analysis. Such definitional restrictions need not necessarily render the study worthless: but it certainly stops it being a Weberian study in the full and original sense. Gusfield's study does, nevertheless, have the value of placing the question of the diverse meanings which social groups attach to drinking practices onto the research agenda. It recognises that social divisions exist, and addresses the question of how groups of individuals sharing a particular structural position may evolve shared perceptions of the meaning and significance of drinking practices.

Gusfield's study is primarily one of the development of social control of drinking practices, but it does also contain a theory of drinking practices per se. Assuming that social behaviour is guided by the status goal of social ascent, he describes contemporary drinking patterns as an example of consumer behaviour that facilitates sociability, and hence ascent:

> Thorstain Veblen, himself the epitome of the rural, middle-class protestant, saw the new society of consumers coming into being. In his satirical fashion, he depicted a society in which leisure and consumption fixed men's status and took precedence over the work-mindedness and efficiency-concerns of his own Swedish-American farm communities. More recently, David Riesman has brilliantly depicted the major outlines of this society by pointing to the intensity with which Modern Amerians are replacing an interest in work and morality with an interest in

> interpersonal relations and styles of consuming leisure. For the 'other-directed' man neither the intolerance nor the seriousness of the abstainer is acceptable . . . One must get along with others and liquor has proven to be a necessary and effective facilitator to sociability . . . In a consumption-centred society, people must learn to have fun and be good mixers if they are to achieve respect. (Gusfield, 1966; 8-9)

This aspect of Gusfield's work provides a useful bridge to discussion of the contributions of the sociology of youth culture, early versions of which also conceptualised social practices in terms of consumption behaviours (see Parsons, Abrams, etc, below). As more recent contributors from the sociology of youth culture suggest, however, social behaviour in the sphere of consumption must be related to the whole life-situation of the social group concerned, including their palce vis-a-vis the relations of production. It is to this literature that we now turn.

Contributions from the Sociology of Working Class Youth Cultures: drinking as male delinquency

In contrast to the studies described above, which attempt a purely 'moral' analysis of drinking practices and of the conflicts which arise around them, there is a broad tradition of sociological analysis which attempts to relate moral phenomena to the material conditions in which they arise. Some studies of youth culture in the USA and, more recently, advances in the UK, have focussed upon the relations between social class background (as a collective attribute of social groups, rather than as an individual 'factor'), the ways in which the state (and especially the educational system) manage the socialisation of working class youth, and the youth cultures that arise as collective responses to shared circumstances. Although none of these studies have been specifically interested in or focussed upon youthful drinking practices, some have touched upon these practices with the context of a broader discussion of youth cultures, use of 'leisure' time, and delinquency or near-delinquency. Generally speaking, these studies have focussed upon lower working class groups, and have characterised youthful drinking, along with other 'problem behaviours', as a specific example of lower working class male delinquency. Discussion of this literature leads into dicussion of the methodology adopted in the 'case study' of youthful drinking in the following chapter, in which we take up David Downes' conclusion that 'the analysis should take into account . . . three areas: work, school, and leisure' (Downes, 1966; 215). But there are considerable problems with the literature on youth cultures insofar as it focusses almost entirely upon lower working class males, and analyses their position from a 'masculinist' point of view. The case study uses a methodology that makes *selective* use of the advances made in studies of youth culture, *reconstituting* these within the context of a methodology that more adequately treats the relations between youth, social class and sexual divisions in society.

The sociological literature on youth cultures has been reviewed by several authors (Downes, 1966, Murdock and McCron, 1976, Clarke et al, 1975, Brake, 1980, Cohen, 1980) and since we are interested in picking out some general principles rather than in refining any specific hypothesis within that literature, we shall simply plot some landmarks. The origins of the term 'youth culture' lie within American sociology: it was originally coined by Talcott Parsons and came into general use in the early post-war period, during which mention of social class was equated with communism and with Stalinism. Parsons' 'youth culture' had two main aspects:- a 'compulsive conformity within the peer group of age mates' (Parsons, 1954; 343), and an extreme accentuation of the values of hedonism, irresponsibility, and consumption (as opposed to routine, responsibility and production). Acknowledging that adults also share these values to some extent, Parsons nevertheless describes the continuities between youth and adult cultures as 'structurally secondary' to the discontinuities between them (ibid; 91-93).

This approach informed attempts, in empirical research, to demonstrate the existence of a youth culture common to all youth, cutting across all class boundaries, and comprehensible in terms of the values of consumption: such research tended to show, however, that consumption tastes of youth varied with social class background (Coleman, 1961, Hollingshead, 1949, Abrams, 1959), though such unwanted findings could be eliminated by the simple expedient of dropping social class from subsequent data analyses (as Abrams did). Furthermore, some research showed that, in working clss areas, only a small proportion of youth became at all involved with the commercial leisure market (Wilmott, 1966), undermining the assumption that youth could be defined in terms of that market.

The first major study of youth in relation to their class origins was conducted by Albert Cohen (1955). He argued that the American educational system discriminates against those with a working class background, and that these youth respond by inverting the school's value-system. Cohen's study protrayed working class youth as working class, but also as cut off from the general working class community: as working class by virtue of origin, rather than by everyday interaction with the parent culture. Other researchers, however, began to stress the links between the values and cultures of working class youth, those of the adult working class, and those of the whole society: Walter Miller argued, on the basis of observation research, that the concerns of working class youth were versions of the 'focal concerns' of working class adult cultures extended and reworked to fit the specific situation of working class youth (Miller, 1958), whilst David Matza described teenage values as accentuated or 'stretched' versions of the dominant values in post-war capitalism (Matza and Sykes, 1961; 717-18). These writers re-inserted youth culture into the broader social order. As Murdock and McCron (p.20) put it:

> Hence in place of Parsons' and Coleman's presentation of 'youth culture' as a self-contained system set over against the value system of adult society, the analysis of Matza and of Miller directs attention to its connections with the two central configurations of class culture – the dominant culture, and the subordinate culture of the (adult) working class – and raised the complex question of triangular relationships between them. (Murdock and McCron, 1976; 20)

Although this 'complex' question is capable of being treated in several ways, we shall describe three, referring (i) to the work of Downes, (ii) of Parker, and (iii) of the Centre for Contemporary Cultural Studies of Birmingham University.

(1) David Downes' 1966 study of East End London youth relied upon a Mertonian theoretical framework, within which social class is seen as mediating the degree of access to culturally prescribed objectives. Within this perspective, Downes' major contributions were to emphasise the differences between the British situation and the situation described in the American literature; and to suggest that youth from the lower working class were disadvantaged twice – once within the scholastic opportunity structure, and once again within the teenage leisure market.

Facing double failure in the available opportunity structures, the lower working class boy dissociates himself from school, and builds a 'teenage culture' based on 'exploits' that embody the values purveyed by the teenage leisure market – status, romance, fantasy, excitement, violence (Downes, 1966; 132). As Downes puts it, he 'arrives at the 'delinquent solution' by pushing the legitimate values ofeeenage (i.e. commercially-offered) culture to their logical conclusion' (p.134). Downes' analysis rests upon two assumptions: that working class boys subscribe to the values of the school in the first place; and that 'teenage culture' is best analysed in relation to the leisure market, rather than in relation to working class traditions. This is 'a theory of ideological incorporation of the working class' in which the process of incorporation (into the values of the school and of the leisure market) have 'gone wrong' (Corrigan and Frith, 1975; 232); a theory in which working class youth culture is seen as a 'collective compensation for those who could not succeed.' (Clarke et al, 1975; 29). Such an approach has not, apparently, been applied to the analysis of youthful drinking in the UK (Downes himself did not research drinking) but, if it were, then it presumably would lead to a protrayal of under-age drinking practices in the lower working class as motivated by a lack of access to other leisure activities, and as structured by the themes made available by the leisure market and by the media (including drink advertisments). This sort of analysis would have to attend to the problem that some youth might like drinking *even when* access to other culturally prescribed leisure activities (eg. films, clothes, music, etc) was open; and it would not be applicable to drinking amongst males in class locations other than the lowest. Mertonian and neo-Mertonian analyses have not generally been applied to girls, perhaps because of a reluctance to analyse girls in terms of social ambitions.

(2) Although Mertonian sociology intends to analyse youth in relation to their class origins, it tends, in practice, to dislodge youth from the the context of working class culture and community, and to portray youth as an empty vessel, drained of class culture, which is then filled up with commercially-produced culture. This problem does not arise in the 'appreciative' sociology of the late 1960s and 1970s, in which the aim is to use observer participation methods of research to investigate a culture by living, as far as possible, as a member of that culture. This approach draws upon anthropology, journalism and the interactionist school of social psychology; it involves a down-playing of theory and of formal testing of hypotheses,

and an emphasis on being open to social and cultural processes as these present themselves to the 'insider'. Howard Parker has done a notable study of this type in Liverpool, and whilst his study does not concern itself particularly with youthful drinking, it does discuss this area in one chapter (and indeed Parker initiated his research contacts within a pub in his study area). Parker looked at lower class working males who indulged in occasional theft in their teenage years and subsequently began to 'settle down' into marriage and relatively continuous employment (Parker, 1974; 209). In this group, pub drinking took place within the general framework of a search for excitment, male group solidarity, jocular chauvinism towards women, and occasional confrontations with authority. These concerns are, Parker suggests, not unique to lower working class culture: they are expressed in a particular way by that culture because of the circumstances of its members. Parker suggests that 'emphasis on certain behavioural themes are consequences or functions of the boys' situation rather than traditional concerns that are simply transmitted to them. Toughness and masculinity, for instance, are concerns of most men at all levels of society. The tendency for the down-town adolescent to express this concern through physical combat may well be related to the lack of control over resources and power . . .' (Parker, 1974; 153). Drinking occasions dominated by these themes are common because 'facility-wise the pubs, with their drinking and socialising, are the only real leisure centres regularly and readily available' (ibid; 154).

One problem with this sort of study is that its vivid descriptions can too easily be generalised to other social groups whose culture and drinking practices may in fact be quite different; this danger is exacerbated by the fact that the leisure situation itself is the point of entry for the observer participant researcher, rather than an empirical or theoretical investigation of the boys' broader structural position.

(3) Workers at the Centre for Contemporary Cultural Studies have been concerned to develop an explicitly Marxian analysis of the wide variety of male youth cultures that have emerged in the UK in the post-war period. Reviewing preceding Mertonian approaches (such as that of Downes) they suggest that 'the situation of the (youth) subculture's members within an ongoing subordinate (working class parent) culture is ignored' in such theories of youth. They suggest that 'the young inherit a cultural orientation from their parents towards a problematic (perspective) common to the

class as a whole' (Clarke et al, 1975; 29). In other words, the culture of working class youth is *primarily* derived from the working class parental culture, not from middle class value systems as represented in schools or in the media. The Birmingham workers specifically, and through them many sociologists in the cultural studies and deviancy fields, have been much influenced by the important work of P. Cohen (1972). According to Clarke et al (p.30), Cohen 'offers a class analysis, but at a much more sophisticated theoretical level, placing the parent culture in a historical perspective, mapping the relations between sub-cultures, and explaining the intra-class dynamic between youth and parents'. Cohen's analysis overcomes the problem of those 'appreciative' studies of youth cultures which

> start by taking groups who are already card-carrying members of a particular sub-culture such as skinheads, bikeboys or hippies and working backwards to uncover their class location. The approach therefore excludes adolescents who share the same basic class location but who are not members of the sub-culture. As a result it tends to draw too tight a relation between class location and sub-cultural responses. (Murdock and McCron, 1976; 25)

Cohen's analysis does not suffer from this problem, since he starts with the whole community or neighbourhood, and traces its history. The area he studied, the East End of London, had been characterised by the stability of the neighbourhood, by extended kinship networks and mutual supports, resting upon an economic situation in which most people worked in the area in which they were resident – hence economic and community interests were intertwined. But in the period of post-war 'redevelopment' of the area work opportunities shifted to large units outside the area, leaving the residents with the choice either of falling into dead-end jobs locally, or of attempting upward mobility into the new elite jobs outside the area. Depopulation and redevelopment caused social isolation, and the break-up of extended kinship relationships caused a compression of problems into the nuclear family. Cohen shows that these changes did not result in the 'disappearance' or the 'embourgeoisement' of the local working-class, but in its fragmentation into different strata. The problems facing the adult community, including a central concern over jobs, were also the problems of the younger generation. Youth subcultures were the result of youth's attempts to make sense of the problems youth shared with its parents:

> The latent function of sub-culture is this – to express and resolve, albeit 'magically', the contradictions which remain hidden or unresolved in the parent culture. The succession of (youth) subcultures which this parent culture generated can thus all be considered as so many variations on a central theme – the contradiction, at an ideological level, between traditional working class puritanism, and the new ideology of consumption: at an economic level, between a part of the socially mobile elite, or as a part of the new lumpen. Mods, parkers, skinheads, crombies, all represent, in their different ways, an attempt to retrieve some of the socially cohesive elements destroyed in the parent culture, and to combine these with elements selected from other class fractions, symbolising one or other of the options confronting it. (Cohen, 1972: 23)

For Cohen, youth cultures and youth styles are an attempt to do symbolically, magically, what youth cannot do in reality – overcome the real problems which it shares with parent culture. This view, however, glosses over the fact that, even though youth may share a general outlook (or 'problematic') with the parent culture, this outlook looks out upon rather different circumstances from those confronting the parents. As Clarke et al. put it, 'over and above shared class situations, there remains something privileged (i.e. unique – ND) about the specifically *generational experience* of the young' (1975;49). What is this special aspect that marks youth out from the adults of the social class? During the late 1970s, this question was generally answered in terms of the transition into the labour market:

> Working-class young people are, in sociological terms, an actual and potential labour force and it is this (not their youth) which determines their social situation. (Corrigan & Frith, 1975;236)

1970s' youth culture research was, like most previous youth research, most concerned with boys, and it did not explicitly recognise housework, i.e. work that is most generally done by women and girls, as work. The 'transition to work', therefore, was generally taken as the transition into waged work in the labour market. Thus it is true to say that whilst youth culture research in the 1970s shed the earlier assumption that 'youth' was a universal social status that manifested itself irrespective of the social class of those concerned, and whilst it began to conceptualise working class youth cultures in terms of the teenage transition into waged work, this celebration of the new-found class character of youth cultures almost completely obscured the fact that half the youth are also female.[12]

More recent work has attempted to situate youth in relation to sexual divisions in society; but sexual divisions have generally been conceptualised from the *perspective of the males*. In the otherwise interesting work of Paul Willis (*Learning to Labour*, 1978), for instance, the concepts of 'masculinity' and 'femininity' are described as arising out of the distinction made by lower working class boys between manual labour and mental labour. For 'the lads' in Willis' study, 'Manual labour is associated with the social superiority of masculinity, and mental labour with the social inferiority of femininity' (Willis, 1978;148). Manual labour is valued because it transforms nature and produces what was not there before (unlike housework, according to Willis, p.151): it is the exertion of the male body in pursuit of such transformation that lays the basis for attribution of tough 'masculine' superiority. The school is rejected by those whose class background makes them likely candidates for manual labour, because the school (as an institution of mental labour) appears soft and sissy; the 'lads' cannot identify with the school's values since these are the opposite of what they need to make positive sense of their most likely future of manual labour. Their drinking, occurring in this context of rejection of the school and associated authorities, takes on a rebellious flavour: drinking and drunkenness are employed as symbols of rejection of the school;

> As well as inducing a 'nice' effect, drinking is undertaken openly because it is the most decisive signal to staff and 'ear 'oles' that the individual is separate from the school and has a presence in an alternative, superior and more mature mode of social being . . .
>
> The point is, of course, that the drinking has to be done at lunchtime, and in defiance of the school. It is not done simply to mark a neutral transition – a mere ritual. It is a decisive rejection and closing off. They have, in some way, finally, beaten the school . . . (Willis, 1978; 19 and 21)

It should be stressed that Willis' remarks were meant to refer only to the social group which he studied, and that his research was based upon the assumption that other class and gender groups have quite different cultures. It remains the case, however, that the focus upon those lower working class boys who exhibit 'defiance' – a focus running all the way through the literature on youth cultures – gives a very partial view of 'youth'. In relation to youthful drinking, such research seems to confirm the worst fears of the moral panic: youthful drinking is closely related to delinquency, even Marxists say so!

Youth Culture Research Before Feminism: Taking Stock

In spite of its tendency to see girls as marginal to youth culture (or not see them at all) and its tendency to define the transition to work purely in terms of entry into the labour market, 1970s' youth culture research made important advances that have direct relevance to our study of alcohol in teenage cultures. The most general of these advances was to see youth cultures as being closely related to parent cultures, rather than being 'a world apart' as the early post-war popularisers of the idea of youth culture had suggested. This similarity between youth and parental cultures does not however necessarily mean that youthful drinking can be understood in terms of the taking on of adult drinking patterns. Working class youth cultures are general frames of reference, or structures of meaning, within which to interpret the world and events within it, and vocabularies of action: youth apply these to the circumstances which face them and which are, of course, somewhat different from the circumstances that faced their parents when they were young, and also from those that face their parents now. This implies that they may develop some norms and attitudes that are different from, or incomprehensible to, their parents. It will not necessarily be the case, for example, that youth and their parents have the same ideas about a specific practice, such as youthful drinking in pubs. This suggests that youthful drinking cannot simply be understood as the wholesale taking-on of the drinking norms of the parents, as Maddox and other alcohol researchers conceptualise it. Instead, youthful drinking has to be understood within the framework of youth's application of a culture that they largely share with their parents, to circumstance which are rather different from those of the parents.

The second major advance with implications for a study of youthful drinking is the attempt to understand the cultures of working class youth, and of their parents, as responses to the circumstances they face by virtue of being working class. The working class is made up of all those who have no disposable assets other than its labour, which it must sell in the labour market in return for a wage. Since this basic condition of and predicament of the class, the questions of the sorts of labour markets that face specific social groups (e.g. the level of demand for labour, the types of jobs, entrance requirements, wages, etc), and of how particular strata of the working class respond to those markets, are important for any understanding of working class cultures. In the case of mid-teenagers, who are entering the market for the first time, the questions of the types of jobs on offer to them, of entrance qualifications (formal and informal), and of the demands of the probationary or training period, are especially important. Teenage 'leisure behaviour' such as drinking takes place in the context of the circumstances of the mid-teens, in which period leaving school and trying to get a job figure prominently. It follows that a study of drinking practices in any teenage group must be concerned with a study of the local labour market as it faces that group.

The third and last major advance, made by youth culture research and having implications for a study of teenage drinking, is the understanding that youth, parents, and labour markets have to be placed within the broader context of the local area and its history (as demonstrated in the work of Cohen, referred to above). Since areas in different regions of the country differ considerably in their economic, demographic, social and cultural histories, it follows that contemporary parental and youth cultures may differ from area to area; and hence that particular youth practices, such as patterns and styles of drinking that form a part of youth cultures, may also differ from area to area. This means that it would be hazardous to talk about youth cultures 'in general', or about teenage drinking 'in general'. What are required are investigations into specific areas, cultures and drinking therein. It should be possible to *hypothesise* that broad similarities exist between the drinking norms and practices of a particular teenage group, and those of similar teenage groups (i.e. similar in terms of social class, gender mix, ethnic background) in areas of the country in which similar labour markets, schools and parental cultures exist; but such similarities can be *demonstrated* only on the basis of comparative research. Still less could it be assumed that youthful drinking in one country is the same phenomenon as youthful drinking in another.

What can be generalised is a method of investigation of teenage cultures and drinking. So far we have identified three contributions that youth culture research can make to a study of teenage drinking. These are (i) whilst teenage cultures may be closely related to the cultures of the parents, specific teenage activities such as teenager drinking cannot be seen simply in terms of socialisation into the patterns of their parents; (ii) teenage cultures and drinking have to be understood in relation to the transition to the labour market; and (iii) this understanding must be sought in a broader understanding of the socio-economic structure and history of the local area and its inhabitants. But, as noted above, youth culture research has been marred by male-centredness. It has generally focussed upon boys and has regarded girls as marginal to or absent from youth culture. When sexual divisions are admitted to be important, these are too often defined purely in terms of boys' conception of them (e.g. in the work of Willis). When the family is discussed – as in the work of Cohen – it is seen in terms of an institution of socialisation and mutual support, and sexual divisions (e.g. in relation to power, in relation to domestic labour) are glossed over. It is therefore necessary, in order to move towards a more balanced view of teenage cultures and drinking, to reformulate the advances of male-centred youth culture research within the broader framework of the relations between youth, social class, and sexual divisions in society.

An Alternative Approach: Housework, Schooling, Labour Market and the Development of Adult Class Relations

In an Annexe, I review some theories of the relation between social class and sexual divisions in society, and take up the position that working class married women can be conceptualised as having a class position different from that of their husbands.[13] The relevant parts of the argument can be summarised quite briefly. According to the materialist theory of Karl Marx and Frederick Engels, there are in contemporary society two main social classes: the class of capital, which has effective possession of the means of production, and the working class, which has no disposable assets other than its labour, which it must therefore exchange, in the labour market, for a wage. (There are also a number of classes or strata intermediate between capital and the working class, but it is the working class – and its youth – which are of primary interest for the purposes of a study of working class teenage drinking). But if the working class is defined as that social group which has possession of its labour, and can sell all its labour power in the market, then any social group that is obliged to expend a proportion of its labour outside the market (e.g. in the home, in domestic tasks and childcare), cannot be part of that class. In most working class families in the UK (indeed in most countries), there is an unequal division of labour within the home: women do most of the domestic tasks including the bulk of the practical work required to maintain the husband and children, and provide the bulk of the emotional support and caring, and men do only a few specialised and/or token tasks. This being the case, women do not have full possession of their labour, in the sense that a proportion of their labour is used up outside the labour market. These considerations suggest a model of society consisting of three main classes: capital (ownership of means of production), male working class (full possession of labour), and female 'underclass' (lacks full possession of its labour). (The theoretical arguments for such a view , and its relation to the classical concerns of Marxian theory and to the more recent concerns of feminist theory, are explicated in the Annexe). In the present chapter, we adopt this three-class analysis, which implies three main sets of *adult* class relations (capital/male working class, capital/female underclass, male working class/female underclass), and explore *youth* as an extended process of taking on, by boys and girls, of those class relations. To do this it is useful to refer to the fact that whilst capital/male working class relations and capital/female relations are set up within the labour market (i.e. not until the teenage years in our society), the male working class/female class relation is established, at least in outline, quite early in the life of the child. Forms of play and work within the home are quite clearly sex-segregated, little girls being socialised into housework at an early age. Whilst it may be the case that men also do certain types of tasks within the home (carpentry, electrical work, some washing-up, etc), it remains the case that women typically do much more work within the home than men do, and that little girls in most households are socialised into this pattern many years before any socialisation into the labour market. We can therefore say, since female labour power is appropriated from little girls, in domestic work, at quite an early age, that the basis of the male/female class relation is formed early in childhood.

In terms of a class analysis based on whether or not social groups have full possession of their labour power, schooling may be seen as a process which, for a decade of the child's life, appropriates labour power of both boys and girls and therefore places boys into a similar class position to that of girls. In the UK, schooling takes up the greater part of the day for most of the year, and neither boys nor girls are supposed to be able to evade the demand that they be in school and carry out the exact forms of labour prescribed: very clearly, this is appropriation of labour power, as much as is unpaid work within the home, though this is not of course all it is (schooling also prepares youth for participation in the labour market and in other adult social and political relations). During this period, girls are generally expected to continue to work within the home during the evenings, weekends and holidays, hence their labour power is more thoroughly appropriated than boys, and in differing ways. The greater free time of boys gives them more scope, as they grow up, to take part-time paid employment; but the bulk of their labour power is appropriated, as is the girls', until at least age sixteen. The years of childhood and schooling therefore represent a period in which the basis of social rleations between the sexes is laid, but these social relations cannot develop fully in adult class relations because neither sex has full and effective possession of its labour power during childhood.

It is at sixteen years, when most British children enter the labour market full-time, that class relations blossom. Boys, released from school, gain full possession of their labour power and the freedom to sell it to capital for a wage. Most girls also enter the labour market at this time, but their position within the market is weakened by (a) housework obligations within the parental home, (b) more extensive obligations within the marital home if and as marriage occurs, (c) withdrawal from the market for several years to care for pre-school children, (d) capital's tendency to disciminate against women workers and to pay them less than men on the grounds that points (a) to (c) reduce the pay-off that capital obtains from women, and (e) discrimination by and sometimes outright opposition by the male working class to female workers (Hartman, 1979). It is at this point, when males and females enter directly into class relations with capital, that class antagonisms between the male working class and females become most intense. We say 'class antagonism' here in order to differentiate between the strong emotional and personal feelings that arise between many boys and girls, and the class function which these serve: the personal feelings may be highly positive and often of a shared nature, but the longer-term effect of the relationship to which these feelings give rise is the full reproduction of the class relation in which women's labour power is partially or wholly appropriated in domestic work. Only if the bulk of females enter, sooner or later, into the marriage relationship or some equivalent (in terms of the appropriation of their labour power), will the class relation between the sexes be reproduced; and consumerist, familial and personal pressures upon young women, pushing them into the direction of reproduction of these class relations, are intense. These pressures are reinforced by the fact that the existence of these class relations hitherto has supported discriminatory practices within the labour market, offering relatively unrewarding prospects of promotion, wage, etc to women who are considering supporting themselves. How strong these pressures are depends to some extent on the nature of the local economy, and the degree of its discrimination against women. (This point is demonstrated in the case study that follows this chapter).

Hence we cay say that the development of class relations of men and women goes through several stages. In the first instance, little girls are expected to help mother in the house, this often being presented as a form of play, and so the basis of later appropriations of labour within the domestic unit is laid. Secondly, both boys' and girls' labour power is largely appropriated during schooling. Thirdly, boys and girls enter the labour market. Following this some girls do not enter into the marriage relationship (or some equivalent in which part of their labour power is appropriated whilst little or none of the man's is): these single women may be regarded as escapees from their predestined class. They may be regarded, then, as members of the working class (alongside most males), though their treatment in the labour market and elsewhere is affected by application (both by men and by other women) of expectations of their 'femininity'. But most young women do enter into the full class relationship with males (i.e. as a group, not just with an individual male), when they take up the role of housewife (even if also working outside the home). It would take a fully study of the circumstances of each stage in this process – early housework-play; schooling; labour market entry and romantic relations; housewife – to give an adequate account of the forms of youth culture that arise at each stage, and of the patterns, styles and meaning of drinking that may be associated with each, as it occurs in the various social groups and regions in the UK.[14] For practical reasons, it is necessary to restrict the scope of fieldwork quite severely in any one case study. Being most interested in mid-teen culture, we have focussed upon aspects around the middle of this extended process – school-leaving, labour market entry, concomitant social relations between the sexes, and the significance of mid-teen drinking in this context (see following chapter). But the more general conclusion, about the need to situate not only the drinking of teenagers, but also the drinking of younger children, in relation to social class and sexual divisions in society, is worth making. None of the existing studies of drinking by young children or teenagers, reviewed in this chapter, has attempted to do this.

Conclusion – Justification for a Materialist Area Case Study

This chapter has discussed various developments in youth culture research, and in theories about the relation between social class and sexual divisions in society, and has drawn several conclusions about the way in which youth cultures and youthful drinking can be researched. We can now summarise these implications in the form of 'research guidelines'.

The first guideline is the need to recognise that individuals' ideas and practices about drinking (or any other form of social behaviour) have to be seen as variations on the themes to be found in the culture evolved by the social group to which those individuals belong. It follows that research methods must avoid the danger of stripping individuals from the social groups and cultures to which they belong.

The second guideline is that for the culture to be understood, each social group has to be situated in relation to social class and sexual divisions; children have to be understood as being at a definite stage of taking-on of class relations, rather than being 'outside' relations of social class and gender enjoyed by their parents.

The third guideline is that whilst the parent culture supplies much of the framework for the culture (or general outlook, world-view) of children and teenagers, this broadly shared culture is applied by children/teenagers to cicumstances that vary depending up their stage of development (early housework-play; schooling; labour market entry, etc). And none of these circumstances are the same as those that currently face the parents. This means that the development of children's views and practices in relation to drink cannot be understood as a smooth process of acquisition of parental norms regarding drink. Discontinuities and changes of direction in the development of children's drink-related ideas and behaviour are quite possible, as children apply the general cultural viewpoint, broadly shared with parents, to different stages in the transition to 'adult' social class and gender roles. Not only research, but also health education, should be appropriate to the social position of the child.

The fourth guideline is concerned with the need to understand youthful drinking and youth cultures within the context of the region and local area in which they occur. Labour market and sexual divisions are general frameworks, not structures which impose themselves identically upon all teenagers in all localities in all countries: the forms which these structures take and the cultures which youth construct in response, differ somewhat according to two (linked) circumstances. In the first place, the basic material conditions (environmental, 'natural', geographical, etc) of life in a locality may influence the type and amount of wage work that comes to be performed there, and this affects the development of relations in and around the labour market. In the south-eastern English metropolis, for example, material conditions as well as historical circumstances have encouraged small-scale industry and service industry, rather than the large-scale and heavy industry that is more common in coal or iron-rich areas of the country and this, together with the tendency to exclude women from 'heavy' industry, lays the basis for differing labour markets, adult cultures and youth cultures. In the second place, social classes and national and local state agencies (such as the schools) respond to the conditions in which they find themselves, and these responses may differ, for historical reasons, from locality to locality (even when material conditions are quite similar). It therefore becomes difficult to make any but the most general statements about class cultures and youth cultures; one has to examine how local variations in material circumstances, and class and state responses, fill out the general frameworks of labour market and sexual divisions. This can only be done in an empirical manner, by looking closely at particular localities. Findings may then be generalised, as working hypotheses, to other, similar localities; but dissimilar localities would require separate case studies.

These four guidelines are offered as a general contribution towards the development of research into youth cultures and drinking. In the following chapter, we report on an aplication of these procedural guidelines.

5 AN AREA CASE STUDY: SERVICE-SECTOR, SCHOOL-LEAVING AND ROUND BUYING

This chapter reports on a case study of the culture and drinking of a group of boys and girls leaving school and entering the service sector of the labour market in a southern inner city area. The case study begins with a general introduction to the economic and social structure of a declining inner London Borough (called *Servicetown*[1] for the purposes of this study); it then describes the two main sectors of the labour market facing youth – the fast-declining small manufacturing sector, and the relatively favoured service sector; outlines the ways in which local secondary schools attempt to manage pupils in their school-leaving year; and concludes with a discussion of the culture and drinking of a group of teenagers who are in transition from those schools to employment in the service sector. We differentiate this group and their culture – 'service sector youth culture' – from other teenage groups, particularly from those lower in the class structure, who go into small manufacturing and/or domestic housework. The drinking situation of service sector youth is (in contrast to many other teenage groups) characterised by mixed-sex round-buying, and this is analysed as a feature of the culture which these boys and girls evolve in response to their positions in relation to the labour market and sexual divisions. The case study may be seen as an application of the general research guidelines developed in the preceding chapter.

Methods of Investigation

Within the social sciences in the post-war period, and within the sociologies of deviancy and of youth culture particularly, there has been a tendency to abandon quantitative methods, and to take up qualitative methods of investigation;[2] this tendency is illustrated, in the preceding chapter, in the shift from questionnaire-based work to ethnographic studies. From a materialist perspective, however, it is possible to employ either quantitative or qualitative methods,[3] and neither has any *general* claim upon researchers.[4] Rather, the researchers should adopt methods most appropriate to the task at hand. In the present study the aim is to make an initial and explanatory study of a specific object of enquiry previously not researched within a materialist framework – the circumstances and drinking practices of a strata of working class youth entering the service sector of an inner city labour market. The aim is to establish the forms taken by drinking practices in this strata (and hence to be able to compare it with the concept of youthful drinking inherent in the moral panic), and to offer an interpretation of those practices in terms of the group's collective response to the material conditions facing it. Any attempt at quantification would have been premature, since the object of enquiry had yet to be conceptualised in terms of its qualities and social meaning. For this reason, rather than because of any over-riding attachment to qualitative methodology, it was these mthods that were adopted for the case study. Because of the scope of the case study – covering research into local employers, the school, and youth itself – intensive and exhaustive research was possible in none of these areas. Partly in order to compensate for the 'stretching' of fieldwork over such a wide area, and partly because of the advantages obtained by use of a 'mix' of qualitative methods for filling in various aspects of a case study,[5] three qualitative methods were used throughout. In relation to each of the spheres selected for direct study – labour market, schools, and youth (in and out of school) – questions were asked in three ways: semi-structured and unstructured interviews and group discussions, observations, and searches for background material. This approach may be considered an attempt at triangulation', i.e. comparing three perspectives upon complex objects of enquiry.

Such methods, and indeed other methods of empirical research, are useless for purposes of generating basic theoretical assumptions. Generation of 'grounded theory' (Glaser and Strauss, 1968) on the basis only of one's innocent eyes and ears is impossible without some initial theoretical organisation and rules for conducting oneself. But when a theoretical framework is available which clearly specifies basic dimensions of social structure that are taken to permeate all of social life, then qualitative methods *can* be used to 'put flesh on the bones'.[6] The success of their use in these circumstances will depend upon the adequacy of the theoretical framework (e.g. are class and sexual divisions of importance for youth?), upon the adequacy of the fieldwork (e.g. did the fieldwork cover the right areas, addressing the issues posed by the theory?), and upon the general construction and reproduction of the data and the

Diagram 5.1: Research methods

semi-structured and
unstructured interviews
(and some group discussion)

observations of situations,
sometimes as participant,
sometimes not.

all other available 'case-study'
methods of getting 'background'.
E.g. official, council, school and
employer documents, pupils' written
notes, reading local newspapers and
talking to careers office and youth
workers, etc.

quality of interpretation of its meaning (e.g. the overall question of whether the project fairly recorded the process and fruits of research, recognising and exploring unexpected findings). Of these questions, the most fundamental is that of the adequacy of the theoretical framework: this underlies the ways in which particular research techniques (observations, interviews, etc) are employed to generate 'findings'. It is a basic assumption of this study that social practices have to be understood as responses of social class groups to the circumstances that they face. Such understanding necessitates that material circumstances (which lie at the base of social class and sexual divisions) have to be investigated. This assumption is 'unpacked', and its implications for research into youth are discussed in the *Annexe* and in the latter sections of the preceding chapter, in which some methodological principles are explicated. This case study is an application of those principles, and of the theory behind them, to the study of youth in one particular inner city area. This chapter now discusses the area, the labour market facing school-leavers, the schools' management of schol-leavers, and youth's response.[7]

Servicetown: An Introduction

Servicetown, as one of the Inner London Boroughs, grew rapidly in the nineteenth century. This growth, which was most rapid, when measured in population terms, in the decade 1941-51, was based upon small craft industry and upon the services and infrastructure needed to support such industry. In contrast to that period of most rapid growth, the population of Servicetown is currently suffering its fastest rate of decline, caused largely by the continuing collapse of the small industry upon which previous prosperity was build (London Borough of Servicetown, 1978).

It should be noted, by way of contrast, that whilst the growth of industry and population in inner city areas of small industry, such as Servicetown, was indeed rapid during the nineteenth century, it was by no means as explosive as the growth in cities which grew up around large-scale industry. During the decade 1921-31, for instance, the inner city populations of Leeds, Newcastle and Salford grew by around 40%, and Birmingham, Liverpool and Manchester by over 33%, whilst the rate of growth for Inner London was more steady; around 20% per decade throughout the first half of the century (Central Statistical Office, 1980; 40). And, severe as the problems of Inner London are today, they are not so bad as problems in those inner city areas based on large-scale industry: unemployment is worse in many nothern and midland English towns than it is in the southern metropolis, largely due to the greater reliance of the former on fast-declining industries such as steel and textiles. Boroughs such as Servicetown are declining as their small-industry base further erodes, but this process is less drastic than the closure of large works in large-industry towns, and is to some extent compensated for by the relative strength of the service sector of local economies in south-eastern metropolices.

It is the service sector of the economy which has helped, to a certain extent, to cushion Servicetown's post-Second World War decline. About half the paid labour force work in the service sector (shops, offices, distribution, etc). But the service sector has itself been declining recent, albeit not so fast as the industrial sector, (as table 5.1. shows). Professional employment increased during this period, but this was of little significance for the bulk of the working class, except insofar as the professional jobs were often taken by newcomers to the Borough, who added to the housing problem by buying flats and houses, encouraging landlords to sell property, decreasing privately rented housing stock, and increasing the cost of buying housing. The influx of middle class professionals also had consequences for Council policy, providing a new generation of Labour Party Councillors and activists that increased public housing and other welfare service benefits for local consumption (though these are currently being cut back as a result of central government policy).

Table 5.1: Loss of jobs in decade 1961-71

	U.K. as a whole	Inner London as a whole	Servicetown
Manufacturing jobs	−16%	−25%	−38%
Service jobs	(not available)	− 6%	−11%

(*Source:* Borough Development Plan)

Servicetown's economic history has resulted in a number of small firms, rather than a small number of large employing units. The largest employer is a state agency, the Post Office, whilst the largest private employer employs 1,300. Since the workforce is 142,000 this means that the majority of paid workers work in relatively small units (all statistics from the 1978 Borough *Development Plan*). Table 5.2 shows the number of premises employing specified numbers of people. The smallness of most work-units, and the fact that most are in the service sector of the economy which is weakly unionised, explains why trades unionisation is relatively weak in Servicetown.

Table 5.2: Numbers of premises employing specific numbers of workers

Workers	0-9	10-19	20-29	50-99	100-249	250+	All premises
Number of manu-facturing premises	950	450	330	110	55	20	1915
Number of service premises	4850	500	360	140	95	45	5990

(*Source:* Borough Development Plan)

Not included in the Council's statistics are those unpaid workers, housewives, who work in the smallest units of all – i.e. doing domestic work by themselves. Approximately half the married women in the area do not work in the labour market, but at home. The other half do the 'double shift' of housework *and* work in the labour market. According to the 1971 Census, the percentage of Servicetown's married women working was above average for inner London, and may be increasing: it was 52% in 1966, and 53% in 1871, the fastest increase being in the 25-34 age-group. A relatively high proportion of married women entering the labour market is to be expected in such an area, in which the declining small manufacturing sector does not provide the male worker with an adequate 'family wage', and in which the relatively large service sector provides opportunities for female employment, and to a certain extent tends to offset the historical and ideological constraints that keep women out of the labour market. In this respect, women are less disadvantaged vis-a-vis men in Servicetown than they are in London generally; their position in London is better, in relation to the labour market, than in the UK generally; and more women have paid work in the UK than in any other European country except Denmark (Central Statistical Office, 1980; 123). Servicetown is therefore more representative of areas in which a relatively high proportion of women have paid work, than of English or European inner city areas in general. It should be noted that most 'working wives' are expected to do the bulk of domestic work and childcare in addition to their paid work, and that most teenage girls are expected to help mother in the home to some extent, in addition to school or paid work. The position of women in relation to the labour market is of importance for adult cultures, for relations betwen the sexes, and therefore for youth cultures and leisure activities therein, as we shall see.

Servicetown's characteristics have made it an area with a quite large immigrant population. The post-war population decline produced the relatively cheap rented housing which immigrants could afford on the wages paid at the bottom of the job market, where they are most acceptable as employees. The 'sweatshops', producing clothing and like articles, where pay is especially poor, employ a high proportion of coloured immigrants and children of immigrants, who commonly also find some work in the lower parts of the service sector (shops, distribution, warehouses, etc). The area also has a proportion of people with an Irish background. Racial discrimination is quite considerable, but the degree and duration of influx has been such as to make it clear to whites that coloured people are a permanent part of the local community. Some ethnic groups – especially those from Asia and India – have set up shops, restaurants and other units in the service sector of the economy, but the bulk of coloured people are employees rather than self-employed or employers, and are paid relatively poorly. It is they, and their children, who are most at risk of unemployment as the recession deepens and redundancies increase.

The strains put by the world recession and by government policy upon small business of the type common in Servicetown lead to bankruptcies, redundancies and unemployment. This especially affects ethnic minorities and women from the lower strata of the working class, many of whom work in firms that are mostly likely to fail. The shrinkage of the job market also makes it more difficult for school-leavers, especially those from the bottom of the working class, to find work. An unpublished Council document correctly attributes the increase in unemployment to an increase in redundancies:

> School leaver unemployment at the present very high level is a relatively recent phenomenon – and while, in the past, unemployment among Black people and the unskilled has always been at a higher level than average, overall it was still very considerably lower than it is at present. Four years ago, more Black people, more unqualified and unskilled persons and more women were all able to find work. What has happened in the intervening years does not result from the make-up of our residents (we do not think it has altered signifiantly), but by the decline in job opportunities, particularly manual job opportunities, within Servicetown and Inner London. It is the total of nearly 4,000 notified redundancies per year (almost certainly a very substantial undercount) which leads people to be without work.

The increasing economic decline leads the Council to anticipate that the major problem facing the Borough will in the future be a shortage of jobs, in contrast to the shortage of homes which have hitherto been of greatest concern to the Council. But there is still a considerable housing problem in Servicetown. In spite of the relatively high number of public housing units built during the 1970s, the majority of housing units in the Borough are old and many are in poor condition. Over 40% of housing units were built before 1919; about one fifth lack a basic amenity, such as a bath, or have to share it with other households; overcrowding is common; and a higher-than-average proportion of households are dissatisfied or very dissatisfied with their accommodation than in most other areas of the UK (Central Statistical Office, 1980; 43).

Overall, then, we may characterise Servicetown as a *declining* area, though not declining so fast as some one-industry towns; and as a highly *heterogenous* inner city area, in terms of employment, ethnic groups, and cultures. It is to be expected, in such an area, that youth cultures, stratified by place in the class structure, by sex, and by race, may also be heterogeneous within the general framework of transition into labour market and adult sexual relations. One has to distinguish not only between areas like Servicetown, and dissimilar areas; but also between the various social groups and youth cultures which face various facets of the quite varied material conditions that exist throughout the Borough.

In this case study, we move towards a study of the drinking practices of the (predominantly white) boys and girls, who come from the central strata of the working class and who, as a group, tend to take jobs in the service sector of the local economy. In order to locate this group in relation to other strata of youth in Servicetown, the following paragraphs discuss conditions of work in various sections of the local labour market, in which service-sector employment occupies a relatively privileged position (compared with employment in the declining small-manufacturing sector). We then examine the ways in which the state agency most responsible for the initial job-socialisation of teenagers – the school system – deals with pupils in the school-leaving period. Finally we describe some aspects of the culture that service-sector youth develop in response to their circumstances.

Approaches to Employers

Interviews were conducted with twenty-two local employers. In most cases these contacts involved one or more visits to the workplace premises, taped interviews, and some degree of access to the actual work-area and employees. In a minority of cases the employers or their nominees would only consent, for various reasons, to talk on the phone, whilst some employers were very co-operative and allowed me to spend several hours at a time on the premises. The first contact with employers was by letter,[8] followed up by a telephone call.

Table 5.3 shows the numbers of jobs in each type of employment in Servicetown, and the decreases in employment in each sector since 1961. In accordance with the predominance of distribution, services and small manufacuturing employment in the Borough, the fieldwork concentrated upon such employers, and also included public administration and construction because school leavers are employed in those sectors (some in clerical work, some in skilled and semi-skilled manual work). One immediate discovery was that, of those employers who did actively want to talk, their reasons varied roughly according to sector, and in a way explicable in terms of the last column of table 5.3. Those sectors of greatest decline –

Table 5.3: Industry of People Working in Servicetown

Industry	No. employed in 1971	% change 1961-71
Distribution and Services (retail shopping, wholesale selling, warehousing, Post Office, financial and professional)	58,500	– 3%
Light Manufacturing (mostly clothes, footware, engineering, printing)	45,300	–38%
Utilities and Transport	25,200	– 2%
Public Administration and Defence	7,300	+18%
Construction	5,700	–46%
All	142,000	–19%

(*Source:* Borough Community Plan 'Topic Paper').

construction and manufacturing – are also sectors in which school leavers' pay is likely to be especially low, partly because of traditions associated with training and apprenticeships. Employers in these sectors were often so keen to have somebody to *complain to* (complain about teenagers, and sometimes about the local state) that they replied with alacrity – or else they were so sick of thinking about their problems that they didn't 'have the time'. Complaints about the world in general, and school-leavers in particular, were most marked in the smallest firms in these sectors. In distribution and services, in which profitability has not been so squeezed and decline has been less marked (there have even been some new ventures in parts of this sector), the response of employers was generally more neutural – yes, the researcher was welcome to come and talk for a brief while, as long as he could manage such-and-such a date. These employers, especially the bigger ones, were more circumspect in their criticisms of youth and of the state; they had fewer problems, partly due to their ability to provide pay, training prospects and working conditions better than those prevailing in most of the manufacturing sector. The bigger shops, especially, were fairly pleased with their personnel policies – pleased enough to talk about and display them at some length. Probably the most sought-after jobs were those with the local council itself. Because of the prospects and security offered by the Council, and because of the varied experience provided by its training phase which aims to find the new recruit the kind of work that he or she likes best, there is considerable school-leaver competition for clerical and craft entry. Council officers were pleased to be interviewed. We now illustrate and fill out these remarks with the aid of interview and fieldwork note records.

The Small Manufacturing Sector

If we begin our account with the light manufacturing sector (in Servicetown, this means clothes, printing, some very light engineering), then a first impression of the work process itself must begin with one word – noise.[9] The individual small machines used in light manufacturing are generally noisy, and a number of such machines, all making their various noises, make a racket. This first impression is not, of course, an impression that would escape one in heavy industry or construction – they are also noisy, often more so than light industry. But it is the specific *character* of the noise – a buzzing, whirring, clicking and banging of many machines, each tended by its individual operator, that determines the specific character of the work process in light manufacutirng. *Each worker works as an individual unit.* He or she works alongside any number of other individuals doing the same or similar movements, and individuals are placed under the supervision of a supervisor; the supervisors report to a shop foreman or to a manager. This individualisation of the work process is in contrast to the situation in much of the heavy or medium industrial sectors, where small or large teams of men work co-operatively as one supra-human unit, and do so within a specific work-group identity.[10] In that situation, the work-flow of one depends on the work-flow of all, and the sort of consciousness thus produced tends to be opposed to the individualised consciousness produced by the competitive labour market. In Servicetown industry, however, the individualised work process and the individualisation of the labour market go hand in hand.[10] As one employer said to me whilst walking round his factory:

> Here we have a senior apprentice, a chap who had done four or five years. You (also) have a junior apprentice, that's one that's just started or done about a year, and you have a semi-skilled girl, the girl would do the uncasing and casing, more or less mundane work . . .
>
> This one's a new one on this end (pointing) well he's done about a year with us, but we kept him mucking about because we weren't happy, we used him up the stores for a long while because we were a little bit uncertain about his mentality.
>
> The other one, that coloured (Indian) one up there, a very good lad, he was one who came in, we started him up the stores to see what he would do, how he would handle things, you know if you've got steel screws you don't want them wetting their fingers otherwise they'd go rusty, so we put him up there to see how he'd respond to the elementary training. Now he's doing extremely well, very well. You can see by the way he works, calm . . . methodical, he's not interested in anything that's going on around him. That's the ideal situation.[11]

This brings out several aspects of employment in the Servicetown manufacturing sector. The skilled apprentices and the adults working with them are individualised and supervised to a high extent and the power of the employer to reward or punish him for 'ideal' or 'inappropriate' performance is high. It is clear that, in many of the bigger firms employing skilled labour the labour market penetrates into the firm itself. It is not something that exists purely outside the firm. In those medium sized or larger firms (50+ employees), there are a number of job-levels, with varying skills, requirements, remuneration and prospects. Employees are characteristically moved up or down the job-ladder according to their performance. Young employees, particularly, are advanced and demoted 'on merit'. (This 'merit' is, as we shall see, an interesting and many-sided thing, including much more than simple skill-proficiency). This penetration of the everyday work-situation by the labour market only occurs in those firms which are big enough and have a sufficient variety of jobs to permit discretionary demotion or promotion. (It also occurs in parts of the service sector, but it cannot happen in very small establishment, where there is little scope for promotion or for higher pay, and little effective sanction other than firing). It is in this sense that many school-leavers' first few years in work are rather like a continuous job-interview – with continuous surveillance, continuous examination, continuous record-keeping and the ever-present possibility of the employers' approval or disapproval being translated into changes in one's status, remuneration and prospects. Some school pupils, who know older and already-working teenagers, discover this truth in advance from them before they face it themselves; whilst others, who whilst at school yearn for the 'freedom' of work, discover it abruptly and with disappointment later. It is only when teenagers have been in work several years that they are no longer under continuous re-appraisal for evidence of their 'mentality' – by then they have been judged and positioned on the record of their presentation in earlier years.

The examination of the young worker's worth proceeds along many dimensions. One of these dimensions is body-language. It does not surprise us that women's physicality is generally considered in judging their job-worth: women are expected, even in those manual jobs such as the clothing industry in which 'looks' are not a great advantage, to have a body language of fine and delicate control. Teenager males, on the other hand, especially those seeking manual employment, are expected to move 'like a man'. Learning to appear to be a man is part and parcel of many apprenticeships. This cannot be explained purely in terms of the strength needed for the work, since power tools render great strength unnecessary. And much of the supposedly-softer 'women's work', whether in light industry or in service environments such as shops, involves long hours of exhausting and tedious movements, often standing. No, the requirement to move like a man is primarily a *moral* requirement. That is not to say that all employers are on the look-out for Mr Butch, nor that there are no limits to masculinity's value in the labour market. Here is one employer's description of the sort of worker he likes. This extract follows on from a discussion of the formal and educational requirements that the employer (in light engineering) has:

> I'm always happy if a kid comes into interview with his mother or father or both of them. As soon as my receptionist says Mr

> So-and so's got his mother and father here, I'm much happier than the kid who has come on his own. You'll find the average white lad'll come in quite humble and . . . but you get the coloured lad with the black leather hats and cigarettes dangling out of their mouths and sort of "Are you going to give me a job or aren't you?" sort of thing. Ah, of the two, I much pefer the timid little white lad whose parents say "Look, I want him to learn a trade. We know that if he's learning a trade he's not going to get the money now but he'll get it later." And father's been a trade-man, he's in the print or he's in engineering or something and he wants it . . .

Similar sentiments were expressed by other employers. The discrimination against blacks is not purely an irrational or racist response. It has several aspects. First and foremost it is based in the employer's expectation that the traditions of apprenticeship and the privations of status and remuneration are better understood and accepted in that part of the English working class – the white part – from which generations of such apprentices have been drawn. Especially favourably regarded will be the white teenager actually accompanied by a skilled father or, since he himself may be hard at work, by a wife of such a person. Secondly, the 'attitude' of the boy is important to the prospective employer. Faced with a choice between timidity and belligerence, he chooses timidity. An apprenticeship depends, more than anything, on the willingness to enter communication with, acknowledge the worth of, and comply with the directions of one's elders and betters. Signs of too great an independence, signs which the employer sees in the dress and manner of some black teenagers, threaten this relationship.

Because of the lack of profitability of the declining small manufacturing sector, employers' abilities to provide congenial working conditions or to pay reasonable wages is much reduced. The smaller, least profitable manufacturing firms complain bitterly about young people's lack of 'stickability' and about their 'greediness', and about unfair competition from other, better-paying concerns (particularly in the state sector). Some young males drift in and out of employment with firms at the bottom of the labour market until they are 18 years old, when they are eligible to join the Post Office, which pays well compared with declining manufacturing firms:

> Now being a business where you've got to train people, ah, and obviously, as far as the first two years anybody you get in, as far as working content goes are a liability, you get nothing out of them, you train them; by that time they're eighteen, seventeen or eighteen, Joe Bloggs who's living next door is running a motor bike, and ah, at their training rates of pay they don't get a motor bike, so off they go, and you're £2,000 down. It's rather a disheartening position after you've been here 25 years. In the 25 years we've been here I've retained about three, and I've actually interviewed by the last count about 480 different people and retained about three.

The decline of small industry had produced a situation in which the terms 'training' and 'apprenticeship' have become devalued. For many of the smaller employers, who could not afford to pay skilled rates of pay, and whose work-processes actually demand no more skill than can be picked up in a few weeks (at most), the demand for young people to undergo 'training' is equivalent to the demand that they accept high levels of discipline and low levels of pay, with no formal contract or guarantee that their position will ever improve substantially. Few small manufacturing firms in Servicetown are unionised, and individual workers pressing for increased pay can easily be labelled 'troublemakers' and dismissed. The lack of investment in the worker in the smaller firms, and the ease with which they can be replaced, means that there is little constraint on employers ability to hire and fire at will: the employer quoted above confirmed that many of those no longer in his employ had in fact been dismissed (for a wide variety of reasons, including 'laziness', 'bad influence', and 'greedy'). Employers' attitudes to their employees were in some cases quite contemptuous:

> Well, you tell me, what am I supposed to do? You get them in here, still wet behind the ears, mummy's boys and that, and they say they want a job. What am I supposed to pay them?

A recurring complaint of employers in the smaller firms was that 'the dole's too high'. The work-conditions facing school-leavers entering such firms, the low pay and lack of prospects of improvement, and the employers' tendency to solve problems by dismissal, combine to present a picture that can be made to look attractive only in comparison with unemployment. It is against this background that the service sector can be seen as offering a relatively pleasant future to some school-leavers.

Service With A Smile

Employment in the service sector (shops, offices etc) differs in some respects from employment in manufacturing. This is true even if a particular job-description, e.g. warehouse work, can be found in either sector – the job will be rather different depending on the sector in which it occurs. Warehouse work in a manufacturing firm is, for example, a job at or near the bottom of a particular kind of job-hierarchy, and in a particular (industrial) environment – whilst warehouse work in one of the newer distributive concerns can often be a relatively well-paid job, one that involves reasonable clerical skills and a degree of self-management, and which is regarded by more 'modern' managements as an integral, rather than peripheral, part of the work-process. The status, working conditions and social relations can differ markedly depending on the employment sector, even for 'the same job'. When one considers that the types of jobs available in manufacturing and service sectors are generally *not* the same, even in name, then it becomes clear that the distinction between manufacturing and service employment is quite important if we want to understand the job-market facing teenagers.

One significant aspect of much service employment is the demand it makes upon 'facework'.[13] This is an obligation in shop work, where one is constantly interacting with a stream of outsiders. One well-known chainstore even obliges its staff to wear a badge inscribed with a smiling face and the legend 'Friendly People'. That this may indeed be more of a legend than a reality need not concern us very much – the badge is an illustration of the management's concept of an ideal worker, just as the actual lack of smiles illustrates the difficulty of living up to that ideal. Whilst in manufacturing work the 'ideal solution' is a person who concentrates on his hands and is 'not interested in anything that is going on around him', shop work obliges the worker to process persons as well as things. The amount of facework required depends, however, on the type of shop. The more that a shop approaches the supermarket pattern, the more shelves, trolleys, fencing and exotic tills intercede between shopper and employee, and between employee and employee, relieving them of the burden of eye-contact, facework and body language, and creating a work-environment that approaches 'hand-work'. The more the shop adheres to 'personal service', on the other hand, the greater the 'social' demands, and the more the worker selling his or her labour has to include his or her face, body language and 'general personal presentation' in the deal. More than this, he or she is obliged to give him or her commitment and *enthusiasm.* Consider this statement made by a personnel officer of a large 'personal service' store in the locality:

> There's something, something electrifying about being on the sales floor. If you have a chance to actually advise a customer, and you know that you've done something that the customer wants, that really is quite a good feeling. And in addition, I think because it's a department store, each individual doesn't do just one job, there's a great variety to each particular job title. As a sales assistant, you're a jack of all trades . . .
>
> I miss the battle. On a Saturday I will try not to interview unless somebody can't come in except on Saturday because I want to be on that sales floor. For two reasons. One is the P.R., for example, because I think it's fairly important that they (staff) know that we're (personnel office) not having Saturday off. And two, because, actually, there is that buoyancy in the air. It's great . . .
>
> So many people come back again and again, you can see it, when I worked in the gifts department you saw mums, with the kid, coming round on a Wednesday and having a look, she'd come back on Saturday with the other kid on her other hand, husband and a mummy, to buy . . . And you see it happening. So you get used to people, you get the same customers again to a certain extent, not always . . .

The service sector, and retailing in particular, tries to marry economic rationality and personal relationships and, in so attempting, transforms both into an *instrumental emotionality.* The object is to help the customer to buy. The means are helpfulness, informativeness, genuine interest, expressed with the whole self. This expressive role, once learned, can bring rewards. There may be other reasons why staff are reluctant to take Saturdays off – they may – for instance, not wish to face the recriminations of their short-staffed and over-stretched colleagues - but there are also real emotional rewards to be had in producing a satisfied customer (just as there are rewards to be had, in manual craft occupations, in turning out a good product).

In the more routinised, less 'personal' big stores – especially supermarkets – staff training consists of training rather more in specific routines and rather less in self-presentation, general principles, or 'commitment'. In these stores, however, because the staff are not supposed to be reserving their attentions for the customer, they may interact more freely among themselves. Workers in industry are supposed to interact instrumentally with their product (and to take instructions from supervisors); workers in 'personal service' shops are supposed to interact in an emotionally facilitatory way with customers; and workers in supermarkets and similar shops may react mechanically with the goods *and* with the customers, and are freer to interact emotionally with each other. Because such familiarity is easiest within specific age and/or ethnic groups – and because young women from the lower strata of the working class are least likely to get other, better paid jobs – one often finds that the workforce in such a shop is predominantly made up of young people who are female and from the same ethnic minority group. As I was told by one girl working on the till in a supermarket: 'I think I'd go mad here if it wasn't for my mates'.

Let us now turn to office employment. Office work involves working as an individual, but 'in a team'. As such it requires some specific work skill(s); it requires a certain degree of 'initiative', that is, knowing how to respond to circumstances which do not exactly fit the general rules, and knowing when to ask for help; and it requires the ability to 'get on' with people. 'Friendly office', say the advertisements. In the context of a conversation about black people and employment, a (female) personnel worker in a large office underlined the important of a friendly manner:

> I find that black girls have got dreadful chips on their shoulders when they come in to us. I mean I've sat a girl here before and, I can't remember where she came from now (i.e. how she learned of the job) but I said something to her and she said, 'Ah, well, I won't get this job anyway because I'm black'. And I said to her . . . you know, and I think it was because she was (just) sitting there, she wouldn't smile, I couldn't get her to talk and so on. And I said to her, I had to, 'You won't have any chance of getting a

> job unless you can sit there and smile and chat to somebody and show that you want the job.' And for her, she was here as a matter of course because she'd got the interview booked but there was no way that she was going to get the job anyway because she was coloured. And as far as I'm concerned that wasn't so . . .
>
> . . .I'm trying to think if I've taken on . . . (pause) . . . we took on a school-leaver, you know the Government training, we took on a coloured girl from there and she was tremendous, she came in, she was chirpy, she smiled and as soon as I'd seen her I said she's the one because – she'd come down from Norfolk or somewhere; her parents lived in Norfolk – and I spent about an hour with her. She hadn't got a chip on her shoulder, she was chirpy.
>
> . . .Now if a lot of them were like here – I mean she wasn't particularly good at what she was doing – but she tried hard, and she was always willing, and she did her best. And I think if they do that they've got far more chance.

A somewhat different self-presentation is, however required from boys:

> I suppose with boys, I think, they're looking for more from careers than girls are. I think that's the difference. Girls know they can leave and they can get another job as easy as anything, but boys tend not to be able. They think their first job is where they're going to get their career and training . . . they think that this is my first job, I've got to get the training behind me and so on. Whereas girls seem to flit from one job to another.

Boys are supposed to present themselves as friendly without 'flitting' or being 'chirpy'. Girls, on the other hand, are supposed, even if they aspire to promotion, to present themselves, non-threateningly, as not doing so. A chirp is a sign of being happy with one's present lot.

Clerical work also takes place in places of employment that include one or several other types of department apart from 'the office'. We look now at two such employers – a local warehousing and distribution business, and the Council. These employers share some characteristics – e.g. the ability to transfer employees from one department to another – and they differ in some respects. The warehousing and distribution businesses that form a relatively buoyant part of the local service sector tend to inhabit new buildings and to use modern business techniques. Both the relatively pleasant physical environment and the new techniques such as computer stock control and record-keeping have the effect of drawing 'manual' warehouse work closer to clerical and office work. Yet the distinction between office work and warehouse work remains.

> Um, you see most of the office staff have all come from school, straight from school, er, I can think of at least four or five examples where they've come up with their parents for the interview . . . and I think personally – and I'm talking about the office staff, not the warehouse – on the office staff we've been very fortunate . . . But I think we've had one, two, three down in the warehouse which we've kept. The others we've had problems with.

This firm finds it more difficult to recruit, and to retain, warehouse staff than office staff. This is in spite of the fact that rates of pay for school-leavers are higher in the warehouse than in the office, and in spite of the fact that the warehouse deals with light and clean goods. The warehouse work also contains a high clerical content but, in the minds of both employer and employees, it is still more 'manual' and of lower status than office work, and 'prospects' are relatively poor. The introduction of new technologies into warehousing challenges the assumption that it is unskilled manual work and hence opens up the possibility of employing school-leavers in the warehouse. But, because 'warehouse work' has traditionally been considered to be primarily 'manual' in status and prospects, it is not so attractive as office work, and so recruitment into the warehouse remains a considerable problem. It is in these lower-status, less-favoured sections of the firm that employers have most difficulty in disciplining their workforce:

> Well I would say one thing – I think discipline, er, you know, this is only just recently I've had this feeling but, you know, with the young fellas that we've had downstairs there's, you can see that there's no sense of discipline at all. Discipline in any sense, ah, self-discipline or otherwise.

'Discipline' has two aspects – one centering upon the worker's attitude to work and his subservience to the procedures and authorities at work, and the second aspect, 'self-discipline', which centres upon one's out of work behaviour and personal life. Since most employers consider these two aspects of discipline (also called 'maturity') to be closely linked, both aspects concern them:

> You get a change in attitude about seventeen or eighteen . . . Now we've got a chappie downstairs who has been with us about nine months now and he's quite young, he's not married, he's got a child, just had the child and I had troubles before his wife, his girlfriend was expecting, and I thought, well, probably, when he's had the child he might settle down, but he didn't, he got worse, and I gave him, I think he's had four warning letters . . . Well, he used to go out drinking at lunchtimes and ah, he'd come back and he'd get in trouble with other people working downstairs and that kind of thing – usually with older people. Ah, lateness, attendance . . . but, um, but um, but when he got that last letter he sort of settled down, I hope he has, because I put him back on packing – he was assembling – and he said, 'Well this is degrading'. And I said, 'Until you mature and show your willingness to work there's not much else I can do' . . . But I'm hoping that he is maturing in all senses, with the job, with the family and everything.
>
> (ND: Do you see them as related areas?)
>
> Obviously I do, yeah. You know, I mean, er, it is little things, you can't really get a grip on. You ask me now and the only think I can think of is that Mary, when she opened her banking account, well she did it first and then another one followed suit. It might seem a silly thing but, you know, her attitudes, she used to go out drinking a hell of a lot and I don't think she ever does now. You know, she's got a banking account, she looks after herself.

This extract again illustrates the existence of a hierarchical labour market *within* the firm, which the employer can use to discipline and mature his workforce. Promotion/demotion can take place within the clerical or within the non-clerical departments, and between departments – where these possibilities exist the employer is likely to make use of them, retaining dismissal as a last resort. The structure of discipline in service sector firms with several departments involving overlapping job-skills thus depends very much upon the employee's aspirations and upon he or she depending upon the job for identity and status – the employer tries to avoid hiring employees for whom the job will simply be a job, since he has relatively little control over such employees. Service sector employers concern themselves with 'the whole person', both in recruitment and in management. When a 'whole person' employer has a department of his firm that is traditionally considered 'manual', that employer will find it difficult to discipline the labour in that department. This is a problem many Servicetown employers face – and a circumstance that many of the school-leavers come up against. The newer Servicetown employers want not only your hands, not only your smile – they want your heart too.

From School to Service-sector

This middle section of the case study looks at the institution which feeds the labour market – the school – and especially at the ordinary, run-of-the-mill comprehensives.[14] In order to begin to understand the social space which 'ordinary' comprehensives occupy, it is instructive to look at an ex-grammar school which is now being obliged to come to terms with its new comprehensive status. Social structures become most clear when they shift. A careers teacher outlined the changes in these terms:

> My feeling is that the school is definitely middle class and in fact at the moment is very much struggling to understand the new working class population that is coming in . . . in language, in behaviour and in culture . . . the comprehensive intake is very broad, ah, very mixed.
>
> (ND: Does this cause problems for the staff?)
>
> Yes . . . it's bound to, really. You see, if you've been teaching in a grammar school, um, you've been used to one particular sort of ability. And if they're not of that ability, well, you know, it's only perhaps one difficult person to cope with . . . difficult in the sense of academic difficulty.

(ND: And now you get other kinds of difficulty.)

Yes. There're all sorts of emotional difficulties, sort of . . . er . . . between people in the class as there's much more sort of friction going on, um, a lot more of the . . . er . . . because of the lack of . . . um . . . being able to articulate thoughts through words. There's a tremendous change in the use of bodily language . . .

(ND: You mean the teachers have to cue in to all that?)

Yes. Because if you don't know what's going on then things can get out of hand. I think the school's actually coping amazingly well. I mean I've always taught in comprehensive schools, so I'm fairly used to a comprehensive intake and all that that brings with it.

One type of school that continues to escape the 'very broad' or 'mixed' comprehensive intake 'and all that that brings with it', is the Roman Catholic school. Roman Catholic schools tend to draw upon a particular ethnic group – the Irish. This ethnic group has established its own occupational history, and this tends to stabilize the expectations of its teenage members and to provide a relatively high level of cohesion between home and school. The Irish community pre-socializes many of its teenage boys into apprenticeships in the construction industry, sometimes to the chagrin of teachers who feel particular boys could 'do better'. But teachers appreciate the ease of discipline in Roman Catholic schools which have a close and long-standing link with an ethnic group that is not at the bottom of the labour market:

I feel that in a classroom situation, teaching, there's no problems, no discipline problems. That's a personal point of view, I mean there are discipline problems . . . there are ten or twelve who are a continual trouble, problem. But its certainly, I don't feel its a sink school, but at the same time we do have, uh, we haven't got any, ah, well a great number of West Indian boys, of course, its mainly Irish, and very much a working class background . . . and I think that the background being a church school, we have got the support of the parents. And I think that's probably our greatest asset.

(ND: So you've got the support of the parents. The support of the parents in terms of discipline, isn't that really the issue?)

Yes. Well, yes, but from the point of view of using work as a discipline, in that I want to teach, now whether I'm teaching good things or the things that they want to know or not, but at least I am teaching in a classroom situation, I'm not just, I feel, childminding. And if a boy isn't responding, then at least I can – it may be my fault – but at least I can contact parents and I can talk to them. And in the majority of cases then with the boy we'll talk it through . . . Now that might not apply to everybody in the school.

(ND: Not to everybody, but its more of a general thing?)

I think it would be, compared with the schools outside.

This is so. Many comprehensives have a continual problem of control,[15] and have to construct strategies for dealing with this central problem and for preventing it moving to the centre of the stage and obliterating their 'educational' tasks. Continual staff effort is expended in the creation of a classroom atmosphere conducive to scholarship. The majority of Servicetown schools seem to have a fairly continuous internal debate over whether or not the situation should be described as a 'discipline problem'. Staff consensus on the existence of a discipline problem signifies the ascendency of the less liberal wing of the staff, since it rationalises a more hard-line pupil control policy and a tendency to lay the blame upon 'minorities' in the school. The more liberal staff generally try to fend off recognition of a 'discipline problem', finding it more congenial to continue their efforts to achieve control as a by-product of the main project of helping each pupil to fully explore his or her unique potential. For the liberal element, a disciplinary orientation is incompatible with an educational one, whilst for other staff, it is prerequisite. Because it is too exhausting for staff to be fighting continuously amongst themselves, as well as with the pupils, the school generally seeks to adopt a relatively stable control situation – and that depends crucially upon the resources that it can deploy both from within itself and within the pupils and the local area.

Work-experience schemes are an important and increasing element in the schools' practice, and one that solves many of the immediate problems that pupils and schools face. For the pupil, work-experience gives money, facilitating their leisure lives; it gives a broader identity than that of 'school-kid'; it relieves them of the monotony of a schooling that seems scarcely relevant to the present or future concerns of many; it can advantageously position him (and it is generally a he) vis-a-vis the job market on leaving school. Employers often see advantages insofar as they obtain cheap labour and may presocialise teenagers into work in their firm. For the schools, work-experience helps to solve control problems – teenagers not orientated to school work can be shunted out on work-experience, converting what would otherwise be either truancy or classroom disruption into legitimate training, and leaving the more 'interested' pupils in the classroom to get on with their school work. Many pupils float between school and work during their fifteenth and sixteenth year: this has significant consequences not only for those pupils, but also for the whole school environment, and hence for other pupils, their transition to work and their leisure pursuits. A teacher in a large local comprehensive explained the origins and development of work-experience schemes in these terms:

> The idea behind it was that, uh, boys should *taste* the world of work . . . the whole purpose was that the boys should taste some type of work, whatever it was, and the idea, the underlying idea was that if he didn't take a fancy to that particular type of work then he might try something else and ultimately settle down, after he's got his CSEs and O levels . . . That was the original idea, its supposed to be still, but something's happened in the last two years because it gets round the grapevine. I started it by sending boys out to banks – the big five pay expenses which amounts to £5 a week or maybe £6, and that covers lunches and it also covers fares – and then for some reason the first break into the supermarket work-experience things was the L.C.S. because they've been running it for years . . . and there, it varied from supermarket to supermarket, how much the students would get, in the north of London they still get about three to five pounds a week. If the boy's working hard and there's a part-time vacancy on Saturday the boy gets it so he might knock it up to £8 or £10, so it gets round the grapevine, through the grapevine rather, that its possible to get quite a bit of money on this. So then, I sent a few to Tesco's, and Tesco (branch) paid a certain boy for three months – he was one of the permanent truants – and, ah, he was

> getting £30 a week because the manager was rather sympathetic to him, he had no father, just a mother and the mother was over the moon – he was getting thirty quid a week for three months or four months. And after that, of course, he must tell his friends who still go to school once he's left, that you can earn quite a bit on this work-experience project 'lark' as they might say and therefore the first thing boys ask me about six or nine months ago was "How much?" I said, "Well, its not a question of 'how much?', you're going there for work-experience and you're getting experience." But, it got round the school I suppose and then boys started saying "Can I get £15-£20?" and then, of course, there's no end to it. And now they want money otherwise they won't go . . .

Whilst work-experience schemes were intended to facilitate teenagers' recruitment into the 'better' jobs in banks and similar work-environments, this school (and others) is now using work-experience to release boys into the secondary (lower) job market, and the boys are taking this up more for money than as a step in building a career.

> It's really making it, ah, a four-years stay at school from eleven to fifteen, then the last year is work, in the normal sense, except its legalised, and they're still 'going to school' and getting their register marked. So it has, as you say, subverted the original principle. On the other hand, something else has happened which is quite important, because, it doesn't apply to the whole of the fifth year, it only applies to a relatively small number. That number could grow considerably in the years to come. Maybe not in other schools, they'll just be faced with empty rooms, perhaps . . . because as you've seen, you've seen, have you? As you go round the school, well I don't know if you've consciously looked for this, but if you go into a fifth year group, I mean there should be twenty-eight in the group, at least twenty-five, twenty-six. And if you counted heads you'd find eight, ten or twelve. That means sixteen are not there – at least sixteen don't go.

The process of getting release from the school in order to work for part of the week has become relatively simplified, quick and easy in some schools. During a period of less than two hours spent with one careers master (not the one quoted above), two 5th form boys sought and obtained permission to work for two days a week. The first boy brought his father (who supported himself by selling vegetables from a barrow) to see the careers teacher. The boy wished to take up an offer of part-time portering work, and this was agreed. After an hour, another boy came in, unaccompanied. The transaction went as follows:

T: Yes?
B: I've been set up to you by Mr –
T: Oh. What about?
B: About a job.
T: About a job?
B: Yes, he said that you could try to get me three days (off school) a week.
T: Not three days a week.
B: The firm sent this (hands over a printed form).
T: Huh. When are they going to start you, my boy?
B: Just until just after Easter, cos they thought I could start (full-time) after Easter, but my birthday falls wrong. (Name) said she would try to get me three days a week. I've got in contact with the firm and they say they've never done it before but they will . . .
T: Uh. I wouldn't say three days . . . possibly two days.
B: (muttering) . . .
T: What's your date of birth?
B: Twenty-sixth of February.
T: February. Good God, you've got to suffer (until the end of) the year. What exams are you taking?
B: None.
T: You're not going to take any. (Fills in form, tells boy to take it to his house head so that he knows to mark him 'present' in the register).

In this study, these male pupils are called 'early workers'.

Girls' Truancy and Domestic Labour

Because of expectations less favourable to girls working, work-experience schemes are less commonly operated in relation to girls. Girls do sometimes, therefore, truant in order to work, but their participation in the labour market is more commonly *indirect.* That is to say, many girls truant in order to work in the *home.* Their labour releases hard-pressed mothers to sell *their* labour in the market or helps the mother cope with a large and difficult family. This is most likely to be the case when the family is large, when the girl has several younger brothers and sisters, when the father is absent or unwaged, when the family is poor – and it is virtually the only solution open to many families. Girls' long-term truancy is therefore no more 'emotional' than boys', and it has just as much economic rationality. The difference is that whilst the boy regards his earnings as 'his', and hence keeps at least some part of them, the girl does not become a wage-earner. Even in truancy, then, we see the continuing differential socialisation of boys and girls, their preparation for their class-roles. This differential socialisation is most rigorous in the lower part of the working class, since it is here that the objective pressures upon girls to truant in order to do domestic labour are most strong:

> The more able girls don't do anything around the house. I talk to them a lot about that, say, "do you do the washing-up?" – "No" – they don't feel, nobody obviously asks them to and they don't see any particular reason. I think they probably do to help every now and again but its not part of their duty.
>
> While less able girls, you know you talk to one or two of them and they say, "ah, don't give us too much homework tonight" – "Why" – "Tonight's my ironing night", and they'll do the ironing, or they'll go down the launderette, or they'll do the shopping. I have a couple of girls who quite often ask me to look after the post office book and about twenty-five quid, um, which parents have obviously asked them to put into the post office. Um, so on the whole, the less able girls . . . Actually, when I say "less able", that sounds awful, I've just realised what I've done, I've done a terrible thing, and that is to equate working class with less able, which is not true . . .

As far as could be ascertained from interviews with teachers, the school are quite tolerant of non-attendance on the part of girls from the lower strata of the working class, it being understood that family duties come first. The schools seem quite ready to bow to local class traditions when it comes to girls, and this readiness is enhanced by curricula and by staff attitudes that fall short of a full commitment to sexual equality:

> It has been remarked on in several staff meeting when we were doing the curriculum, that it was odd that we had a very female-stereotype curriculum, um, and its regarded as a great joke if you say why don't we do woodwork. This brings the house down, I don't quite see why, it annoys me - well, I've stopped getting annoyed. But, so, I thought that a female staff – the majority of staff are females, and an all-girls school, would be straight into the feminism, but no. Um, again I think that this is partly from people at the top, who have very strong ideas. I mean, people that get married, for example, have to change their name, they're not allowed to retain their maiden names, at least they do, they can try, but its a difficult thing to fight against . . . (personal detail).
>
> And members of staff that have got children, ah, you know, there's a certain amount from the top of feeling that if their child is less than two that they perhaps ought to be at home looking after it, even if they've got husbands that are prepared to do, or they've got some sort of arrangement . . . So, there's that there, within the system.

Sexism from the top severely limits the ability of female teachers to act as role-models or curriculum-planners encouraging a questioning of traditional sexual imagery and roles. Teachers who wish to do fairly modest sexual-equality education find this reaction limiting. The smaller number who wish to go beyond simple sex-equality, and question male and female roles more fundamentally, are severely constrained by this and by the hostile, anti-feminist reaction of many male members of staff which it sustains and supports. Teachers have considerable impediments to overcome *within* the educational system before they can come fully to grips with the problem of helping pupils to combat sexism *outside* the schools. One consequence is that most working class girls are still being set up for the double shift of waged and unwaged work which dominates the lives of the majority in Servicetown.

'Fixed Up' and 'Perpetual Students'

With the non-attenders, be they working in the labour market or in the family home, absent from the school, class size is considerably reduced. Fifth year (i.e. leaving-year) classes of less than half of their total roll size of about twenty-eight are not unusual in Servicetown comprehensive schools. Apart from those regularly absent from school (on particular days or continuously), there is a floating population which 'bunks off' depending on the lesson and on alternative attractions. Amongst those remaining, several groups can be discerned. One group of school-attenders consists of those who have got some kind of apprenticeship or on-the-job training 'fixed up' for when they leave school at sixteen. Having their future fixed up, and that arrangement depending more upon a record of discipline, orderliness and attendance than upon exam results, these pupils are simply marking time. This is one group for whom the hazards of truanting (boredom, cold, being caught, getting a poor school record, etc) outweigh the tedium of school. Sometimes recognised by teachers as 'underachievers' (they have no reason to 'achieve' in school), these pupils make up a high proportion of Catholic schools, and a smaller proportion of many other comprehensives.

The 'fixed up' pupils, who so obviously 'lack motivation' in their school work, can be *contrasted* with a large group within which there is the opposite tendency. Some groups, particularly members of ethnic minority groups who have been led by their parents to aspire to a good, often self-employed artisan or professional-level job, put their hope in the educational system. They regard the education system as a kind of class-mobility conveyor belt – just sit on it long enough and you'll get there. Several teachers were concerned with racial minority groups parents' tendency to expect 'miracles' from the educational system. When told that their offspring might have to stay in the sixth form for several years, painstakingly collecting exams, or that the professional qualifications sought might not be obtained until the offspring was over thirty years old, the parents simply said 'fine'. A prospect of eventual success was often more acceptable to them than the prospect of their (male) children following in their own rather humble occupational footsteps. In West Indian groups, in particular, boys share with their parents the desire to escape the bottom of the labour market, though they may often be less patient. The mismatch between black boys' aspirations and the means for and likelihood of such success is, together with other issues already touched upon, a major headache for teachers:

> Every heads of department meeting we seem to be discussing the same issues, time and again, we don't seem to resolve these massive problems. The main ones are under-achievement, truancy . . . truancy mainly in the latter years, four and five, especially five, especially Easter leavers. And the rot for the Easter leavers sets in, I think, in year four when they see how unattainable are the goals which we have set them. And then fifth year boys have such fantasies about what they want to do . . .

It is extremely hard for teachers to say to any pupil that he or she should give up his or her apsirations and settle for what is within grasp, since this 'realistic' advice flies in the face of much of what many teachers believe education is about. Such advice is particularly hard to press upon a ethnic minority already discriminated against in many ways. Boys therefore often stay on into the sixth forms (where they try to improve on their CSEs or O levels and maybe attempt an A level or two), and/or they go to a College of Further Education. This latter course gives the status of 'student' – a considerable social support for those aspiring to professional status. For many black students in Servicetown, the promise which their culture draws from the educational system is not made reality – they have eventually to settle for much less than that to which, at fifteen or sixteen, they aspired.

Service-sector Youth

We have now, on the basis of the ways in which material conditions and cultural resources shape the transition to waged work, identified four groups of pupils - 'early workers'; 'domestics'; 'perpetual students'; and 'fixed up'. This brings us to the group recognised by teachers as being relatively 'good' pupils. Unlike the truanters, those on work experience, and members of minority groups, these pupils are not from the bottom of the working class. They are from the middle or 'respectable' sections of the working class. But unlike those relatives of artisans or of supervisors in small firms who have got themselves 'fixed up' with an apprenticeship or other job-training, these pupils must rely upon exam results, school reports and a 'respectable' self-presentation to prevent themselves slipping into the lower small manufacturing sector of the labour market. Few white teenage members of the respectable working class aspire to the kind of student status and the class mobility dreamt of in some ethnic minority groups – but they do regard the educational system as a means of holding or slightly bettering their class position. The pressure to do reasonably well in academic terms comes not only from the 'respectable' working class family, but is also generated by the pupil himself when he sees the circumstances faced by friends from a similar class background who have already left school:

> I've got a friend who's at the London College of Furniture, um, a couple of friends, one works for a carpet factory, you know, delivering carpets, laying them, but he isn't a fitter or anything like that. And, um, er, a friend is a clerical officer, a senior clerical officer. But they don't talk very much about work. I think they find that a depressing subject.

Such friendship groupings within the middle parts of the working class, and containing teenagers of both sexes below and above the school leaving age (sixteen years), form a coherent youth culture in relation to which I shall later discuss drinking and the pub. The point for our present purpose – and this is a point drawn not only from interviews but also from participant observation work and from simple eavesdropping – is that 'work' is indeed an uninspiring subject of conversation for participants in such groups. Work is discussed – but generally in terms which present it as having reward only in the pay packet, not in the content and meaning of the job. Indeed, the job content seems often to be defined in terms of avoidance of negatives[16] – not in a factory, not stuck in an office all day, not stuck at a till, not outside all the time etc. These negatives are drawn up on the basis of hearing about their friends' and acquaintances' dissatisfactions.

> I've no idea what I'd like to do . . . I don't think they've ever designed a job which involves going out, and staying in. I'd like to be able to sit down behind a desk and do something, but I'd like to get out, and do work, do-you-know-what-I-mean-I'm-not-sure.

It is upon the culture of such teenagers, who are in transition into some part of the service sector, that we now focus. 'Service-sector youth culture', as we shall use the term, refers to a number of loosely-articulated groups of white boys and girls from the middle sections of the working class. This is a *service-sector* culture because the participants come from the working class and are in the process of finding their own places within that part of its occupational structure. It is a *youth* culture because it is organised around age as well as class, and because it recruits teenagers aound age sixteen who share the characteristic of being in transition from childhood status of school-attendance to adult status of being settled in the labour market. Because of their anticipation of moving into the labour market, and because of their continuing concern over their place within it once they have entered it, this transition is an extended *process*. It provides common ground for those working class boys and girls who neither jump into a pre-arranged apprenticeship or other slot nor attempt to use education in an attempt to escape the working class altogether. We use the term culture rather than 'subculture' because the latter term implies a more socially restricted membership (in terms of gender or age range or 'style') and a more autonomous (autonomous from the adult working class, from occupational concerns, etc) social process, than is here involved. 'Service-sector youth culture' is a social space in which children who know that they have little chance (as a group, in an area like Servicetown, in times like today's) of escaping the working class but have yet to finalise their exact occupational and social position within the middle strate of that class, negotiate with each other the meaning of such a life as it confronts them day-to-day:

> We don't do a great deal. Usually we just sit on the park wall, smoke and talk . .for hours on end.

The main activities of the service-sector group observed were 'hanging about', playing street games with younger kids, establishing the whereabouts and activities of others in the group and, sometimes, going to the fishshop, pub, or each other's houses (or, more rarely, to the cinema). The pre-teens and younger teenagers spend more time in the streets in the immediate neighbourhood of their homes, whilst the older teenagers (16-20), who come from further afield, meet in or at specified spots, such as the pub.

Members of the middle age range (around 13-16 years old) tend to oscillate between the street games of their youth and the more 'adult' set of older teenagers. The street games of the younger teenagers have an exuberance and untroubled appearance absent from the activities of the older boys and girls. The street congregations and games are also marked by a high degree of playful shouting ahd physical contact. Boys and girls run about in the road (the area is a partial cul-de-sac), interacting first with one individual or small group, and then with another. Games of 'chase' are common, and quickly shifting allegiances and 'sides' are formed to determine who will chase whom. The younger and smaller boys and girls frequently appeal to the older ones for attention, and this atention can take the form of trying to lift one another, the older twirling the younger one around, or chasing. In this group, the degree of physical touching of boys by girls is in sharp contrast with the reserve that occurs in older groups. Girls under ten may hurl themselves in a mock attack on a teenage male, who then fends them off with elaborate displays of being wounded by their attack. The young teenage girls may command the attentions of mid-teenage boys by grabbing them, sometimes round the neck. These encounters are safe because they are not 'sexual' – the girl is too young to be a 'girlfriend', she's just a friend. It seemed that street play with such younger groups was well enjoyed – at least for period of an hour or so – by mid-teen boys, who often exhibited signs of strain when talking of or sitting with older groups. Mid-teenage girls, however, rarely joined in the more physical side of street life. Those teenage girls who did 'hang around' outside did so in the more settled mid-teenage groups that formed later in the evenings when the younger ones had gone home.

'Class' and music

Music provides a topic of conversation, and an activity, inside and outside the pub. In its most marked form, the interest includes playing an instrument.

> Usually round me mates' house having a jam or sitting round the park . . . electric guitar, six string. I've also got a six-string acoustic, and there's me mate's bass guitar as well so I can play all three.

The more frequent level of interest involves talking about music, recording each others' (and brothers' and sisters') records onto cassette, and arguing about the merits and demerits of various groups.

> I like Dylan and they like Led Zeppelin so we're forever arguing . . . Pink Floyd, yeh, they like Pink Floyd, Zeppelin, that mob, and I like Dylan, so we argue a lot on that point, um . . . there's a . . . whose doing what, and how they bunked off today and what lessons they bunked off, its general crap, you know, we often sit there in silence, insult each other.

It is significant that all musical discussions and arguments took place within a consensus that excluded punk rock from serious consideration.

> I've listened to a bit of punk. I admit one or two things are funny, you know, bits and pieces of them. But, um, it seems silly, you know, somebody sticking safety pins in and out of their earholes and things like this, running around and spitting at each other and into each other's mouths, it just seems vulgar.
>
> (ND: What sort of people do like punk?)
>
> I don't know. — School of Girls is supposed to be a pretty good school and everybody in there runs around looking like a punk.
>
> (ND: Why do you think that is?)
>
> I don't know – I was round (local area) one night and a family at a corner house, like, was having a party. There was a couple of us there (in the street) and this lady came out and she said "excuse me, you three", she goes "do you like punk rock?" and we said "no", she goes "don't move, don't move, stay there", and she ran into this party and brought this bloke out. He was a . . . a journalist or something, for a newspaper. And she goes "look, I've found three people who don't like punk rock." And he was going on about punk rock was the thing of the kids today, you know, you should listen to the words and get their meaning.
>
> (ND: And what is their meaning supposed to be, according to him?)

> According to him it was, it was, er how did he put it, he said something about describing kids of today, you know, life, death opinions on life, sex, drugs, stuff like this . . . he said punk was the music of kids today, it was written by kids today . . and you know, that is the kind of stuff we should like. My friend said, "I can't stand it". He goes "What kind of music do you like?" He said "Emerson, Lake and Palmer, Pink Floyd", stuff like this. And he said "But that's not your music, that was the music of kids years ago . . ." He said, "I've been straight through that", he said, "and then it was good stuff, then I liked it, but now I like punk". Punk is the in thing (ironically).
>
> (ND: Did you think he was an idiot?)
>
> Not so much an idiot. If he wants to believe that he can believe it by all means. I didn't agree with it. I mean I don't like punk. I don't see the point in it . . . We take the mickey out of it. Like, in Mike's house we'll just pick up a guitar and strum it, make a terrible racket, and you'll say, "Oh, you're playing punk rock I see". "You can play guitar – you'd be a good punk". It seems like, the words they write, you know, the words and music, there's not style, no class, no . . . no thought in it. That's probably why I don't like it.

Punk rock is, in the eyes of this group, OK for middle class teenagers and middle class adult trendies.[17] Middle class teenagers are assured of their class position, and can even celebrate this security by flirting with cultural forms that appear to have 'no class'. Hippie culture in the 1960s and punk culture in the 1970s are by no means similar in content, but they both represent a degree of 'going native' that can be safely indulged in only by the middle class. For members of service-sector youth culture to take up such 'unrespectable' and 'vulgar' forms of self-presentation would be to imperil their chances in the labour market.

Relations Between the Sexes

The position of girls within this culture is of special interest. Girls are visible and long-term members of service-sector youth culture.[18] But, as in the general population, there are powerful sanctions against girls achieving too dominant a position within the group. Such sanctions are sometimes expressed in the form of 'jokes', as recalled by one boy:

> There's a joke which is often brought up a lot now, on John and Debbie . . . but John can't stand Debbie at the moment, you know, he's for ever calling her names and whatever. And the joke was that whenever you wanted to find John, just look for Debbie, and if ever you wanted to find Debbie, look for John 'cos John would always be right behind Debbie. But something changed and he can't stand her now. But he was never actually going out with her. I mean . . . she's a very nice girl, but um, she'd be difficult to get along with on a one to one basis, like that.
>
> (ND: Do you mean she is independent?)
>
> Very! . . .

Such independence on the part of girls is not welcomed by the boys, who prefer to conceptualise the social group as revolving around its male members:

> One night I happened to meet a girl I used to know about three or four years back, and um, I started going out with her and I brought her in and she brought in a couple of her mates, but then a few weeks after that I decided I didn't like her a great deal, and we stopped going out with each other, and she immediately split and the other girl that she'd brought in with her went with her . . . Every so often she'll come through, like go through (locality name) and stop and talk and that, but she doesn't particularly stay around now she doesn't come down there as much as anybody else. And, um, you know, just kind of like girlfriends who come in, maybe they'll stay if those two split up, she might go out with another boy in the group, or er, she might just split the scene altogether.
>
> (ND: So the nucleus is male. Can you imagine it being the other way around? A group formed predominantly by females with men drifting in and out?)
>
> I wouldn't want to imagine it the other way around!

Whilst there are few signs in this group of things being 'the other way around', the material and cultural conditions of the area were, during the study period, beginning to erode the dominance the boys had over the girls. Some girls could gain temporary dominance over some boys within mixed groups. This may be associated with trends portrayed in the national media (increase in numbers of female singers, stars of TV series, etc) but is also grounded in local conditions. In an area such as this, in which there is a large service sector, school-leaving girls (especially white girls from the middle or upper parts of the working class) can easily get work in shops, and also in offices. (The young woman referred to as Debbie had a job, at 18 years of age, as a senior clerical officer). They therefore achieve independence in the labour market and a wage at least equal to that of most boy school-leavers. Furthermore, the wage obtained can be used to finance the clothes and other props used in the projection of 'feminine' attractiveness and desirability. So working class girls are able, *for a few years of their life and in some circumstances,* to occupy a position of independence plus 'femininity' that evens up the hitherto unbalanced power relationship with males. In the paragraphs that now follow, we discuss the pub and the associated mixed social group in which this 'sexual equality' is played out.

Work, Sexuality and the Pub (i) Entry

The area in which members of the group congregated during some evenings and over parts of the weekend was within a few minutes walk of several public houses (as is the case in most inner London residential areas). Most of these pubs were equipped with juke boxes and some bad amusement machines (such as 'Space Invaders') and/or a television; but most were relatively small public houses, patronised by a quite regular, adult, mostly male, lower working class clientele. One pub, by contrast, was relatively large, having tables arranged around a central 'island' bar staffed by between three and six persons (depending upon the amount of custom) and opening up into a larger space at the back, which could be used to house a dee-jay and other entertainments. The pub was quite typical of a number of inner London pubs which have become increasingly oriented towards a younger clientele: several similar existed in the Borough at the time of research. Not simply the music, but also the relatively large bar – too large to be 'claimed' by any one group – set the scene for participation in the pub by a number of loose groupings of young people, of which the service sector groups researched was one.

Some memers of the group could be found in this pub on any given night of the week, and many (up to ten) were present on Saturday and/or Friday, albeit sometimes for only part of the evening. People would generally start arriving, either singly or in small groups, after seven o'clock: coming as a larger group rarely happened as it was the pub itself that was the meeting place. Reasons given for leaving during the evening included doing something together (cinema, playing records, etc) or individuals going off to attend a pre-arranged meeting elsewhere. Conversation amongst the over-sixteens almost invariably included their work, and this conversation was frequently an early one. Because the service sector (shops and offices) that dominates employment is more favourable to job-changing by girls than by boys, it was the girls who talked most about changing their work. They compared notes on each others' jobs (pay, conditions, travel arrangements) and related hearsay about other peoples' experiences in employment. In one conversation, for instance, two girls compared their shop jobs and considered the advantages in applying for jobs at a new shop shortly to open just outside the area. This conversation was listened to by the males, who offered fewer comments on their own work. In general, the males spoke more of the possibility of moving in a few months time than of any immediate plans. Males talked about their jobs in ways that ranged from depression and desperation to cocky assurance, whereas the females' job-talk seemed more instrumental, more concerned with fine calculations of satisfactions and dissatisfactions and with ways of slightly improving the balance by a calculated move. These are not simply 'cultural' differences or differences in teenagers' attitudes to work – they are an accurate reflection of the opportunities facing these boys and girls. The service sector allows girls to change job relatively frequently but a relatively dim view is taken by employers of boys who don't 'settle down in the job': a boy who attempts to change jobs often finds himself discriminated against, considered 'unreliable', and destined for the bottom of the labour market. Boys and girls yet to leave school find pub conversations a more real window on 'the world of work' than any careers lesson, and listened with evident interest.

The pub supplies music from a juke box and from a disco (some evenings only). The music supplies a stream of cues for conversation, comment, and discussion, and gives the means for 'doing something' when one is not directly engaged in conversation – one listens to the music. This music is one of its main attractions. The pub is also a place in which various forms of sexual imagery are projected. The first form of sexual imagery is that alluded to or declared by the music.[19] The second – a stripper – confirms the sexist role of woman as something to be looked at, rather than someone to talk with as an equal. The strip occurs only on some evenings, and towards the later part of the evening. The disc-jockey announces 'the lovely' who-ever-it-is, and puts on a record. 'Lovely', who is usually a girl around twenty years, then goes through her routine in a manner that is both explicit and controlled. It involves removal of a wrap to display panties, girdle and stockings, a slow strip accompanied by fast dancing, many undulations and the rubbing of the breasts and crotch, and finishes with the girl squirming on her back on a raised stage with her legs towards the audience. Owing to the crowding round of males, those not at the front of the stage cannot see the details of this latter part of the act, and it is possible for couples who are talking or dancing to give appearances of disregarding the act. Girls in the group under study generally referred to the act as 'disgusting' and 'embarrassing'. Boys feigned indifference, giving the explanation that 'once you've seen one you've seen them all' when with other males. Whatever the exact meanings of the strip for members of the group, it remains that the strip introduced a highly explicit hetero-sexuality into that part of the evening and, by extension, into the pub in general. The management of this sexuality cannot have been too painful for members of the group, otherwise they presumably would not go to that pub.

It is in terms of these two sets of social relations – those of the labour market, and those between the sexes - that we now analyse this group's involvement in the pub. In the first place, these relations are important in understanding the group's *entry* into the pub and, in the second place, they underpin the *form taken by drinking practices* in this group.

Entry into the pub should, according to the strict letter of the law, have been impossible for many members of the group, since they were too young. As bar-mats and notices displayed in this and other Servicetown pubs declare, the management 'will refuse to serve' anybody who 'appears to be under eighteen years of age.' In fact, this pub is by no means exceptional for having under-age drinkers. The over-18 rule is not vigorously enforced in most pubs in the area and, when efforts are made to enforce it, these efforts restrict themselves precisely to the level of appearances. This means, first, that it is only those boys or girls who *look* young who are likely to be refused service. One boy in the group who was especially small (at sixteen) was able to go into the pub and drink alcohol as long as he did not attempt to buy drinks himself, and as long as he kept a lemonade by him so that he could pretend to be drinking that when bar staff were in his immediate vicinity. (During the study period he was, however, challenged by an off-duty policeman who was drinking in the pub and, following this, the bar staff made active efforts to exclude him, whilst other teenagers under eighteen continued to frequent the pub without challenge). At a quite basic level, therefore, the ability to 'pass' as an adult in the pub relies upon being not too small. Additionally, apparent age rests, in the teenage years, upon possession of recognisably adult sexual characteristics; voice-pitch in the case of boys (many of them were too young to grow convincing facial har), and breast development in the case of girls. The ability to pass in the pub was not, however, simply a matter of such physical appearances. Indeed many of the group aged sixteen or under looked no older than their age; the girls were generally qute sparing in their use of make-up (in contrast with another group of girls in the pub – see below), and the clothing commonly worn – casual jackets, pullover, jeans and so on – did not make them look any older. The maintenance of the appearance of having a right to be in the pub depended to a large extent upon an adult *manner*, and on the confidence to maintain such a manner. One source of confidence was particular to the girls:

> Well, I've been in pubs when I was quite young. It helps 'cos if you're a girl you can go round with blokes, older blokes not boys, and they can take you into places. They (the bar staff) don't chuck you out if you're with a bloke, 'cos he'd be narked, not unless you're *really* young . . .

It thus seems that bar staff in Servicetown and similar areas may have been socialised into an acceptance of young female teenagers accompanying older males, and that they thereby become desensitized to girls in the pub. As a man serving in another Servicetown bar put it, in the course of a casual conversation, 'It's up to him, isn't it, if he's taking a young girl around; good luck'. Somewhat at right-angles to this sexist reasoning is the fact that the mid-teenage service-sector girls consistently conducted themselves with independence in the pub (this is discussed in some detail below), and that they had a quite 'steady' confidence that did not rely upon the males present. It is to the basis of this confidence that we now turn.

Entry into the pub is only the preliminary step in participating in it; to buy drinks for oneself and/or others, money is needed. Most of the group were given some pocket-money by their parents, although not all received a regular sum and, of those that did, the amount varied widely (between fifty pence and two pounds a week). Most of the groups who were still at school relied upon some form of part-time employment (such as working in a shop on Saturdays), or an occasional job in the school holidays. Most, therefore – and this is of considerable significance for understanding their drinking practices – were already at least partly involved, in the labour market, selling their labour for a wage. This material fact facilitated a confidence about entry into the pub that, on some occasions, became expressed in quite militant forms:

> Look, we work for it, so why shouldn't we spend it?
>
> (ND: In a pub?)
>
> Why not, other people do. Its up to me whether I want to spend my money on this or that. Its my money. I work for it. Who's going to tell me how to spend it? (Girl)

The part-time and temporary jobs that many of the group had not only gave them the money required for buying drinks – it gave them the sovereign right of the consumer to spend the money in that fashion. For these teenagers, the question of entry into the pub was not simply a matter of 'getting away with it', but of right. This is the basis of the confidence that drapes the physically not-fully-mature boy or girl with adult manners in the pub. We turn now to the form taken by drinking in this group.

Work, Sexuality and the Pub (ii) The Round

Within the pub, the buying and drinking of alcohol by groups of service sector youth typically proceeded in accordance with the round system. That is to say, each person, irrespective of age, gender and financial circumstances, strove to take his or her turn in buying a round of drinks for the group with whom he or she was sitting and did so readily and willingly, rather than dutifully or resentfully. Any explanation of drinking patterns in service sector youth culture should be capable of explaining this drinking norm and practice (the mixed-sex round) as a feature of this youth culture.

> Say we go in, someone buys the first drink(s), you drink up, talk and that, then its up to someone else . . . No-one wants to be slow to offer.

This remark, made by a member of the group, accurately represents the group's behaviour as observed in the pub. Boys and girls made equal efforts to 'stand their round', in spite of the financial burdens that this necessarily placed upon those of them not working full-time. The group quite frequently included teenagers who were still at school and those who were working full-time, and the consequent differences in financial resources introduced an element of strain into the round-buying situation.

> (ND: I remember, when we were in there last, a couple of people made a couple of jokes about the fact that you weren't working and so didn't have very much money. It was all in very good humour, and everything.)
>
> It's usually accepted as such, um, I know a lot of people might call it bullying or whatever, but we always take the mick out of somebody on something, anything, you know. As far as I can see its always a sign of affection, never meant to be a grudge . . . (Boy) (street interview)

Observation of the group's behaviour in the pub confirmed that such affectionate joking was generally accepted as a means of coping with, and defusing a potentially embarrassing situation; and as a means of reassuring those with least money that their predicament was well understood. In no case was there any pressure upon individuals to buy 'their round'; indeed each individual gave every appearance of wishing to do so.

It is of course true that round drinking is not peculiar to this youth culture. Government social surveys of the general adult population in England and Wales indicate that 87% of males and 98% of females do most of their pub drinking in groups of two or more, rather than by themselves; and about one half of adults' pub drinking occasions are characterised by the round (Wilson, 1980; 18). These data show that the round is a widespread social institution: but they also show that it is by no means universal, and this underlines the need to understand why it is taken up by some social groups, and not others. This differential take-up of the round cannot, as was realised early in this research, be attributed to a general 'pub-culture', since even within one pub, some social groups may operate the round whilst others do not. In the pub frequented by the service-sector group, for example, and in which they adhered to the principle (if not always the strict practice) of the round, there were other teenagers who did *not* operate the round system (discussed in subsequent sections of this chapter). The adoption of the round by service sector youth cannot, therefore, be attributed either to the dominance of a national norm, nor to any generally accepted norm about behaviour appropriate to particular pub milieux: what has to be explained is the adherence of mid-teen service sector youth to the round system.

Not only was the round system the general framework for pub drinking amongst groups of service sector youth; the round as practiced by these youths also had specific features not found in some other round-buying groups in this and other pubs in Servicetown. The first specific feature was the full participation of girls in the round, whenever they were present in a drinking group of service sector youth: yet within the same pub, and in other pubs in the locality, there were other social groups in which only the males went to the bar. The second specific feature of round-buying in service sector youth was the adoption of various strategies for dealing with the practical problem of shortage of money. We shall discuss both of these specific features of the service sector round in greater detail in subsequent sections: the purpose at this point is to indicate that what has to be explained is not only the adoption of the round, but also its adoption in a specific form, in this particular youth culture.

The following explanation of the mixed-sex round in service sector youth culture follows the framework set out in chapter 4; it assumes that specific norms and practices, such as those related to round-buying, can be understood as part of the collective response of the group concerned to the material conditions (specially local labour market and sexual divisions) which it faces. We shall first focus upon round drinking as part of a culture that acquiesces in, indeed celebrates, entry into the middle strata of the labour market; then, in a later section, we shall show how the temporary equality that the service sector accords girls, and the relatively light domestic duties expected of them, makes possible a youth culture in which mixed-sex round-buying is the norm.

Taking the more general condition of entry into the labour market first: we have already drawn attention to the way in which the service sector group (and perhaps others) sets up a culture that is much orientated toward and much concerned with the transition into waged work. In this context round-buying provides a means for affirming the formal relations of equality and independence (upon which the wage-labour market rests) which these teenagers are in the process of taking on. Round-buying provides a reflection and proof, within the sphere of consumption, of one's (actual or anticipated) position within the sphere of production. Work in the labour market involves acceptance of the wage relation – i.e. involves acting *as if* one were a free and independent agent, equal to all others in the market – and the round provides a means of affirming and celebrating this relationship. This underlying basis of the round relationship in commitment to the wage relation comes out indirectly in answers to the question, what sort of person doesn't want to buy rounds?

> Spongers . . . like its alright to cadge a fag off somebody but you don't want to go on doing it. Its like that with drinks, you want to show that you're as good as them.

And the thought of breakdowns in the assumption of independence elicits generally-formulated statements of dis-ease: 'I don't like obligations', as one boy put it, eliciting emphatic nods around the table. Obligations are incompatible with independence. It needs however to be stressed that what is being celebrated in the round is not some 'value' of independence-in-general, but the specific form of independence that correspond to aspirations and commitment to the labour market. In the context of an orientation to the social relations of the labour market, the round system has two advantages over the alternative possibility of each person buying his or her own. In the first place, round buying demonstrates the independence and *equality* of each party, since it involves full reciprocity; whereas buying one's own indicates independence, but not necessarily equality (of status, and of means). Secondly, buying a round of drinks is an action that demand the attention of all those involved, and draws attention to itself in a way that buying one's own need not. Every time a round is bought, each person in the round must signal his or her preference for type or size of drink, or, if type and size of drink is fixed custom, must at least signify whether or not he or she agrees to accept another drink; and each person acknowledges the drink, on receipt of it. The round therefore necessarily involves repeated *public* acknowledgement of the social relations of equality in the round-buying group.

Work, Sexuality and the Pub (iii) Service-sector Girls and the Round

There are circumstances when the round is not expected to operate:

> Well, say you were trying to get off with a girl. Then you might be glad to buy her drinks, and hope for your luck.
>
> (ND: You'd hope that she would feel under some kind of obligation to you?)
>
> Yes. Mind you, it might not work out that way. She might just drink what you gave and then go off (laughter).

In the context of drinking in pubs, buying drinks for a girl unaccompanied by a male is generally read as the first step in making a pass at her. This reading is reinforced by the particular features of this pub. Firstly, the disco and dancing provide a context for 'being together' without continuous talking, and for some physical contact (particularly towards the end of the evening, when the music slows down). Secondly, in this particular pub emphasis is placed upon the sexuality of the situation by provision of the overtly sexual stripper act – 'feminine' sexuality which is paid for by patrons in the price of the drinks. In this context, having drinks bought for one implies sexual obligations towards the buyer.

Within service sector youth culture, however, the girls do not generally afford the boys such opportunities. As we have shown, the character of the local economy, with its large service sector in which girls from the middle strata of the working class are temporarily equal with or even sometimes advantaged over boys, undermines the material basis for male chavinism within service sector youth culture. The girls often seem as 'independent' as the boys, often to the chagrin of the latter. This temporary independence is reflected in the form of the characteristic pub drinking occasions for members of this culture – round-buying is shouldered equally by girls and boys. Sometimes working girls even seemed to buy more than their share, thus further reducing the possibility that their open friendliness with the boys would deteriorate into sexual compromises not of their choosing. This independence on the girls' part is viewed with some ambivalence by the boys – whilst relieved of additional financial burdens, they are also relieved of the power such burdens confer.

Within the pub upon which the fieldwork focussed, there were however groups of females whose class background and age range differed from those of the mid-teen service-sector girls. There were, in particular, groups of girls who appeared younger than sixteen, and who, judging from accents, dress and manner, came from lower strata of the class: the 'domestics'. These girls do accept drinks without reciprocating. These younger girls have, in their ability to flirt and giggle amongst themselves and/or with the older teenagers and men, a cashable resource which the boys do not have, and one which the older, service sector girls also have but generally refrain from using. These circumstances lead to 'norms' governing relations between the sexes in the pub. One of these norms is the requirement that girls over sixteen years, who can afford to buy their own drinks, shall not act in such a way as can be interpreted as 'eyeing up' males upon whom the younger girls are dependent for sexual attentions and drinking. A female polytechnic student on placement who acted as a fieldworker on one occasion found herself in breach of this norm. She 'got stared at, pointed out and noted – clearly a threat to the girls' blokes'. Whilst the young girls 'don't blame the blokes for looking at older girls', the sort of 'looking back' which this student routinely does threatened the younger girls in this pub. In the lavatory, she was angrily approached by a young girl who upbraided her for 'looking' at her man. The student felt acutely uncomfortable, feeling that she could easily handle the men present but not the young girls who, unlike her, relied for their participation in the 'adult' milieu of the pub upon male patronage. Any unwaged female who fails to discourage males from eyeing them up threatens to take away from a younger girl not only the man – which may or may not be a serious setback – but also, with him, the resources necessary for the younger girl to stay in the pub. This is 'unfair' and its ever-present possibility leads to maintenance of a high level of vigilance and to clear displays of 'keep off' signs by the younger teenage girls.

The fact that the younger girls are reliant upon male patronage is appreciated by males, as is the fact that this does not necessarily put individual men into a position of power over individual girls. A male can generally affect an introduction to a young girl with the offer of a drink – and such introductions often seemed to be elicited by a flirtatious manner on the part of the younger girls ('cattle market' as my female fieldworker opined) – but the fact that the younger girls *have* to accept such offers in order to stay in the pub means that no special significance can be read into acceptance of any particular offer. As the male interviewee quoted earlier pointed out, 'she might just drink what you gave and then go off', subsequently to get another drink from another male. At the end of my fieldwork period, I spent an evening exploring who would and who would not accept an offer of a drink, and found no problems in spending money on younger girls. This caused some amusement to other males over twenty at the bar, on the grounds that 'you're wasting your time there, mate'. Buying drinks for service-sector females over school-leaving age was, however, virtually impossible. Since they were able themselves to support their presence in the pub milieu, and since they knew that men knew that, all parties were aware that an acceptance of drinks was a *choice*, not a necessity. Accordingly, acceptance of a drink was, for the older ones, some sign of acceptance of the person offering, and implied that stilted conversation, at the least, was involved in exchange. Any conversation that occurred in the context of an acceptance, by the older females, of a drink, falls into the category of 'a chat up'. Acceptance of a second drink would imply rather more – though few of the older girls would accept a second drink even if they did think the offerer was 'nice'. After all, to accept a string of drinks would imply that she was a young girl without resources, independence and character of her own.

Thus between the pub behaviour of girls who are in their lower teens, and those who are in their upper teens, we see a difference much greater than that between the younger girls and the older males. The younger male teenagers behave, whilst they are in the pub, as much like the older ones as they can – entering fully into the round. No boy – whatever his class background – displays social dependence within the pub. Some young girls, on the other hand, do. Their presence in the pub is contingent not upon their financial resources (part-time jobs, full-time jobs, etc), but upon the use they can make of their group 'femininity' – flirting, giggling, and relying upon friends to get them out of sticky situations. Young girls are dependent upon other people – men – whilst in the pub. The older teenage girls look down on such behaviour, since *their* sexual identity is bound up with their transition to the labour market and the independence it confers. Thus whilst there is only one kind of 'masculinity' in the pub ('independence'), there are two types of 'femininity', and a sharp divide between them: 'Silly little girls, why don't they grow up. They really annoy me' as one of the older girls, who was in no way being directly inconvenienced, put it. The point is that the older girls feel that the younger ones' behaviour in the pub undermines their own position as independent agents not reliant upon male favour and patronage. Underlying this age division is a social class difference. Girls from the lower strata of the working class generally have extensive housework (and sometimes childcare) responsibilities, job-chances much inferior to those of the boys and to those of girls from the more privileged strata, and hence insufficient material resources to develop a culture involving 'independence'. For them, entry into the pub is an opportunity to invert their domestic role, to use their gender to get men to do things for them for a change, and to have a good laugh about it. The relatively privileged service-sector girls from the middle strata of the working class are prevented from acting in such a manner (a) by their own aspirations to independence and equality, expressed in the pub by round-buying and (b) by the censure of other teenagers (especially girls) from that class background: neither of these penetrate far into the culture of the less privileged.

Regulation of the Round: Everyday Constraint Versus 'Getting Paralytic' at Weekends

Pub life is the non-work sphere within which service sector boys and girls celebrate their adult rationality as independent workers. Wanting to take part in the round is not just precociousness – it is part and parcel of their aspirations to be fully working class. It is within this framework that the collective regulation of the round – sometimes encouraging the level of consumption of the group, and sometimes discouraging it – has to be understood.

When viewed from the perspective of the most commonly observed drinking occasion, the round appeared to act as a means of limiting the size of the drinking group, the number of drinks consumed, and the expense thereof. The most common drinking occasion for service sector youth involved entry into the pub fairly early in the evening, drinking in a small group (two or three at most), and leaving sufficiently early to have time to do something else with the remainder of the evening. Halves of bitter were generally chosen in this situation, and efforts were made to avoid setting up a lengthy round. This was done in two ways: a person coming into the pub and finding two or three others already drinking might quite often go directly to the bar and buy his or her own, and then come and sit down with the group, hence avoiding an extension of the round; or an offer from the new-comer might be refused on the grounds that one or more of the group was 'alright, thanks, 'cos I'm just going'. One some occasions the haste of individuals to leave the pub when faced with newcomers was sufficiently evident to be remarked upon: 'He's in a hurry not to be caught for a round'. Such remarks were, however, saved until people had left, and were made with evident amusement and understanding of the predicament, rather than as personal criticism. In these circumstances, the round system seemed to place clear limits upon the amount drunk – indeed upon the time spent in the pub – rather than encourage drinking.[20]

In other, less common circumstances, however, the round becomes the vehicle for relatively heavy drinking. One important consequence of the position of fifteen and sixteen year olds in service sector youth culture is the collective phenomenon of 'getting paralytic' at the weekend. Tightly engaged in a culture which, in the individualism of its social relations of exchange, prescribes the round system of buying drinks, those who are as yet unwaged (or have only part-time jobs) have not the funds to very often risk entry into the pub and the subsequent expenditure. As noted above, this can lead to going into the pub only in twos and for a short while only, (although even this remains quite expensive). Another solution is to forsake the pub on most evenings, thus avoiding frittering away one's funds in a way that does not allow participation in the round system. Come Friday or Saturday night, one has money enough to participate fully in the round system in a medium-sized or large group. This is the social basis of that highly enjoyable ritual – 'getting paralytic'.

> Everybody, like, hangs out in (area name).
>
> (ND: Hangs out? I mean, what do you mean, what do you do?)
>
> Precious little.
>
> (ND: Lean up against street posts, walk about with a fag, walk the dog . . . ?)
>
> No, it's . . . usually we sit about and have a fag. Over the weekend we go down to the pub, you know, for a drink, and get paralytic.

Getting paralytic is a 'normal' part of the youth culture of those social groups which aspire to, but have yet to attain, the status of the wage. It is because an occasional binge is a satisfactory resolution of the contradiction between the obligations of the round and the lack of resources to meet these obligations on a continuous basis that occasional bouts of relatively heavy drinking occur. Better to participate in the round occasionally but fully and for an entire evening, than to participate more frequently but at the cost of having to depend on others' charity and/or creeping off home early. Most teenagers who drink within the round are thus likely to become experienced in getting paralytic occasionally. The question of the exact social processes whereby some of them, on becoming waged, step up the frequency of drinking whilst maintaining the amount consumed on each occasion, whilst others reduce or vary the quantity consumed as they increase the frequency of drinking, remains unanswered by this project, which focusses upon school-leaving age. It would require a study of the economic and cultural relations of older groups (late teens, twenties), to establish the ways in which getting paralytic may in some circumstances become a frequent routine.

Socialisation into the Round System: In Transition to the Pub

Within the working group of those who have left school, some care is taken to ensure that everyone 'pays their way'. Reciprocity of round-buying is enforced more by the desire of each boy or girl to show his or her standing as independent, equal and 'adult', rather than by any external pressure exerted by others in the group. But when the group contains those both older and younger than sixteen (as it quite often does in the group observed), then all have to take cognizance of this situation and adapt the round system in some way. There are limits to the extent to which philanthropy can be stretched without making the giver and receiver uneasy. The danger is that too great a generosity will result in a 'grudge' or will become an issue over which the banter and jocular name-calling which forms a normal plank of group interaction will descend to 'bullying'. One direction which this bullying may take depends upon the ascription of childish status to the offender – his or her lack of round-buying ability is focussed upon, rather than being smoothed over. Such 'jokes' assert the demarcation between the child and the waged man, and police the extent to which the collective wage is redistributed to the unwaged. Service sector group members who are still at school and have sufficient funds to take their independent and unsupported place in the round are generally careful to avoid getting too many 'obligations'. This acts as a brake on school-attenders' pub attendance. We look now at how the round system is adapted in ways that preserve the underlying ideal of equality and introduce this ideal to younger children who have yet to experience the inside of the pub.

When the drinking group includes several non-waged teenagers, and especially if it consists of a majority of non-waged, then it is accepted that the non-waged cannot be expected to pay as much as the waged. This is particularly so when the group is quite large, when a round of drinks is clearly beyond the means of the unwaged. There are two systems for coping with this situation – splitting up, and having a 'whip-round'.

Splitting up consists simply of going into the pub in groups of two or three, or by oneself. This allows one to escape the embarrassment of facing a lot of empty glasses when sitting in a group. It is the case that the small groups generally congregate into larger groups whilst in the pub, but these larger groups are quite fluid as people get up to go and 'have a word' with others in the pub and those who have just come in or to go to the lavatory. In the event that a group of, say, six waged and unwaged are sitting together, no one expects the unwaged to 'stand a round'. In a group this size, a fragmentation of the round system tends to occur and buying a drink for one other person is quite frequent and unremarkable. In these circumstances the unwaged can often manage to 'stand a round' for him/herself and one other, and such a gesture is often the occasion for particularly appreciative thanks on the part of the waged recipient. Although the round system is not strictly adhered to, its spirit has been adhered to and the buyer has shown evidence of good character.

The other method of coping with a mixture of waged and unwaged is to have a 'whip-round'.

> Rather than everybody walk in we had a whip-round at the beginning and everybody gave in a pound or whatever. We sat down and drank for as long as that lasted. And then everybody gave in the last of the money they had, and Neil and Donald – they're both working – Neil's working full-time – like, put whatever was left, or whatever else was needed to finish off the round.

It is significant that such transactions are generally negotiated *before* going into the pub. The situational norms of round-buying are assumed to apply once one is inside the pub unless these norms have already been suspended by explicit agreement. This only happens when it is evident that the situational norms cannot be applied, without modification, to the social group (e.g. including a high proportion of the unwaged); I found no evidence of such arrangements when the group consisted only, or predominantly, of waged teenagers. It is by such means that the mid-teen boys and girls are introduced to the round-system within the pub environment. Such 'whip-rounds' *establish the norms which they temporarily displace* precisely because they are negotiated as *temporary expedients* for the purpose of overcoming an otherwise problematic situation. It is through learning that certain procedures, whilst being quite acceptable and even advisable in certain circumstances, are not the *normal* procedures than one learns what the norms are.

Just as the round system is 'taught' in this way to the mid-teen boy and girl who is not yet (fully) waged, so the mid-teen person teaches the norm of reciprocity to younger pre-teen and teenage children. In order to understand this we need to distinguish clearly between the social circumstances of childrens' first contacts with and experiences of alcohol, and the social circumstances and norms and relations into which their drinking is subsequently absorbed. Available research suggests that most children's first exposure to drink is within the home (Jahoda and Cramond, 1972). Jahoda found that very young children could distinguish those bottles which are used for alcohol. He also found that children developed increasingly negative attitudes to alcohol as they approached ten years of age, and hypothesised that these attitudes were the result of parental prohibitions. By the mid teens, however, as Davis and Stacey (1972) have shown, attitudes to alcohol are much more favourable and alcohol use is becoming quite frequent. In the social group observed in the present study, there were two social processes that explain this reversal. Firstly, most parents were content for mid-teen boys and girls to drink within limits. Some parents offered drinks to their teenage offspring within the home, some took them along to a pub occasionally, and some supervised parties at which drink was available to those in their mid-teens:

> Lorraine had a party, and I was invited, Julian was invited, and that mob (under fifteen years) that were hanging (around) there were invited, and a couple of others from Lorraine' school . . .
>
> (ND: And what happens over the drinks, are people expected to buy things).
>
> No, not unless you are specifically asked, or you run out of drink. It comes from parents. There's pretty tight laws (rules). Like at Lorraine's party, I was allowed to drink, Julian was allowed to drink but he doesn't, Gary, Peter, Michael, Ray were allowed to drink but not very much and they were kept mainly to the shandies. There was about twenty-four, no, there was about thirty cans, and . . . that lot they drank about eight (each), and I drank about twelve, for some unknown reasons – I just sat there and kept drinking. And, um, they (parents) were alright up to

> ten o'clock, at ten o'clock the parents said 'alright you lot, you'd better stop drinking, you know, you stick to shandies', but most of the time they were allowed to drink.

This is the non-moralising parental attitude that some alcohol educators advise in the hope that teenagers will learn to drink in a 'responsible' way, rather than learning to drink in possibly less responsible ways outside of and perhaps in opposition to parental constraint. The fact is, however, that by the time that parents permit this supervised drinking, most children (in the social group researched) are already participating in a street culture which, whilst it does not stand in an oppositional posture to parents, does introduce cigarettes and alcohol within a different set of social relations. Whilst parents make age the criterion for alcohol (and sometimes cigarette) use, the early evening street culture, involving the pre-teens, younger teens and mid-teens, makes possession of money the criterion:

> Usually everybody puts in a bit of money, right, go down, pick up a couple of bottle of Pomagne, couple of cans, and come back and sit down and drink. But if, say (names) were all there, then they'll put in some money, and . . . supposing everybody was here one night, right, something like thirteen or fourteen of us everybody would put in some money and everybody would be allowed to drink. There'd be arguments on about how much compared with how much they'd put in – you know, 'you only put in so much so you're only getting so much' – but, um that often happens with cigarettes. You know, no one's got any cigarettes and no one's got enough money on them to buy a packet, so someone will say 'alright, how much have you got . . . alright, chip it all in', and go down and when the cigarettes are back and someone says right, these three are yours, that's your two, you didn't put any in so if there's one odd you get that one, and you get these two and you get that one, and there's one left, here you are'. In a whip-round as such, unless you put in you rarely get anything out of it.

Unless you put, you rarely get anything out – one receives according to one's contribution. It is striking that this procedure, most common in those groups which include a proportion of younger teenagers and pre-teens, involves a much stricter principle of exchange than is found in the whip-rounds of the older teenagers and young adults. In the pub-going group it is the *principle* of *formal equality* of the persons involved that is honoured, permitting a relatively relaxed and generous practice in which the obligations of the round are deemed to have been fulfilled as long as each person has made some 'reasonable' contribution within his or her means (whereupon the older and waged persons will 'top up' the round or will buy their rounds slightly earlier than would otherwise be required). The younger groups, most of whose members have yet to enter the labour market, are organised around a *recognition of inequality* – people are unequal being of differing ages and having differing resources, and they receive only what they pay for. The younger children, therefore, are operating with a 'pre-capitalist' culture, revolving around the social relations of a market in goods, in which social inequality is manifest and is determined by differential resources.

In the culture of those who have entered the labour market, whilst there may be actual inequalities between the resources of the teenagers, social relations within the group typically proceed on the basis of an assumption of formal equality. (In the labour market, everyone is formally equal since every person has only his or her own labour to sell). The mid-teen person is in transition from the younger group to the older, and his or her consumption is structured by one or other set of relations depending on the social circumstances (age-spread of group, etc) in which he or she situationally finds himself. As a group of teenagers grows older, its culture is decreasingly marked by the social relations of the market in goods, and increasingly marked by the social relations of the market in labour. A mid-teenager finds himself now in a group in which the prior relations dominate, and now in a group in which the latter relations dominate. The transition to work and associated identity changes is an extended process, but the few months around school-leaving and the entry into the first job is the pivot, and probably the time of quickest change, after which participation in the games of the pre-teens and lower teens declines rapidly. By the time they have entered the labour market, boys and girls are formally enmeshed in the culture of the round, and are in the process of socialising their younger, mid-teen, brothers and sisters into that equalitarian culture. These mid-teenagers are, in turn, providing the spectacle of the round to the street audience of younger children – using 'rounds' of reciprocal offers of cigarettes, and managing whip-rounds that modify the equality of the round system to take account of the inequality of resources. In this way, cigarettes and alcohol become the goods around which the ideology of equality within the labour market is passed down to children yet to enter it. Hence, learning to drink is also learning to labour, and vice versa: youth culture is closely articulated to the world of work.

Summary

In this chapter an attempt has been made to describe the labour market into which most teenagers in the case study area move at age sixteen, the ways in which schools attempt to manage the school-leaving process, and the culture and drinking practices that one particular group of teenagers construct in response to their experience of the transition from school to labour market. The case study area experienced a rapid growth in small and craft industry and in population in the nineteenth century, but the economic base of small industry (small engineering, clothes, shoes, etc) has been declining since the turn of the century, and particularly since the second world war. An increase in size of the service sector (professions, distribution, shops, offices, etc) has occurred since the war, but this has not sufficed to compensate fully for the decline of small manufacturing. Hence the labour market, and with it the Borough's population, are both in decline. The decline of craft industry has meant a reduction in the size of the skilled manual working class, whilst the remaining industrial units (e.g. clothing manufacture, 'sweatshops') pay poorly. Women and immigrant groups form a high proportion of the workforce in these poorly-paid, non-unionised firms. However, the employment policies of firms in the service sector of the economy provide employment opportunities for girl school-leavers that equal those for boys – at least during the immediate school-leaving years. Girls are generally considered well fitted for jobs involving personal and social interaction, and since this is an important aspect of work in the service sector, the market position of those school-leaving girls that seem most suitable for such work is relatively good (compared with areas in which agricultural or heavy industrial work predominates). This case study is especially concerned with service sector youth – boys and girls from the middle strata of the working class who leave school at the normal school-leaving age of sixteen to enter the service sector – and with their schooling, with the culture constructed in response to the transition to employment, and with the significance of drinking practices within that culture.

The schooling of service sector youth is conditioned by the fact that they are of several groups of pupils whom the schools have to manage in their final years. In addition to those boys and girls from the middle of the working class who are in transition to the service sector, most local schools also contain representatives of four other groups: 'early workers' (truanters and 'work-experience' pupils who have quite long stretches of paid employment – these pupils are generally from the lower working class, white and male); 'domestics' (truanters who stay home to look after younger family members so that mother can go out to work – generally from the poorest parts of the lower working class, female): 'perpetual students' (school attenders whose ethnic background is a disadvantage in the labour market, who wish to escape their most probable fate of obtaining poorly paid employment or being unemployed, and who stay on at school or at F.E. gradually being 'cooled out' – generally black, male); and 'fixed up' (school-attenders who are 'fixed up' in relation to a job with training, and simply have to wait out their time at school – generally male, artisan or 'good' working class background, often Catholic-Irish). Each of these groups pose specific problems for the school: truanters because they are missing the benefits of an education that might increase their otherwise low occupational expectations and opportunities; those with high expectations because it is unlikely that these will be met; and those who are simply waiting to leave school because they seem to 'underachieve'.

In comparison with such groups, those relatively ordinary boys and girls who attend school fairly regularly, who aim at the one or two exam passes which may be required by service sector employers, and who leave school at the appointed time to enter service sector employment, present relatively few problems to the schools. The school are largely taken up with the problem of how to respond to the other social groups, and the management of the service sector pupils is a relatively routine, uncontested process. Service sector youth culture consists of boys and girls of school-leaving age and those in the two or three years above and below that age. The culture transmits to the younger teenagers information about employment in the service sector, and boys and girls become aware of their relatively privileged employment position (compared with that of ethnic minority groups and white boys and girls from the lower strata of the class). The culture provides an opportunity for mid-teen boys and girls to make sense of their economic circumstances and of the social relations of service sector work, and it is within this context that their drinking practices may be understood:

(i) The normmal and accepted practice is the *'round system'* of pub buying and consumption of drinks. Entry into the labour market not only provides the financial resources to buy drink, but also provides a model of socio-economic relations that emphasises independence and equality between individuals. This model is accepted – indeed celebrated – within service sector youth culture, and epitomised in the observance of the round. Service sector round drinking may be regarded as a celebration, within the sphere of consumption and lesiure, of the social relations of production in which these teenagers are becoming actors.

(ii) Because of the social and economic structure of Servicetown, and particularly because the relatively prominent service (shops, distribution, office work) sector of the labour market offers work involving social and affective skills that girls' socialisation is considered to provide, some teenage girls are relatively well-placed in the labour market. Girls from the middle sections of the working class, who are generally less weighed down with housework obligations than are girls from the lower strata of the working class, are for a few years in a competitive position. This position is echoed, within the youth culture, as a collective social confidence of girls vis-a-vis boys, and has consequences for the construction of drinking occasions. The pub and the round system provides a cultural context in which girls celebrate the sexual equality conferred, for a few years, by the economic structure of the area: they buy drinks not only for themselves but also for boys. Such temporary sexual equality is sometimes resented by the boys, who would prefer that the economic facts were more congruent with chauvinist class traditions of establishing sexual possession through the purchase of drinks.

(iii) Younger teenagers aspire to the round system of drinking but generally achieve it only in relation to (cheaper) cigarettes. In relation to alcohol, there is the obvious difficulty of entry into the pub, but also the embarrassment of lack of funds. In these circumstances they often have to content themselves with the inequality of the 'whip-round' and with unequal sharing of drink bought from the off-license.

(iv) Another way of reconciling the ideal of equal participation in the round, and the reality of insufficient funds to do so on a regular basis, is to save up and enter the pub infrequently, whereupon the savings are expended on 'getting paralytic'. Such episodic binges are by no means simply a result of internal and personal motivations, but result from the contradictions thrown up by the slow process of transition to independence in the market.

The process of transition from school to service sector employment and the development of drinking practices is summarised in diagram 5.2.

Diagram 5.2. Development of Economic Independence and its Reflection in the Mixed-Sex Round in Service Sector Youth Culture

Socio-Economic position of service sector teenagers:	*Up to 13 years;* dependency on parent	*Up to 16 years;* partial dependency on parents, and holiday/part-time	*Over 16;* entry into labour market, independence
Form which recreational alcohol use takes:	The whip-round: getting out what you put in, unequal shares	The whip-round, plus occasional pub rounds, leading to 'getting paralytic'	More routinised pub visits and round-buying by boys and girls
Cultural meanings of drinking situations:	Acknowledgement of dependency on others, of childhood	Foretaste of 'adult' relations of equality, of equality, independence	Celebration of social relations of independence sex-equality

This case study has shown that the mixed-sex round in service sector youth culture may be understood as an integral feature of that culture, and that this form of drinking practice does not generally occur in some other youthful social class and ethnic minority groups in the same locality. In considering how widely the findings of this study might be generalised to other groups of service sector youth in other localities, regions and countries, it is important to recognise that the association observed in the present study between (a) a local economy with a relatively large service sector, (b) a transient sexual equality within that sector, (c) a youth culture that accommodates itself to the social and sexual relations of that sector and, (d) the mixed-sex round, is a contingent association, not a necessary one. That is to say, there is no necessary reason for all these circumstances to recur together in other localities, regions and countries. The precise manner in which cultures and practices arise as collectively constructed responses to structural conditions in particular localities can be established only on the basis of research, and there is considerable scope for comparative studies of service sector (and other) youth cultures and drinking practices in various regions. Government statistics on social and economic structure may be found useful in indicating which regions and local areas of capitalist countries are characterised by service sector employment open to young women,[21] but such statistics do no more than indicate that the material prerequisites necessary for some kind of service sector youth culture exist. It seems reasonable, in the absence of corroborative research, to suggest that the present analysis of mixed-sex round drinking within service sector youth culture in Servicetown might be extended to other similar teenage groups in other, similar areas in the UK – but only as a working hypotheses, not as a conclusion.

What can be claimed as a conclusion, arising out of this study, is that I have domonstrated the need to distinguish clearly between the variety of drinking styles that arise within the cultures that are constructed by particular strata of youth, facing specific circumstances. This demonstration has been achieved on two levels. (1) Within the case study, I have contrasted differences between the drinking styles of service sector boys and girls, with those of less privileged youth (eg. the girls referred to as 'domestics'). (2) A comparison of my observations with those of other investigators (eg. Willis, 1978, Parker, 1974) reinforces the point that youthful drinking styles differ from group to group. The drinking styles adopted by Willis' 'lads' fit their anti-school, overtly masculinist culture, just as the mixed-sex round forms an integral part of service sector youth culture. This raised the question of the range of drinking styles that it might be possible to document if a greater variety of social groups were researched.

In table 5.4, I present a typology of youth, describing boys and girls as being in transition into various levels (or grades) of

Table 5.4 Youth and the Labour Market: an incomplete typology

	SECTORS OF THE WAGE ECONOMY		
	Service Sector	**Manufacturing, mining, construction, etc**	**Agriculture**
STRATA OF YOUTH			
Working class youth			
Middle strata			
Boys:	Service sector youth	Semi-skilled (eg assembly)	–
Girls:	Service sector youth	Semi-skilled	–
Lower strata			
Boys:	Hotels, catering, etc	'Unskilled' (eg packing).	Agricultural labour.
Girls:	Cleaning, etc.	'Unskilled'	Seasonal
Upper strata			
Boys:	Supervisory	'Skilled'; supervisory.	–
Girls:	Supervisory	Some skilled 'new technology' employment.	–
Middle class youth			
Various strata			
Boys:	Professional and various managerial positions in all sections of the economy.		
Girls:	Some professions, especially in welfare system.		

Notes: Where employment opportunities do not generally arise (eg there is little opportunity for girls' paid employment in agricultural areas of the country), this is indicated by a dash in the table. Ethnic minorities are not evenly distributed across educational groups, as could be shown in a more complex table. Involvements in household labour and the informal economy are not shown (see text).

employment in three sectors of the wage economy. A fuller typology would have to describe the involvement of each group in non-wage areas of the economy – households, and the informal economy. Both these non-wage areas will become increasingly important for understanding youth cultures as youth unemployment perists or worsens. The wage economy will, however, remain as a major structural determinant of the material position of all groups of youth – as an area of participation, or as a negative reference point, as a zone of exclusion. It follows that the number of distinct groups of youth, each of which may be expected to have its own characteristic culture and associated drinking style, is much larger than that hitherto documented by the sociology of youth culture.

Now it might possibly emerge that several of these disparate groups have similar styles of involvement with alcohol. On the available (and admittedly limited) evidence, however, we are more justified in concluding that youthful drinking styles are quite heterogeneous. This is our most general conclusion: there is no such general phenomenon as 'youthful drinking'.

PART III

ALCOHOL AND EDUCATION – SOME IMPLICATIONS

6 EDUCATIONAL IMPLICATIONS

This chapter attempts to synthezise various aspects of the study and to draw out implications for health and social education related to alcohol. In order to achieve this objective, it is necessary to recognise that *general* conclusions about alcohol-related education and policy cannot be drawn from a study of only *one* group of pupils. As is made plain in the case study, the circumstances, cultures and drinking practices of youth in differing structural locations are likely to differ considerably. That case study focussed upon a mixed group of teenagers whose backgrounds were in the middle strata of the working class and who were in transition to the relatively favoured service sector of an inner city labour market. This group was not approached with any expectation that their culture would be characterised by themes of rebellion or resistance. What is described in chapter 5 is, indeed, a culture that is broadly acquiescent to the requirements of labour market and schools. This, it is suggested, results from a collective appreciation of the relatively privileged circumstances of these school-leavers, in relation to the circumstances of lower working class boys, girls, and ethnic minority groups (who face employment in the declining small manufacturing section of the economy, and/or heavy housework obligations, and/or unemployment). Drinking practices in service sector youth culture are structured by the general concerns of that culture. The mixed-sex round, the characteristic drinking practice, is a collective and public affirmation, on the part of these girls and boys, of the social relations – socio-economic independence, sociability, (temporary) sex-equality, facilitated by service sector employment.

The findings of this case study may be generalisable to other service sector youth in similar parts of England but do not, in and of themselves, carry any implications for the development of health and social education strategies that are able to engage the cultures not only of this youth culture, but also of others. Such education would depend upon the development of a *general model* of the processes involved in the construction of youth cultures and drinking practices and the relation of these to the offerings of schools and the media. It is the task of this chapter to attempt a first approximation to such a 'model', and to make some suggestions about its applications inside and outside schools. This requires a step back from the details of the case study, and a return to the methodological details, developed in chapter 4, that underlie it and could equally well underlie research into other youth cultures. This task is approached by way of a review of the various conceptions of youthful drinking that have been bequeathed by various stages of English history and discussed in chapters 1 to 3 above. The contrasts pinpointed by this process of review help to illuminate the essential features of the theoretical approach which was applied in the case study, and these features are then incorporated into a general model of youthful drinking practices. This then serves as the basis for some suggestions about educational strategies in schools containing youth from a variety of backgrounds and involved in a variety of cultures.

Four distinct approaches

The work carried out in preceeding chapters allows us to distinguish between four approaches to the analysis of 'alcohol problems', which we can call conservative, social democratic, leftist, and materialist. The conservative conception of youthful drinking focusses upon the possibilities of a relationship between drinking and delinquency. Chapter 1 of this study has attempted to show that the historical origins of the conception of youthful drinking as a disciplinary problem lie in the history of state regulations of the economic and political behaviour of the working class. Licencing legislation arose within the context of early vagrancy statutes concerned with the suppression of those public meeting places which became foci of political agitation and organisation. Subsequent legislation sought to suppress those leisure customs, such as extended feasting and drinking, which (because of the time they took up and because the social attitudes they supported) impeded the imposition of the work-disciplines required by the new class of merchant capitalists. Nineteenth century reformers, inheriting the historically-constructed view of collective public drinking by the working class as a threat to political order and to workaday discipline, regarded such public drinking as particularly hurtful to the proper development of the child – with the result that children were increasingly excluded from pubs throughout the nineteenth and early twentieth century. Throughout the first half of the twentieth century health education curricula developed on the basis of this history, and portrayed youthful drinking as a vice to be avoided through the cultivation of firm self-discipline of the individual. This approach was temporarily occluded by the adoption of Keynsian social and economic policies as the basis for post-war settlement between social classes, but has recently reasserted itself.

The mainstream of social science research related to youthful drinking arose in the post-war period and bases itself in the social democratic assumptions underpinning the political order of the period. Youth cultures and drinking patterns are ascribed to norms, values or attitudes, and it is suggested that health education can reduce or restrain youthful drinking by changing attitudes and, in particular, by encouraging a self-reliant mentality in the individual, thus innoculating him or her from peer pressure (which is assumed to favour heavy drinking). Drinking patterns are considered primarily from a quantitative point of view (how much alcohol? how often?), and the question of differences between the social form of drinking practices in social groups is largely neglected. This neglect is related to the failure to locate youth in relation to social class and sexual divisions in society: social class and sex are treated as 'factors' that may contribute to the 'dependent variable' of level of drinking, rather than as given structures to which groups respond by constructing specific cultures and practices.

During the 1960s and 1970s a self-consciously leftist sociology constituted itself as a critique of the social democratic mainstream. The main achievement of this sociology was the acknowledgement of social class and of collective cultures and practices as important analytic concepts for the understanding of youth cultures. It also drew upon neo-Marxian studies of working class culture, sometimes adopting the most unhistorical method of projecting onto contemporary working class youth cultures the class consciousness of their forbears. This sociology was indeed particularly fascinated in signs of working class resistance to capitalist disciplines, and sought to give voice to the spirit of defiance and rebellion that social democratic researchers preferred to integrate into the consensus. It recognised, however, that full-developed anti-capitalist consciousness was uncommon in working class youth, and fell back upon the explanation that certain social practices could be seen as vestigial or symbolic forms of class resistance. This approach, if applied to youthful drinking, comes close to conforming conservative conceptions of that activity, and offers few clues to health and social education practitioners.

Each of these approaches suffers from serious methodological inadequacies. The approach embodied in the mainstream of the literature on youthful drinking neglects the relationship between material circumstances which are *given* (i.e. the child's structural location in relation to social class and sexual divisions as manifested in labour markets, families and schools), and the cultures which are collectively *constructed* in response to those circumstances and which provide the context in which particular practices (such as the round) 'made sense'. The more recent sociology of youth culture represents a methodological advance since it recognises the importance of material conditions, but the manner in which it specifies these conditions (playing down the relevance of the division of labour within the home) is open to criticism. Other methodological objections to be made against this sociology are its tendency to fantasize about class resistance, its almost exclusive focus upon lower working class boys, and its disinterest in mixed-sex and girl-focussed youth cultures. The conservative, disciplinary vision of youthful drinking is clearly inadequate since it derives not from any actual study of youthful drinking practices *per se* but from an *a priori* proposition that the working class and its youth are disorderly and in need of firmer discipline, imposed both through external agencies (eg police) and through the cultivation of self-restraint.

A specific feature of this study is the underlying conceptualisation of women married to or living with working class men as members of a class other than that of their menfolk. Chapter 4 makes selective use of the work of Christine Delphy and others to suggest that the extensive housework obligations 'normally' expected of and enforced upon married women mean that some proportion of womens' total capacity to labour is expended in the home. This implies that they do not have full possession of their labour power; they cannot sell it, on equal terms with men, on the labour market; since the working class is defined in terms of having full possession of its labour (and of no other alienable commodity), it follows that women with housework obligations are members of a dispossessed 'underclass'. It also follows that the system of social classes toward which youth is in transition has to be considered as a system of social relations involving not simply capital and labour (plus other minor classes), but capital, working class, and female underclass. It is against this general background of adult class relations that the specific situation of service sector youth culture (and other youth cultures) has to be seen. The social relations between the sexes in service sector youth culture represent a *specific* and *temporary* departure from the general case. For the relatively short (considered in the span of a lifetime) period in which girls from middle strata of the working class in an area characterised by a large service sector begin to take up employment in that sector, yet refrain from 'settling down' with a male, their housework obligations are not pressing. Girls from lower in the class system are expected to do more domestic work, as a matter of routine, in the parental home (often filling in for a mother who has a part- or full-time paid job); and it is the norm in most working class homes for women married to or living with males to service the household, as well as having major responsibility for childcare. As soon as service sector girls 'settle down', they find themselves in this position – members of an underclass. If they continue to work outside the home, in addition to unpaid domestic work (about half Servicetown married women have part or full-time paid jobs), they do so at the cost of considerable strain and exhaustion and, as they get older, sexual discrimination increasingly shows itself in restricted chances of promotion to more satisfying and well-paid positions. It is only in the years between school-leaving and 'settling down', and only in areas with a large service sector (or other job market favourable to young women), that some girls, temporarily, escape their underclass position. This temporary redressing of sexual inequality is reflected in the specific youth culture researched, and in drinking situations therein: it is not a general feature of youth cultures: indeed service sector youth are atypical in this important respect. Such atypicality has to be appreciated against the general circumstances of class relations between the sexes, outlined above.

Some features of this study are quite unexceptional when viewed against the mainstream of youth culture research – for example, the insistance on starting, in theory and in fieldwork, with material conditions facing adult groups in a specific geographical area, and working 'downwards' to youth. This is exemplified in the paragraph above, which starts from the question of the social relations between the parents of the youth. It is also exemplified in the order in which the fieldwork is presented in Chapter 5; first reporting on the local labour market, and then looking at the schools and at school-leaving and labour-market entry, and, later in that chapter, looking first at pub round buying in the mid-teen years, and then at the 'whip-round' and at other strategies that substitute for it in younger age-groups. Another feature of this study which ties in quite closely to the tradition of sociological youth culture research is the concern with the social *form* which behaviour takes. Throughout the study, the emphasis has been upon the form of the youth culture and upon the ways in which this shapes the form, or style, of drinking practices – within service sector teenage culture, the mixed-sex round. The question of the *amount* of alcohol consumed within this social form has been neglected. Any *general* model of drinking practices would, however, have to look both at the social form or style, and at the amount, of alcohol consumption within particular social groups. But it is correct to begin investigations of drinking with a consideration of the social form which it takes, and then ask about amount drunk, since social behaviour can only meaningfully be quantified within the framework of the social form which it takes. For a member of service sector youth culture to drink three pints of beer in the mixed-sex round situation is, for example, a social act quite dissimilar from that of a member of a different culture who drinks an equivalent amount of alcohol within the context of the drinking form or style current in that culture. Service sector youth drinking together in their local pub, are, for example, likely to be perceived (by themselves and by others) quite differently from either a motorcyle gang entering that pub, or a group consisting solely of young women. Accepting that such differences exist, how can we move towards a general model that might be able to articulate them? Not only the social origins of these acts, but also the consequences in terms of their meanings for participants and observers, will most probably be quite different in differing class cultures.

Towards a General Model of Youthful Drinking Practices

A general model of youthful drinking would locate discussion of individual choices within the context of the cultures which members of social groups collectively construct in response to shared material conditions. The following paragraphs amplify this general statement by drawing upon the theoretical position advanced in this study and by developing a general model of the relations between material conditions, schooling and youthful consumption styles and practices (eg. of alcohol).

The model should meet a number of criteria. In the first place, it should be firmly based in a sociological analysis of the position of youth in relation to social class and sexual divisions, as outlined above (and supported by the theoretical considerations argued in the Annexe). This means that it must locate social practices such as youthful drinking within cultures which are constructed in the context of the transition of social groups from school to the labour market, against a background of continuing involvement in the socio-economic relations of the family. Secondly, the model should outline the ways in which consumer goods and services, and imagery made available through the media, may be taken up within youth cultures. Thirdly, the model should distinguish between, on the one hand, the social forms which drinking practices take within youth cultures and the ways in which these may be conducted and, on the other hand, quantitative variations within each form (eg in the case of service sector youth culture, the frequency and duration of participation in round-buying), and factors that may influence such quantitative variations. To be useful to health educators, the model should refer to the complex relations between schooling and the qualitative and quantitative aspects of leisure practices; it should be capable of being presented in a fairly brief and clear manner, and this means that visual aids, such as diagrams, might usefully accompany the text. The model should, of course, provide a general framework, within which the case study findings of the preceding chapter may be seen as a specific instance, and which could equally be applied to other groups of youth in the localities.

Diagram 6.1 (following page) and paragraphs that follow provide an opportunity for conceptual integration of preceding discussions of sociological theory, fieldwork, and health education. In the diagram, a distinction is drawn between the preconditons of class cultures – the labour market, the family, the state (and its institutions such as schools) – and the construction by social groups of their cultures and consumption practices in response to those preconditions. Social groups construct the general frameworks of their cultures in response to the conditions they face – eg. the transition from school to a local labour market where this transition takes place against continuing reliance on and participation in the parental family system. Within the broad framework of the culture so constructed arise some specific consumption practices (eg the mixed sex round) whose social forms 'fit' the social relations that constitute that culture. Social groups make *selective use* of themes

Diagram 6.1: A General Model of Youth's Circumstances, Cultures and Consumption Practices

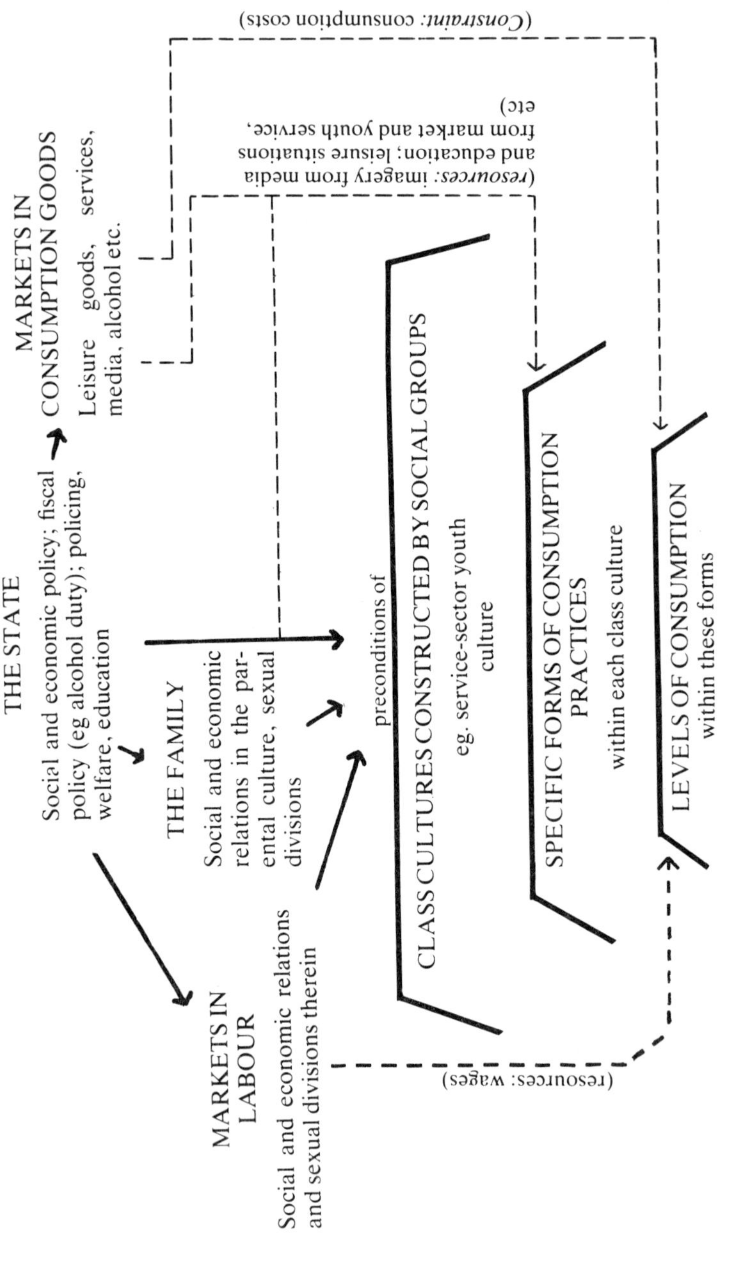

and imagery made available by the media and by the leisure market (styles in music, clothing, speech, choice of drinks, etc) insofar as these available resources make sense within the context of the culture constructed by social groups in response to their situations vis-a-vis labour market, family and state institutions.[4] The potential of in-school and public health education about drinking (and other practices) may be considered within this framework: rather than impacting directly and causally upon drinking behaviour, themes and imagery contained in health education lessons and propaganda may be considered as *resources* which may or may not be taken up within the cultures of particular social groups depending upon the relevance of such times and imagery within each culture.

It is within this framework that we now come to the question of the quantity of each specific consumption practice (eg. quantity of round-buying). The quantity will be constrained by the cost (which in the case of round-buying depends upon conditions in the consumption market, which is in turn open to influence by the State's policy on taxation), and higher levels of consumption will be facilitated by remuneration from part-time and full-time waged work. The last twenty years have seen retail prices of alcoholic drinks rise more slowly than disposable incomes, and consumption of beer, sprits and wine has increased (see table 6.1). The retail price of beer products has shown the greatest increase (though still below the rise of disposable income), and consumption of beer has risen much less slowly than consumption of spirits and wine. There is no reason to believe, however, that consumption level is directly determined by the balance of available wages and consumption costs:[2] a shift in the balance may cause a social group to change its consumption level somewhat, but only within the range of consumption that fits within the drinking form (eg. the round) as it 'makes sense' within the particular culture.[3] There is no way to establish the relationship between a change in, say, the availability or the price of alcohol, and changes in the quantity of alcohol-related practices within any particular culture, except by research into the social group concerned. Any changes in government policy that effect the availability or the cost of alcohol offer opportunities to conduct 'natural experiments': researchers could establish contact with members of specific social groups before the policy change comes into effect, investigate the forms and quantity of drinking practices within the cultures constructed by those groups, and then see what changes in practices follow the implementation of policy

Table 6.1: Comparison of the growth of disposable incomes, 1962-80, with increases in prices of, and consumption of, alcoholic drinks

Indices of incomes, retail prices and alcohol consumption (1962 base = 100)

	Disposable income per capita	**Retail prices**		**Per capita consumption**		
		Beer	Other alcoholic drinks	Beer	Spirits	Wine
Year						
Year	100	100	100	100	100	100
1974	297	198 / 111*	155 / 107*	129	194	257
1980	786	291*	222*	132	229	323

Note: This table is based upon data from the Brewers' Society *UK Statistical Handbook,* some of which are specially calculated for the Society of the Central Statistical Office. Note that the retail price index was reset at 100 in early 1974, hence the figures marked * should be multiplied, by factors of approximately 2 and 1.5 respectively, to make comparison with 1962 prices meaningful. The figures show that, taking the period 1962-80 as a whole, disposable incomes increased faster than prices of alcoholic drinks, and consumption increased, with the greatest increase being in consumption of spirits and (especially) wine. Indices of alcohol consumption are approximate, because they have been calculated from 'rounded' decimal data.

changes. The suggestion is, of course, a variation on traditional experimental 'before-and-after' research, with the important proviso that neither the before nor the after situation can be understood if the population is sampled on a 'random sample' basis. In researching change, as in researching the current position, it is necessary to quantify data in forms that correspond to the various practices to be found in the cultures of the various groups making up the society – rather than attempting to quantify on the basis of 'technical' categories (eg. consumption of millilitres of ethyl alcohol) that 'makes sense' only within the professional culture of alcohologists.

The recognition that the social order is made up of diverse social groups each with their own cultures and drinking practices implies a recognition that there can be no *single* model of alcohol use by a society. The nearest one could get is to place alongside each other a number of models each of which represents the circumstances, culture and drinking practices of a major population group. It should be recognised that the groups might respond variously to any given policy change (propaganda, cost change, etc.). The number of groups (and hence of models) would vary with the complexity and heterogenity of the society in question, but a minimum list would have to include the following:

- male waged workers within each sector of the labour market (agriculture, manufacturing, services, perhaps sub-sections of these – see table 5.4 in chapter 5);
- females in each of these sectors, married and unmarried;
- unwaged workers (primarily married women without work) in geographical areas dominated by each type of waged work (i.e. in areas of heavy industry, etc);
- others in transition into or out of particular sectors of the waged and unwaged economy – i.e. youth, old people, the unemployed.

A barely adequate representation of drinking practices in 'developed' capitalist countries would, therefore, require consideration of at lest ten or so models (each corresponding to a major social group). Such a representation is of course more complex than any model which aggregates the drinking of all individuals regardless of social class and cultural differences, but it is less of a mystification, and hence more adequate as a basis for the formulation of public policy.

Health Education Implications

What are the implications of this model for health education? The model identifies the social relations set up by the labour market, the family, and the State (especially its involvement in schooling) as providing the preconditions of youth cultures. Additionally, both the school system and the market in consumption goods make a secondary contribution, not to the general framework of cultures, but to the detailed forms which social practices (such as drinking) take within them: classroom lessons and the market in goods may provide symbolic resources that are selectively taken up by cultures in ways that 'make sense' within them. Themes and images from health education (for example), brand-imagery from advertisements, and more general portrayals of drinking and drink-related situations in the media (press stories, films, etc.), cannot be expected to have any decisive and general impact upon the cultures that groups evolve in response to their positions vis-a-vis labour market, family and the state – rather, these themes and images may be taken up insofar as they resonate meaningfully within such cultures.[4]

From this analysis it follows that the prospects for school health education are two-fold. The grander possibility is that developments within the economy or within education might have wide consequences for the whole institutional practice of schooling, changing the relations between the school, the family and the labour market, and hence changing the preconditions of youth cultures. The less grand, but still interesting possibility, is that developments within health education might result in new alcohol-related imagery being made available to youth, and that the assimilation of this imagery into existing forms of youth culture may lead to modification of drinking practices.

Let us examine these two possibilities in the light of the proposition that a health education practice corresponding broadly to the research methodology of this study can be developed. A health education curriculum based on a materialist approach to youth cultures and health-related practices therein would involve an investigation – carried out jointly by pupils and teachers – of the material preconditions and forms of local youth cultures. Let us restrict the discussion to the school-leaving, mid-teen years investigated in this study. The essential features of a course for school-leavers would include out-of-school project work, and/or visiting speakers, allowing investigation and discussion of the material preconditions of school-leaving cultures – i.e. of the local labour market and of local variants of the family – as these will face boys and girls after sixteen. Since many localities will, like Servicetown, the case study area, be heterogeneous in social and economic structure, it is likely that any classroom group will contain pupils drawn from a variety of social backgrounds, and in transition to a variety of positions vis-a-vis labour market and family; hence a variety of pupil cultures, and of drinking styles (and other leisure pursuit practices) will be represented within the one classroom. One way of dealing with this problem is to break up the class into working-groups, each formed on the basis of pupils ideas about their most likely future 'occupations' (ie within the labour market, and/or in the home, on the dole etc); in many cases, such groups will correspond quite closely to friendship groups within the class. Each working group (divided into sub-groups if large) could then conduct a short project of interviewing older teenagers or young adults who currently occupy themselves in ways in which the pupils anticipate that they themselves will probably be occupied within a few years; pupils would then report back to the whole class. This pupil-research might involve a variety of methods, ranging from short discussions with parents, friends or other adults, to tape-recorded interviews, and the taking of short biographies. Additional evidence could be collected in the form of visits to the homes and work places of those interviewed, photographs, etc. The sophistication of the project methods could vary with the motivation and interests of the pupils, and a balance struck between such out-of-school project work and contributions from young adults (young wage workers, young mothers, the unemployed, etc) invited into the classroom as outside speakers, depending on the conditions within particular schools. Class records could be compiled in the form of large scrapbooks and/or pin-boards into which all 'evidence' collected by the pupils could be placed. The teacher could then begin to explore with pupils the ways in which their cultures might be seen as collective strategies for managing the expected transitions to 'occupations' and the satisfactions, dissatisfactions and uncertainties involved. Having identified pupils' cultures, discussion could then move on to the ways in which health-related social practices – involving not only drinking, but eating, sexuality, etc – arise in each culture. In a prototype teachers' manual of thirteen lesson guides, Bente Nortoft and myself have outlined a number of practical suggestions for the construction of such a health education course for school-leavers.[5]

Let us now turn to the question of the possible consequences of such a course. The course represents a break with normal teaching practice, insofar as normal practice (a) excludes any overt recognition, within the classroom, of social divisions of class, gender or race and (b) excludes project work into material conditions and social groups in the locality. Indeed, the suggestions outlined above are sufficiently out of tune with normal teaching practices as to be described, by a sympathetic senior health educator, as 'non-educational'.[6] Cutting across the assumptions of child-focussed education in its individualist form, the materialist suggestion not only recognises social groups within the classroom, but also relates them explicitly to social divisions as these are represented in the locality, and proposes the investigation of these as relevant to the child's knowledge of him or her self, and to health. Insofar as some teachers (a minority, no doubt) are able to introduce elements of such an approach into schools, so the whole relationship between schools, family and labour market would be changed. The school is at present a space marked out from both labour market and family – indeed that is its primary structural characteristic. Use of school time for investigation of local labour markets and families, and reproduction, within the classroom, of the social relations of these, might possibly (for some groups of pupils, in some schools) change the preconditions of youth cultures sufficiently to provoke a collective re-appraisal of, and changes in, these cultures. This might in turn, have implications for changes in drinking and other social practices: what these changes might be would presumably vary with regions, social groups and youth cultures, and is a question for empirical investigation.

Secondly, there is the less drastic possibility that health education might offer new themes and symbols that might be employed by social groups, in ways that resonate within the framework of their *existing* cultures, so as to affect slight modifications in the forms which drinking practices take within those cultures. This possibility raises the question of the ways in which health educators might wish to influence drinking practices in youth cultures – the question of *aims* of health education. The problem here is that no general consenus can be reached over the precise definition of and criteria for 'health'. This is because the meaning of and value attached to 'health' will vary from social groups to social group in ways explicable in terms of the cultures constructed.[7] Any health education message or discussion that seeks to appeal to a social group's concept of 'health' must take cognizance of the ways in which 'health' is conceptualised in the culture of that group. This requires a minimum of teacher 'chalk and talk' about alcohol, about health, and about 'healthy drinking' (or 'sensible drinking choices'), and a readiness to listen to pupils describing the ways in which their cultures structure their drinking practices in ways that seem 'healthy' and/or 'sensible' within the terms of those cultures: the teacher's aim should be to build upon existing features of cultures, rather than promulgating an unrelated set of rules or guidelines. This sensitive listening would be facilitated by a greater appreciation, on the part of teachers, to the material preconditions of and forms taken by youth cultures within the locality of the school.

It is one thing to propose changes in teaching practice, and quite another to implement them. The possibilities depend partly upon the commitments of those working in those branches of the state that are responsible for health, welfare and education. Many of these workers are currently being radicalised by the urgency of the struggle against the 'cuts'. Some also have been influenced by the women's movement, and are looking for ways to transform the services so that they correspond to the needs of working class men and women, instead of simply defending services in their existing forms.[8] Health education, which expanded as a professional field in the mid-1970s, is one area in which these tendencies are visible: many of the younger Health Education Officers, Health Visitors, and Health Education Advisory Teachers who have recently entered this field would agree with the broad aim of this study, whatever reservations they might have over particular aspects of its underlying theory, its implementation, or its findings and suggestions. The same might reasonably be said of some teachers, social workers and youth workers. The commitment of those working in and around the state is, however, only a part of the story. All such persons have to develop their practices in the context of being employees of the state: they have to be able to argue their point of view, and be able to de-legitimise opposing points of view within the authority structures that surround them. It is rarely possible to do this very successfully as an individual, and collective organisation and support is necessary. This can take three forms: close collaboration and working class groups amongst colleagues in particular health, education, and related institutions; formation of health education groups within relevant trade unions; and more loosely-organised groups for collective self-education and mutual support. Of these, it is trades union activity that is probably least well developed, and the expansion of existing health education groups within those trades unions whose members work in education and training schemes for the young unemployed would be especially useful. Such schemes are generally intended to include some 'social skills' training (which is however at the present time not well developed), and it is in this context, especially, that approaches that link material conditions, cultures and health may be able to flourish.[9] Given present signs that trainees on youth opportunity schemes are beginning to become unionised, there may be opportunities for trainees and trainers to develop health and social education along collectivist rather than individualistic lines. Thus such schemes may be a more promising arena for development of materialist health education than schools, especially given the greater degree of hierarchical control in the latter. Both sorts of institutions are however important – many school-leavers will at some time go on a work-expense course – and there should, therefore, be an interchange of ideas, experience and support between them.

Cultures of the Unemployed

A particular feature of the case study area is its relatively well-developed service sector, and the rapid rate of deterioration of the other main sector of its economy – small manufacturing. The expansion of the service sector has not however been sufficient to completely offset the decline of job-opportunities in manufacturing, leading to increasing unemployment. In most other parts of Britain, manufacturing is also in rapid decline, and the service sector less developed than in Servicetown. The shape of the labour market in coming years will reflect these trends. If manufacturing continues to decline, then it will become a quite minor sector, and the labour market will be dominated by two main sectors – service sector employment, and unemployment. This will have considerable consequences for the development of youth cultures and social practices such as drinking. Not only will youth cultures associated with the transition to employment in manufacturing industry decline in membership; new mass youth cultures associated with unemployment, episodic employment and training schemes may also emerge. Furthermore, service sector youth cultures will probably not remain unaware of or unresponsive to these developments. The stage is set for substantial changes in the size and shape of youth cultures and hence in teenage drinking practices.

Such changes should be taken into account in relation to future research and to health and social education. There is considerable scope for research into the cultures of the young unemployed. Since the lower strata of the working class – i.e. the strata in which unemployment is concentrated – is made up of boys and girls from a variety of ethnic groups, it is not necessarily the case that there will be one homogenous culture of unemployed youth: a variety of cultures is more likely. The situation is further complicated by the as-yet unresolved question of the educational and training provisions that will develop out of existing further education and Youth Opportunities Programmes; and by the pattern of selective recruitment of social groups into such programmes. Increasingly, however, young people will be spending more time outside the formal frameworks afforded by waged work and state-provided work-substitutes. In these circumstances, what they do will not only be a form of leisure – if indeed that term retains its original meaning when used to refer to activities not undertaken as a respite from and reward for obligatory work – but may also, in many cases, evolve into activities that provide some of the benefits of waged work. The most obvious of these benefits are money, and a sense of identity derived from work. Some of the sociological work on the 'informal economy' may be useful in understanding the 'economic' activities of unemployed youth, whilst the broad tradition of sociological delinquency research may, if reformed to take proper account of sexual and other divisions, offer insights into ways in which identity and excitement may be combined with pecuniary gain.[10] A working-together of these research traditions may offer one useful direction for future research on youthful drinking practices.

Health Education via the Media

There is growing interest in the mass media as a carrier for health education, the 'first international conference on health education and the media' being held in Edinburgh in 1981 (Leathar et al,

1981). Government-funded mass media campaigns have been initiated on a regional basis in parts of Scotland and England (Plant et al, 1981). Government-funded mass media campaigns have been initiated on a regional basis in parts of Scotland and England (Plant et al, 1979, Budd and McCron, 1981), and the DHSS-funded Health Education Council has recently commissioned research that goes beyond the customary questions of campaign awareness and 'effects', and takes up more fundamental questions of the relationship between mass media campaigns and the processes whereby they are appropriated within local communities (McCron, personal communication). Given the context of increasing unemployment and a failure to expand training and educational facilities sufficiently to absorb all the young unemployed, neither the workplace nor the educational system is going to offer a comprehensive channel for health education. Only the mass media offer a means of communication with the mass of the population. It is this characteristic of the mass media, rather than any proven efficacy as a channel of health education, that is likely to lead to a continuation or expansion of mass media alcohol education exercises.[11]

There are two main problems inherent on the use of the mass media for purposes of health education. The first problem applies particularly in the case of television and radio which, unlike printed media, are truly *mass* communications insofar as they address a *mass* audience, with little attempt at audience segmentation. It is difficult to reconcile the need to engage the cultures and material condition of specific strata of the working class, with the media's need to homogenize those strata and to construct a consensus of debate assumed equally applicable to all. It is difficult to see how health educators might surmount this problem within the context of television and radio programming at 'peak' hours, and it may therefore be preferable to restrict health education to relatively 'slack' times (such as the early morning, daytime or late at night) when it is possible, in the absence of the mass audience, to programme for 'minorities'. Local radio stations may be able to adopt such an approach to health education more easily than can regional or national networks.

As far as printed media are concerned, the degree of market-segmentation is relatively high, with magazines and comics directed towards boys and girls of various ages, ethnic minority groups, adult special-interest groups, members of trades unions, and the unemployed.[12] The most promising forum for development of mass media health education exercises sensitive to the material circumstances and cultures of specific social groups may therefore involve co-ordination between local radio (or regional television at off-peak hours), and printed media. Such co-ordination would not, however, resolve the contradiction between the mass media as something *received* by individuals amid small groups, and the need to make health education into an *active* investigation of material conditions, cultures and practices. The Open University, in association with a London Health Education Department, is currently investigating ways of combining a local community development approach to health education with use of television.[13]

A more general problem about the use of the media in promoting culturally sensitive health education about alcohol relates to the historically-constructed perception of a link (discussed in chapters 1 and 2) between drinking and indiscipline. The shift to the right in British (and other countries) politics, which has brought this historical legacy once more to the fore, shows little sign of being reversed at the time of writing (mid-1982). The response of the labour movement has been muted, with trade union militancy undercut by fears of unemployment, and the advance of a rather economistic leftism within the Labour Party being halted by an equally unimaginative reaction. Both the Labour Party and the new Social Democratic Party, formed by breakaway members of the Labour Party, are committed to a degree of reflation of the economy. Were one or the other of these Parties to form a government, then future development of alcohol-related policies and associated welfare and health education practices would proceed in the context of a return to more liberal (even, possibly, leftist) atmosphere. But, even were this to be the case, the problems of maintenance of work discipline, public order and political acquiescence would remain, irrespective of changes of government. Indeed, these problems may deepen for several years, given the time-lag between changes in state policy (eg reflation) and their effects in terms of out-turns such as employment. Recent economic studies indicate a continuing decline in the performance of the British capitalist economy over the next few years.[14] This may or may not provoke a recurrence of intensification of the riots that occurred throughout Britain in the summer of 1981 – but it will certainly ensure that the state will continue to be concerned about the possibilities of such breakdowns in social discipline, especially amongst the swelling number of young unemployed. In this context, the historically-constructed association between vagrancy, lack of capitalist work-discipline, public disturbance and drink will continue to fire moral panic over youthful drinking, and to structure the consensus of concerns within which health educators and broadcasters work. The historical analysis and the contemporary case study presented in the preceding chapters is intended as a contribution to the process of questioning the assumptions of a link between youthful drinking and social indiscipline.

CONCLUSION

This study concerns itself with three substantive issues: the historical origins and nature of currently dominant conceptions of 'alcohol problems' and of the policies brought to bear upon them; the quality of drinking practices as these arise within the culture of specific strata of inner city youth; and whatever implications may be drawn for the future development of alcohol-related policies and health education.

Alcohol Policies: Embedded in Social and Economic Policy

The study's conclusions about the historical origins of alcohol-related controls fall into two separate, but connected areas: those touching upon alcohol *production*, and those touching upon control of the *consumer*.

The history of English legislation bearing upon the production of alcohol shows that only in the national emergency occasioned by war requiring full mobilisation of the economy and the prioritization of armaments manufacture has the state intervened in the process of alcohol production and, even then, the intervention was limited (see Chapter 2). At other times the state has actively encouraged alcohol production, albeit for different reasons at different times. During the middle ages the state legislated to keep the pices of drink and of other victuals low, in order to reduce price inflation and subsequent wage demands, and mercantilist legislation also concerned itself with reasonable pricing and with standard measure. Subsequent capitalisation of the industry was an integral part of the development of the broader capitalist economy. During the early nineteenth century, at the very zenith of the rise of the manufacturing classes, free trade in beer was introduced, encouraging a proliferation of production/retail units. Throughout the century, the commitment to liberal political economy militated against any interference in the production process – in spite of widespread and increasing fears about working class drinking and indiscipline. J. S. Mill's distinction between the sphere of production (subject to economic laws of notion) and that of distribution (subject to human intervention) enabled the commitment to capitalist production to continue alongside an increasing reliance on social welfare interventions (housing, public health, welfare) in the sphere of distribution of the product; when alcohol controls were tightened at the beginning of the twentieth century, they were restricted to licensing controls in the sphere of distribution. Following the adoption of Keynesian economic policies, the state sought to stabilise the economy by expanding demand. As the alcohol industry was an important sector of the economy – providing opportunities for profitable investment of large capital sums, for export earnings, for employment, and for tax revenue – the state's post-war policy towards the industry reflected its commitment to these objectives, rather than being determined by 'alcohol policy alone' (C.R.P.S., 1979; 17).

It follows from this analysis that the prospects for the future development of polices bearing upon the production of alcohol will be determined not simply by the findings of research into alcohol-related problems (though such research may play an important legitimising role) but, more fundamentally, by the general economic policies adopted by the state.

A parallel conclusion may be drawn from the history of the development of social controls touching upon the consumption and use of alcohol. Chapters 1 to 3 take as their point of departure the development of the economy and the expansion of a market in labour, and show how state policy relating to the public consumption of alcohol derived from dominant classes' concerns about the labouring classes. These chapters show how successive problems of restraining labour mobility and wage militancy, of discouraging public meetings at which seditious words might be uttered, and of inculcating the labour disciplines required by merchant capital, provided the framework against which each ascendent class evaluated the social significance of public drinking amongst its inferiors, and elaborated upon existing controls on public drinking. The consistent theme running through the resulting legislation is discipline; social, economic and political. The politically unstable conditions prevailing in the early and mid-nineteenth century provided the context wihin which middle-class consternation over working class indisciplines generally, and gin drinking particularly, led to the formation of a police force. Disciplinary themes were subsequently carried by temperance campaigners into alcohol education.

The development of alcohol education in the post-war period has been mediated by the ideologies of the two branches of the state – the health service and the education system – that carry it. Within the health service, alcohol-related problems in the individual, hitherto seen in terms of moral failing and indiscipline, became redefined as a form of disease. Producers of health education materials drew upon medical metaphors as well as upon temperance themes to illustrate the dangers of over-indulgence. Such approaches were, in the absence of alternatives, embraced by many teachers in the post-war period, but came to be seen as inadequate when measured against child-centred teaching approaches, nurtured in sex education, 'education for personal relationships', and other branches of the 'soft curriculum'. These approaches favoured a de-emphaisis of medical 'facts' about alcohol and alcoholism, and a return to the earlier, moral concerns of temperance education. Contemporary health education curricula and public prevention campaigns draw upon these traditions – the medical, and the moral/disciplinary. Both of these approaches share a concern with the individual and the development of his or her knowledge and behaviour, the main difference being that whereas the 'factual' or medically-orientated approach emphasises knowledge of alcohol and alcoholism, the moral approach emphasises knowledge of oneself and of one's personal values as a basis for independent decision-making. Current approaches to health education are not, it is argued, adequate as a means of communication with pupils or adults who, whilst being individuals, are also members of a society stratified by social class, sexual and ethnic divisions, and for whom the construction of cultures and social practices is a *collective* endeavour on the part of *groups* of individuals sharing particular structural locations. In Chapter 6 above, an alternative basis for health education sensitive to the material basis of social life and to the cultures constructed by social groups was outlined. Whereas currently dominant approaches to health education either ignore the rooting of social practices in cultures, or else characterise cultures purely in terms of peer pressures towards delinquency and over-indulgence, a materialist and collectivist health education would aim to identify and facilitate those existing aspects of cultures that might be regarded, by members of social groups themselves, as healthier or otherwise preferable to other aspects. But the proposition that education should recognise, respect and build upon working class cultures takes on a problematic appearance when viewed against the background of the historical development of alcohol-related policies. It is difficult to reconcile the anti-collectivist, anti-working class theme inherent in alcohol-related policies and health education, with an approach that takes as its starting point the material positions and collective endeavours of working class men, women and children. The recognition of the possibility of fundamental disagreements and conflicts over the scope, methods and forms of knowledge legitimised within alcohol education brings this branch of health and social education into line with that broader field, in which such problems have been acknowledged (Beatty, 1980).

Research into Youthful Drinking Practices: Problems and Prospects

The history of alcohol-related policies and alcohol education illustrates the processes whereby general concerns about social, economic and political discipline of the labouring classes became focussed upon the *specific* issue of public drinking, creating a conceptual framework in which youthful drinking becomes perceived as a failure of self-restraint and discipline in the individual. Such conceptual legacies, if applied *carte blanche* to all sections of youth, may mislead us, since there is no necessity for contemporary youth practices to embody historical problems. It may well be that there are some specific groups of youth amongst whom drinking is an integral part of an inchoate rebellion against society, a form of 'resistance through ritual'. But as the material presented in the area case study illustrates, there is at least one major group of youth for whom drinking does not have this significance – quite the reverse.

The group of school leavers upon whom the case study reported above focussed were in transition to the service sector of the local economy in an inner city area. The material circumstances around that transition are the consequences of the development of the economy, the decline of the main branches of manufacturing industry, and the encouragement, by post-war Keynesian policies, of full male employment, of expansion of demand, and of the service sector. The service sector is not unique to the study area, indeed it is represented to various degrees within all modern economies. Yet the sociological treatment of the service sector as a backcloth for the development of youth cultures has been extremely patchy. Early post-war studies of youth culture, did, it is true, lay considerable stress upon the influence of the service sector in providing opportunities for conspicuous consumption: in their crudest form, such studies portray youth culture as an 'effect' of consumption themes presented in the media and of commercially-produced fashions in clothes, music and other non-durables. This view of youth may be regarded as a specific instance of the more general thesis of embourgeoisment of the working class, in which the increasing subscription of that class to middle-class value systems was assumed. More critical theorists elaborated a more pessimistic approach, characterised as a theory of 'embourgeoisment gone wrong'. This approach retains the assumption of working class subscription to middle class values, but suggests that class inequalities and disadvantages might make it difficult for working class children to 'succeed', and this might lead to disappointment, retreat, disaffiliation or delinquency. More recently, researchers have pointed out that there is no necessity to assume that working class children subscribe to values very different from those embedded in the culture of their parents: any oppositional attitudes might be the result of initial class socialisation, rather than of disappointment at failure to achieve middle class goals. This approach reaches its most advanced expression in the work of Paul Willis, in which the male chauvinism of working class culture is credited with socialising working class boys into a glorification of manual labour and a rejection of all 'sissy' institutions, such as the school, that question the value of such labour. For all such theorists, leisure behaviour (such as drinking practices) is neither a reflection of middle class consumption norms, nor a reaction following disappointment at failure to reach those norms, but an expression of working class consciousness (albeit not developed in politicised forms). Youth cultures are a form of 'resistance through rituals', drinking is a form of 'defiance' (Willis, 1978: 21). Such approaches, ironically, confirm historically-generated fears about the working class, drink and indiscipline.

The two main problems with this sociology of youth culture, and with the opportunities it offers to students of drinking practices, are its masculinist bias and its treatment of the service sector. The neo-Marxian insistence that, whilst consumption imagery is a part of youth culture, the ways in which it is appropriated are mediated by youth's responses to its entry into the social relations of production, represents an important advance in cultural studies. Had this approach been carried through in a consistent manner, then it might have resulted in the realisation that, since an increasing proportion of youth were gaining employment in the service sector, this sector was attaining a *double significance* – as an arena in which relations of production, as well as of consumption were formed. But the sociological focus upon male perspectives, and the persistent tendency to focus attention upon those arenas in which males were most clearly visible, and to ignore areas in which womens work (the service sector, the home), subverted this possibility. The service sector has been conceptualised by both 'bourgeois' and neo-Marxian researchers as a source of consumption styles which are appropriated, developed or subverted (see Hebdige, 1981) but – since it is not exclusively peopled by the lower working class males with whom sociologists of youth culture have been pre-occupied – it has been ignored as an arena of work.

The paucity of work on service sector youth culture is one symptom of the problem of sexism in sociological theory and practice (Oakley, 1974), and also an omission that will become more glaring as this sector increasingly becomes the only one in which large numbers of youth can find employment.

The substantive findings of chapter 5 contradict the assumption, derived from a history marked by successive struggles to impose discipline upon an emergent proletariat, about youthful drinking and indiscipline. Contemporary servce sector youth culture is not one of insurgency and rebellion. It is a culture structured by positive anticipation of the wage relation, acceptance of the social relations of production in the service sector of the economy, and gratitude for its relatively privileged position (compared with those of the lower working class and ethnic minorities). The mixed-sex round is described, in the case study reported above, as a celebration of the social relations of independence, sociability and temporary sex-equality that characterise the service sector. Acceptance of the labour market does not, for these school-leavers, imply rejection of other institutions such as the school (as it may for some school-leavers lower in the class spectrum), since there is no fundamental contradiction between the 'official' values of the school and the work-values of the service sector.

A number of possibilities exist for further research into drinking practices in the variety of youth cultures to be found in inner city areas. It is clear that social class, sexual and racial divisions are important for understanding youth cultures and social practices.

This study however provides some evidence for the proposition that it would be hazardous to generalise about sexual divisions as represented within youth cultures, since these are differently expressed at different levels of the class structure: it is in the lower strata of the working class that young womens' housework obligations are most pressing, and differential sex-roles within youth cultures and drinking occasions most clearly delineated. Within marriage, however, women from all strata of the working class undertake the main burden of housework, whether or not they undertake any form of waged work. It would be illuminating to study the ways in which drinking practices develop, within lower, middle and upper strata of the working class, as boys and girls who have been working in the labour market (or on youth opportunity programmes, or unemployed) for several years grow up, and as many of them reproduce the family unit or some alternative. Such work could provide the context within which could be conducted the sociological study of individual biographies and drinking careers.[1] The opportunites to carry out and apply such research in practical ways will, however, be at least partially dependent upon future trends in state policy, to which we turn in speculative manner in the closing paragraphs.

Prospects for Alcohol-related Policies

We have argued that the development of policies relating to the consumption and production of alcohol are not autonomous of broader developments in social and economic policy. It follows that the opportunities for social research to make practical contributions to the development of alcohol-related policies and to health education are constrained by such broader developments. These closing paragraphs outline three possible alternatives for the development of alcohol-related policies.

One possibility is that the current government's attempts to reintroduce the free market economy by cutting back all state activities and institutions other than those required for law enforcement may continue or even become more pronounced. Such policies provide an atmosphere conducive to temperance sentiments insofar as these relate to the maintenance of social discipline:

> This sentiment always has been, and is still, greater than its advocates. Its origin is in the literature of the ancient Greek

> philosophers and in the New Testament. What began as a philosophical concept of 'self-control' evolved under the influence of Christian doctrine as the basis for the disciplined life. Perhaps its identification with abstinence from alcohol limited its more general application. Nevertheless, its use in this way was vindicated by the results, and since the conditions which lead to its application to the alcohol problem obtain once more, there seems to be no valid reason for abandoning it. If it is argued that the term, is a hindrance to the cause, it must be said that this is how it seemed in the 18th and 19th centuries when the first Temperance societies were formed. If the remnants of temperance organisations have not the capacity, and if others have not the stomach, for initiating a recovery of this fine sentiment, then the cause is big enough to raise its own resources and leadership.
> (Brake, 1981; 26)

But Conservative policies are not conducive to the placing of restrictions upon any branch of free enterprise, including the alcohol industry, as Ministerial statements make clear:

> *Jenkin calls for more collaboration to fight alcoholism – Build on the common ground*
>
> Mr Patrick Jenkin, Secretary for Social Services, today called on the drinks industry to join in concerted action with the voluntary bodies to tackle the growing problem of alcohol misuse. Speaking at the annual general meeting of the National Council on Alcoholism in London, Mr Jenkin said: 'There is much more common ground than is often supposed between those who earn their living from the manufacture and sale of alcoholic drink and the bodies concerned with the dangers of alcoholism. The time has come for this common gound to be turned into common action. All of us – and this is particularly true of Governments – who are connected with the problems created by the misuse of alcohol have to renconcile two facts. The first is that in the eyes of millions of folk, alcohol is a pleasurable and perfectly acceptable part of social life and that, if sensibly used, it causes no harm. The second is that the *misuse* of alcohol is causing health and social problems which it is not an exaggeration to say are of epidemic proportions . . . I believe that the time has come for the representatives of the drinks trade – both manufacturers and retailers –

> and representatives of the bodies concerned with the misuse of alcohol, to sit round the table in a common forum. To continue as if there was open warfare no longer makes sense. All involved must seek out the common ground and work together to find solutions. Of course, the issues concern many more than those two groups. Doctors, teachers, employers, trade unions and the advertising industry – all will need to be involved. Is this a hopeless quest? I do not think so. There are many indications that different interests and different points of view are converging. Let me give you an example. The Licencing (Alcohol, Education and Research) Act has just become law. The Act is the outcome of a long process of discussion and negotiation between this Council – the National Council on Alcoholism – the Brewers' Society, the National Union of Licensed Victuallers and other interested organisations. I would like to pay tribute to the patience and good sense of all concerned. As a consequence of helpful attitudes and painstaking negotiations, we have now enshrined in law the charitable purposes of the Alcohol Education and Research Fund to be administered by the Council to be set up under the Act. Its purposes include the education of the public as to the causes and effects of alcohol misuse and the promotion of research into the means of preventing it. (DHSS, 1981; 1-3)

In summary then, a continuation of currrent government policies would emphasise the freedom of alcohol producers, and would rely upon education about individual responsibility, and upon policing for the minority unresponsive to such education.

Recent successes of the Social Democratic Party, gained at the expense of both Conservative and Labour Parties, suggest that government policies may, in the longer term, become moderated. The policies of the SDP, insofar as they are visible at the time of writing, appear to involve a return to Keynesian management of the economy.[2] Leaving aside the question of the feasibility of such policies it can be seen that, if implemented, they would provide a political context in which measures to reduce the demand for alcohol would be unlikely to find a place. Alcohol-related policies might well reflect those of the early postwar period, in which restrictions on alcohol distribution were eased. Social Democratic polices bearing upon the consumer and upon alcohol education are a matter of speculation in the absence of any clear indication of social policies.

The picture is not much clearer in relation to any future Labour government, in spite of the existence of an Alternative Economic Strategy (A.E.S.) which is the object of much discussion and some disagreement within the Labour Movement.[3] The A.E.S. involves taking into public ownership a substantial proportion of the manufacturing industry. This would not necessarily involve nationalisation of the alcohol industry, since the structure of ownership of the alcohol industry places it outside the main manufacturing conglomerates: alcohol producers are generally independent firms (in which brewing family capital sometimes has a significant stake) or parts of service-sector conglomerates (Thurman, personal communication). Whether or not all or some producers would be nationalised under a future Labour administration would therefore depend upon the vigour with which such an administration pursued a policy of socialisation of the economy, and upon whatever choice might then be made between nationalising the 'commanding heights' of British industry (including highly profitable producers of consumer goods in the food and drugs sector) and nationalising more of the declining engineering sector (in order to safeguard jobs).The information that would be required to suggest which of these directions of action is the more likely is at present lacking. The future is as cloudy in relation to Labour policies bearing upon distribution and supply. One might expect that such a government would be less likely than the present government to promote health and social education that dwells upon the moral failings and indisciplines of the working class. Referring to the beginning of this century, Harrison records a number of reasons for the decline in Labour Party interest and participation in temperance agitation – including the reason that Labour activists had become suspicious that the middle classes were using the drink debate to 'advertise working class vices' (Harrison, 1971; 397-404). The Labour Movement may one day, depending upon circumstances, re-discover this suspicion.

There is however one 'vice', one form of discipline, emanating from men and cutting across social classes, that should be more closely scrutinised. The problem of male drinking and violence against women has long been recognised in the Womens Movement. During the nineteenth century, sections of the womens' temperance movement 'blamed the drink' for male violence, and agitated for restrictions upon supply (Sebestyen, 1980). Some contemporary feminists, however, locate the source of violence not in alcohol, but in economic and power relations between the sexes:

> The prohibition movement, mostly women, had a point when they said that men got drunk and then came home and beat their wives. It was true, and it still is true. But is the solution to ban the sale of alcohol or to fight for wives to be in a position where we no longer have to put up with it? The source of the problem . . . is real power relations, which is why Women Against Rape has preferred to focus most of our energy on actual violence and on the way that the courts, the law, and womens' financial dependence make us vulnerable to it. (Hall and Butcher, 1981; 3)

The policy implications of feminist perspectives upon drink-related problems are, then, arguable. And the currently limited power and influence of feminism in relation to the political forces discussed above make an immediate impact upon alcohol policies unlikely. But such perspectives identify a dimension of alcohol-related problems that are largely ignored in the mainstream of 'alcohol problems' literature and, it must be admitted, in the present study. This omission may partly result from the choice made to focus our fieldwork upon drinking practices in a youth culture within which young women were, temporarily, economically independent of individual men. It may also reflect the fact that the author is a man, learning but slowly from the Womens Movement. Whatever its cause, however, it is an omission that should be made good in future studies.

In conclusion, we suggest that alcohol-related problems may fruitfully be analysed as aspects of broader problems of state maintenance of social discipline, and drinking practices of specific social groups as aspects of the engagement of those groups with the disciplines facing them. Historically, as we have shown, drink controls evolved out of concern about the maintenance of labour discipline. In contemporary society, some groups of young people are sufficiently favourably placed in relation to the labour market to opt to accept (indeed celebrate) the social relations it offers: the service sector, for example, lays the basis for a self-disciplined youth culture, and for the mixed-sex round. Other groups, differently placed in relation to social class, sexual and ethnic divisions, evolve distinct cultures, think differently, drink differently. Some social groups – particularly, perhaps, those whose integration into the labour market and its disciplines are most tenuous – become objects of a moral panic, and their drinking is then seen as 'a problem'. Production of alcohol itself is not, however, curtailed, because of the state's estimation of the economic importance of the industry within the market economy: state policy in relation to production is itself disciplined by the realities of the market economy. From this perspective, public debate, and health and social education about alcohol problems, may be regarded as a set of contending discourses on broader economic and social problems that have crystalised around the particular issue of 'drink'. The practical possibilities for the future evolution of policies bearing upon the production, distribution and consumption of alcohol will continue to be constrained by broader developments in social and economic relations and by the political shifts that accompany them.

ANNEXE. SOCIAL CLASS AND SEXUAL DIVISIONS

The research into the circumstances and drinking practices of a strata of youth in transition from school to the service sector of the inner city economy, reported in chapter 5, rests upon certain theoretical assumptions about the relationship between social class and sexual divisions in contemporary capitalist society. These assumptions, which are summarised in chapter 4 and utilised in that chapter's critique of the sociology of male youth cultures, are elaborated in this annexe.

The Historical Origins of Materialist Theory

> Once upon a time, a valiant fellow had the idea that men were drowned in water only because they were possessed with the *idea of gravity*. If only they were to knock this notion out of their heads, say, by stating it to be a superstition, a religious concept, they would be sublimely proof against any danger from water. His whole life long he fought against the illusion of gravity, of whose harmful effects all statistics brought him new and manifold danger.

This quotation from Marx and Engel's *The German Ideology* (1970; 37) ironically characterises the idealism against which materialism inveighed. Idealism is the philosophy that ideas rule the world. Materialism is not so much a philosophy as a declaration of an end to philosophies, and an acceptance that ideas are formed through practice, or action. Hence the famous line in Marx's *Theses on Feuerbach* that 'philosophers have only *interpreted* the world in various ways; the point is to change it' (1970; 123). Materialism supplies the practical basis to the social sciences, by pointing out that a real world can never be either adequately described nor changed by the application of ideas: on the contrary, the ideas come from a specific practice, and an idea is truthful insofar as it recognises the practical conditions of its own production.

The objection most generally brought against materialism is that it reduces all social and ideational life to physical or economic causes, linking ideas and their conditions of production in a direct, one-to-one and mechanical manner. This we can denote as 'vulgar' materialism, or reflection theory (i.e. the theory that ideas are simply reflections of material realities). Vulgar materialism arose in specific historical circumstances in the eighteenth century. Frederick Engels, writing in the mid-nineteenth century, said that:

> The materialism of the last century was predominantly mechanical, because at that time, of all natural sciences, only mechanics, and indeed only the mechanics of solid bodies – celestial and terrestial – in short, the mechanics of gravity, had come to any definite close. Chemistry at that time existed only in its infantile, phlogistic form. Biology still lay in swaddling clothes; vegetable and animal organisms had been only roughly examined and were explained as the result of purely mechanical cause. What the animal was to Descartes, man was to the materialists of the eighteenth century – a machine. This exclusive application of the standards of mechanics to processes of a chemical and organic nature – in which processes the laws of mechanics are, indeed, also valid, but are pushed into the background by other, higher laws – constitutes the first specific but at that time inevitable limitation of classical French materialism. (Engels, 1970; 349)

Materialism is, then, like any other method of understanding the world, a product of the world of its time. Early materialism was much influenced by the advances of mechanics used in the industry of the time, and the sciences that arose at that time had a mechanistic character. Vulgar materialism, as a theory fairly accurately reflecting its conditions of production, was the authentic materialism of its time.

Materialism then developed, in the nineteenth century, in more complex ways, leaning on the idea of *process* than on simple, static mechanics. In the sciences, the theory of the origin of the solar system began to gain ground; geology, the history of the development of the Earth developed; Darwin successfully put forward his theory of the origin and development of species of animals and man; and organic chemsitry developed apace (ibid; 350). Advances in materialism, from a static to a developmental view, flowed both from advances in sciences (sometimes associated with the newer production techniques) and also from developments in the class structure within which these techniques were developed. As the rise of the bourgeoisie accelerated, so a picture of the world as stable and as repeating established patterns became less viable, and theories of process became more thinkable. In this context developed historical materialism, which emphasises that a material reality can be understood only as the latest stage in a developmental process, extending over time. This materialism replaces the earlier 'fixed' materialism.

However the accelerating pace of economic and social change of the nineteenth and twentieth centuries has led to so much attention on process and change, that the importance of underlying material realities that change not at all or less quickly (e.g. the human body) has tended to be overlooked. As Sebstiano Timpanaro has observed:

> . . . it has to be said that Marxism, especially in its first phase (up to and including *The German Ideology*) is not materialism proper. Physical and biological nature is certainly not denied by Marx, but it constitutes more a prehistoric antecedent to human history than a reality which still limits and conditions man. From the time when man started to labour and to produce, it appears (from Marx) that he enters into relationship with nature . . . only through work. (Timpanaro, 1975; 40-41)

Noting that Marx wanted to dedicate the second volume of *Capital* to Darwin, Timpanaro suggests that Marx was too taken up with this economic work to develop a full conception of the relation between the person, the economy, and nature. This, I want to add, had specific consequences in that it helped Marx to avoid a fully materialist conception of the social relations between persons of opposite biological sex. It was Engels who, not being personally tied to the mammoth task that Marx's economic works (*Theories of Surplus Value,* and *Capital*) turned out to be, had the opportunity to theorise about the relation between nature, the economy and the sexes. His *The Origins of the Family,* however, was as much a speculative reconstruction of early history than a scientific study, largely due to the paucity of the anthropological work upon which he leant. I shall return to the question of relations between the sexes later.

How, then, can we conceptualise the relation between (a) the natural, environmental and biological conditions, including the physical capabilities of women's and men's bodies; (b) the economic level, at which the labour of men and women provides the economic basis for society and; (c) the cultural level, at which relations between social classes and between men and women are expressed in forms of consciousness and culture, and sometimes in attempts to change the natural and economic conditions? This relationship is generally conceptualised, by materialists, in the form of a base superstructure model, in which culture is the superstructure resting upon the base, the economy – which in turn rests upon the underlying base of nature. Marxists have, however, generally emphasised the role of the economy, and played down the role of biology. As Timpanaro (1975; 44-45) characterises contemporary Marxism:

> The position of the contemporary Marxist seems at times like that of a person living on the first floor of a house, who turns to the tenant of the second floor and says: 'You think you're independent, that you support yourself by yourself? You're wrong! Your apartment stands only because it is supported by mine, and if mine collapses, yours will too'; and on the other hand to the ground-floor tenant: 'What are you saying? That you support and condition me? What a wretched illusion! The ground floor exists only in so far as it is the ground floor to the first floor. Or rather, strictly speaking, the real ground floor is the first floor, and your apartment is only a sort of cellar, to which no real existence can be assigned'. To tell the truth, the relations between the Marxist and the second-floor tenant have been perceptibly improved from some time, not because the second-floor tenant has recognised his own 'dependence', but because the Marxist has reduced his pretensions considerably, and has come to admit that the two apartments 'support each other'. But the contempt for the inhabitant of the ground floor has become increasingly pronounced.

This emphasis upon the economy is to some extent reasonable insofar as nature and biology change relatively slowly, compared with the economy:

> When Marxists affirm the 'decisive primacy' of economic and social structures, and therefore designate this level and not the biological level underlying it as the 'base' of human society and culture, they are right in relation to the great transformations and differentiations of society, which arise fundamentally as

> consequences of changes in economic structures and not of (changes in) the geographic environment or physical constitution of man . . . (Timpanaro, 1975; 43)

But as Timpanaro points out, the fact that nature changes slowly does not mean that, as a relative constant, it has no conditioning power upon nor consequences for the 'superstructures' of economy and culture that arise upon it. Immediately there should arise the question – unfortunately dodged by Timpanaro – of the consequences of the human species being divided into two sexes. How are sex (anotomical) differences mediated by economy and culture; how are they related to the sexual division that arises in society?

Now the question of sexual divisions cannot be answered within the classical Marxism of *Capital,* since this fails to theorise sexual relations, fails to get beyond a moralistic appreciation of women (see, for example the discussion of women's work, morality, and the Factory Acts, in chapters of volume 3 of *Capital*). This failure is connected with the over-narrowness of a political economy which tries to define classes purely in terms of their place in the system of production and circulation of 'value'. The Marxist-feminism that has been developed using political economy as a starting point has engendered 'the domestic labour debate' (see Malos, 1980, for a collection of relevant articles). This represented a step forward insofar as it recognised that housework was indeed a form of labour, as much as is labour outside the home; but a step back insofar as it tried to deal with sexual relations purely within the context of political economy, pushing biology and culture to the side. Whether or not housewives contribute, through their labour in the home, to the creation of 'value' in the capitalist economy, is a question that addresses only one aspect of their labour. 'Women's work' in the home takes the form not only of general housework duties but, more specifically, of childcare. More than this, females, due to their biology, actually produce children in the first place. Procreation is an act of labour and a fact of biology. This is a fact not overlooked by the generally anti-Marxian radical feminists today (e.g. Firestone, 1971); but neither was it overlooked by Engels.

> According to the materialist conception, the determining factor in history is, in the final instance, the production and reproduction of immediate life. This, again, is of a two-fold character: on the one side, the production of the means of existance, of food,

> clothing and the tools necessary for production; on the other side, the production of human beings themselves, the propogation of the species. (Engels, 1972; 71)

What we require, then, is some way of conceptualising social relations within and between these two spheres.

Feminist Theories

Marxian theory has in recent years been challenged by feminist theory, itself a systemisation of ideas current in the Women's Liberation Movement (WLM), which arose in the 1960s and spread in the 1970s. Women's politics is, of course, not new, and can be traced through the seventeenth, eighteenth and nineteenth centuries, in spheres of religious freedom, suffrage, and employment (Mitchell, 1974; Rowbotham, 1979; Alexander, 1980). In the post-second World War period, however, women's politics was muted up until the late 1960s, women's energies being channelled either into the family, or into individualistic achievement in the labour market (the 'career woman'), or into subordinate positions in left groups. Out of the experiences of women in the left groups, and out of various forms of community action, arose the WLM. Dissatisfaction with hierarchical and sexist political organisations (Rowbotham, 1979), uncertainty over how best to organise within the community and to provide services meeting the social needs of women (Segal, 1979) and dissatisfaction with personal relationships with men, were explored through discussion and 'consciousness-raising' groups. Given the backgrounds of many of those involved in the WLM, it is perhaps not surprising that one of the most persistent questions posed within the movement has been that of the relationship between social class (and working class politics) and sexual divisions (and sexual politics, where this refers both to struggles at the level of national policies, at the level of everyday life at work, and in 'personal relationships'). The early consciousness-raising groups often developed into arenas for discussion of the relation between social class and sexual divisions (Wander, 1978: 111), and this question remains a prime focus of enquiry today.

There are four main tendencies within the WLM, each with a characteristic analysis of the relation between social class and sexual divisions: the feminist-psychoanalytic, the socialist-feminist, and two tendencies laying claim to the title of radical feminist (one mainly American in origins, one French). The feminist-psychoanalytic tendency, represented in the work of Juliet Mitchell (1974) and the journal *m/f*, builds upon Althusserian and post-Althusserian Marxism and upon Freud and his French interpreter Lacan. Whereas deterministic readings of Marx interpret ideology as the effect or reflection of occurrences in the economic level of the mode of production, Althusser's early theories granted to ideology a 'partial autonomy' from the economic level, although ideology still served the requirements of the capitalist economy by reproducing the required social relations of subordination (Althusser, 1971). This 'half-way house' explanation of the relationship between economy and ideology was attacked by those subsequently recognised as founders of the post-Althusserian approach (e.g. Hirst, 1979), and ideology defined in relation to the specific conditions of its production and appropriation, rather than in relation to the general features and requirements of the capitalist economy. In other words, ideology was to be analysed in relation to the specific material practices that produced it; and a work of art or literature would, for instance, be regarded as having meaning only in relation to the ways in which it was 'read' by specific social groups in specific conditions, rather than being regarded as an effect or 'instance' of the social relations of the capitalist economy. It is in this context that psychoanalysis is offered as a medium for understanding patriarchal ideology (Coward, 1980): Freud's accounts of the reaction of little girls and little boys to realisation of anatomical sexual differences suggest how boys and girls might form attachments with and identifications with fathers and mothers, and construct their own sexed identities on the basis of repression of the primary attachment with the mother. The value of this sort of account for feminists is that it suggests that, since sexual identities and relations are *constructed* in response to observation of anatomical difference (rather than being a determined effect of anatomy), the possibility of de-construction and re-construction of identity, and by implication of social relations between the sexes, arises. But the drawbacks of such an approach are that psychoanalysis gives no clear clues as to *how* to reconstruct sexual divisions on a mass level (as opposed to an individual level), and does not relate the process of early acquisition of sexual identity with the later material realities of sexual divisions within the domestic and capitalist economies. Sexual divisions in this account are articulated only at the level of ideology, and this ideology is developed only in relation to early childhood: it is also implied that psychoanalysis can account for sexual identities in all societies and at all times, without reference to the material basis of social organisation in society. This ahistorical psychoanalysis, and the difficulties of relating it to a broader analysis of the material basis of society, lead to difficulties of theoretical coherence. It is acceptable only to those who are prepared to hold unrelated theories – an ideological theory of patriarchy and a materialist theory of capitalism.

Socialist-feminist analysis do not split the world into an ideological sphere of patriarchy and an economic sphere of class relations; they tend to subordinate patriarchy to capitalism, by suggesting that, whilst patriarchy may benefit men, its greater significance is that it underpins capitalism. This, it has been argued, may be true in three ways. In the first place, women's work in the home allows them to be used as a reserve army of labour, being alternatively drawn into and expelled from the labour market according to the needs of capital for labour. Secondly, it is suggested, women's physical and emotional caring work within the home helps to reproduce the capability and willingness of males to sell their labour in the labour market. Thirdly, it has been argued by some economists, women's work in the home is directly productive of surplus value: hence housewives are to be regarded as members of the proletariat, whether or not they work directly for capital outside the home (see Hartmann, 1979, for a review). In each of these three ways, sexual divisions are analysed as of primary benefit to capital. Hartmann and other feminists have pointed out that the effects of such analyses have been to incorporate sexual issues so much within classical Marxian theory that the former have tended to be represented as an incidental and marginal effect of capitalism. Hartmann suggests (1979: 1) that:

> The marriage of marxism and feminism has been like the marriage of husband and wife depicted in English common law: marxism and feminism are one, and that one is marxism. Recent attempts to integrate marxism and feminism are unsatisfactory to us as feminists because they subsume the feminist struggle into the 'larger' struggle against capital. To continue our simile further, either we need a healthier marriage or else we need a divorce.

It is in this context of increasing criticism of the socialist-feminist (and male socialist) tendency to subsume patriarchy to capitalism, and of the acknowledged difficulties of reconstructing Marxism so as to acknowledge that patriarchy may not only predate capitalism, and not only have an autonomy from it, but may actually have some determining power over its historical development, that more attention is being paid to radical feminist analyses. There are two basic streams of radical feminist thought, and both claim to be materialist in type. The term 'radical feminism' is most commonly associated with their theories of Shulamith Firestone and her followers (Firestone, 1979) who, from the two options posed by Hartmann (above), go for the option of 'divorce'. According to this analysis, the primary benefits of women's subordination accrue to men, who are able to maintain that subordination because women are the one's to bear children.

> Nature produced the fundamental inequality – half the human race must bear and rear the children of all of them – which was later consolidated, institutionalised, in the interests of men. Reproduction of the species cost women dearly, not only emotionally, psychologically, culturally but even in strictly material (physical) terms: before recent methods of contraception, continuous childbirth led to constant 'female trouble', early ageing, and death. Women were the slave class that maintained the species in order to free the other half for the business of the world . . . (Firestone, 1979: 192)

Whilst this view is often described as too reductionist – in that it attributes all aspects of women's subordination to biological roots – it nevertheless represented, for most of the 1970s, the only alternative to socialist feminist analyses that tended to reduce the importance of sexual divisions by reducing them to an aspect of capitalism. This sort of radical feminism provided a theoretical justification for a women's movement not subordinated to socialist political groups, made connections between women's everyday lives and the undeniable facts of biology (largely ignored in socialist feminist theory), and provided the prospect that science and technology could help to end women's oppression by making procreation possible outside the female body. It acted as a total theory for those women able to believe that their biological condition formed the basis of their oppression: it was often these women who were most sharply critical of what they saw as socialist feminist's capitulation to 'masculine' Marxian theories.

The second type of radical feminist analysis, put forward by Christine Delphy, Diana Leonard and, more recently, Mica Nava, focusses upon women's unpaid domestic work rather than upon their (equally unpaid) procreative activities (Delphy, 1977 and 1980, Nava, 1980). But whilst they share the focus upon domestic work with the socialist feminists, their purposes and analyses are quite different from those of the latter. Where socialist-feminists discuss the various ways in which women's domestic work may be functional for capital, causing women's oppression almost as a by-product of the needs of capital, Delphy and her followers analyse women's domestic labour first and foremost as a basis for women's oppression. They point out that all labour within the family, whatever its nature, is given without wage remuneration. Such benefits as the housewife does obtain, over and above her subsistence needs, depends upon the resources and discretion of the wage-earning husband. The household, in distinction to the broader economy, is a sphere of non-exchange, within which women's labour is appropriated in a manner similar to the appropriation of slave labour. Delphy's analysis was worked out in relation to the agricultural sector of the French economy, in which wives work on the smallholding without payment, producing produce some of which is exchanged (by the male) in the broader economy, and some of which is used to reproduce the labour power of the family. But her analysis extends to any situation in which the wife works for the husband without remuneration. It applies even to those housewives who also have a waged job, indeed it is in these circumstances that it becomes most clear:

> The situation of the married woman who has a job clearly reveals the legal appropriation of her labour power. In fact her provision of domestic work can no longer be justified by the economic exchange to which the servitude of the housewife is often assimilated. It can no longer be claimed that domestic labour is performed in return for her keep, and that this upkeep is the equivalent of a wage – and that therefore her work is paid. Women who go out to work keep themselves and therefore perform domestic work for *nothing*. (Delphy, 1977; 12)

On the basis of such considerations, these radical feminists say that the contemporary social formation contains two modes of production, the industrial (or capitalist) mode, and the patriarchal.

> There are two modes of production in our society. 1) most goods are produced in the industrial mode; 2) domestic services, child-rearing and certain other goods are produced in the family mode. The first mode of production gives rise to capitalist exploitation. The second gives rise to familial, or more precisely, patriarchal exploitation. (ibid: 13)

Social relations in the capitalist mode are those of independence and exchange, and those in the family mode are of dependence and non-exchange. Male socialisation is a process of transition into exchange relations and independence (as I have suggested in my review of youth culture research, above), whilst female socialisation is more complex, taking place largely within the family mode, but often also involving participation in the exchange economy.

In assessing this position, it may be useful to refer to an analogy suggested by Mica Nava. The two modes of production are like two semi-detached houses, side by side. In the basement of one house is the exchange economy of capitalism, with its ideological and other super-structures above it; whilst in the other basement is the non-exchange economy of the family, with its patriarchal ideologies above it. There are many interconnecting doorways and corridors between the houses, through which complex relations and contradictions arise between the two systems. Now, this crude analogy may be compared with that employed by Timpanero (1975) and cited above – three-storey house with biology in the basement, the capitalist economy in the ground floor, and ideologies and super-structures above. From a strictly materialist point of view, I suggest, there is something wrong with both of these models. Timpanero is clearly at fault, together with the mainstream of Marxian theory, for his neglect of patriarchal relations both at the economic and at the ideological levels. Followers of Delphy, on the other hand, are as much at fault as are socialist feminists in failing to elucidate the ways in which biological differences relate to the division of labour between the sexes (i.e. to their differential involvement in the exchange and non-exchange economies).

Social Classes

I believe that the way forward from these diffiiculties lies in the direction of taking *social classes*, rather than mode of production, as one's central analytic category. There are conceptual difficulties in relating together two differing modes of production (industrial and family) without making one of them subordinate to the other; and the very concept of mode of production has been severely criticised. Cutler et al (1977, especially volume 1, chapter 9) point out that the strict concept of mode of production rests upon (sometimes implicit) assumptions of determination, by the economy, of all aspects of social life, and that this is a functionalist concept in which political and ideological occurrences necessarily serve to reproduce the conditions of existence of the economy. Furthermore, the strict concept of mode of production requires that if there is more than one mode of production in a social formation then one shall be dominant over the other(s) – a condition that is incompatible with Delphy's two-mode model. In place of the concept of mode of production, they suggest that a social formation can be defined as a definite set of class relations of production, together with the economic, political and cultural forms in which the conditions of existence of those class relations are secured (Cutler et al, p. 222 et seq.). Within any social formation, social classes are differentiated from each other on the basis of differential 'effective possession' of the material prerequisites of life. Effective possession refers to that property which the agent in question (e.g. the male working class) has effective possession of insofar as he/it can exchange it for something else. In capitalism, the male working class has effective possession only of its capacity to labour – i.e. of its 'labour power'. Since the working class does not have effective possession of the means of production and exchange (which are possessed by the capitalist class and by enterprises), they can produce the necessities of life only through selling their labour in the labour market to capitalist enterprises (or to the state, which pays them by means of taxes on the whole working class and on enterprises). The male working class is defined, according to this schema, as a class having effective possession only of their labour power (and not of other essential aspects of the means of production and exchange).

The pertinence of this approach to the problems noted above are quite clear. The adoption by Delphy and her followers of a mode-of-production model of the social formation, and of two modes of production, is actually quite redundant to a discussion about women's class positions. Married women occupy a definite class position that can be defined without reference to any mode of production: women work within the home without payment, which means that much of their labour power is appropriated from them, leaving them only a proportion of their total possible labour power to offer for sale in the labour market. Whether it is the husband or capital which most benefits from this appropriation of women's labour power is no doubt a significant question; but irrespective of one's answer, it remains the central fact that labour power *is* appropriated from married women (and, at least to some extent, from all female family members), leaving them not in full possession of their labour power. Since the working class is defined as that class which possesses its labour power (and not the means of production), this means that women married to working class men are not of that class, but of a dispossessed and subordinate class. It is this consideration which, for Delphy, defines married women as a class, and it is this aspect of her analysis that we can adopt.

So far this definition of class refers only to the level of the economy, and of labour other than in childbirth. Immediately that we recognise the need to include the biological level in any discussion of male and female working class definitions, then we have to refer to a form of possession which men do not enjoy – the capacity to procreate. Women's bodies, not men's, give birth, so as long as procreation continues, women have possession of the process; and whether it should be regarded as an asset or as a cross to bear, is not at issue here – the point is that women possess the ability to labour in procreation and men do not. In capitalist societies, this biological capability of women has been turned, after considerable struggle between men and women, into a justification for making women primarily responsible for all domestic work. The biological fact of procreation has been made a justification for a division between men and women in the economic sphere: women are made responsible for looking after children, husbands and other male relatives. This domestic work covers the reproduction of the male worker's labour power (their ability and capacity and willingness to enter the labour market), and the welfare and maintenance of those excluded by age, infirmity or competition, from the market. Now, the significance of this domestic work lies not simply in the fact that it is unpaid, but in the fact that the obligation of performing domestic work weakens women's ability to enter and to compete equally with men in the labour market. Within the bulk of the working class, women *have* to labour in the domestic situation, and any out-of-home, paid participation in the labour market is *additional* to domestic labour. But this means that, since a person's labour power is not inexhaustible, and since part of it (or, in many cases all of) woman's labour power is used up in domestic work, they cannot freely offer their labour, on the same terms as men can, on the market. Because of this they do not have full possession of their labour power in the sense in which men do; their physical and emotional exhaustion from housework and childcare drains their ability to sell a 'full day's work' on the labour market, and also supplies 'justifications' for job discrimination practiced by employers and by male working class organisations. Thus we have the following *main* social class groups and divisions:

capital	:	owns the means of production, employs those who don't
male working class	:	owns its labour power
female underclass	:	does not have full possession of its labour power

These are not just 'theoretical' divisions, as the fieldwork will show. These social class groups are clearly represented in my study area, with the proviso that, in the teenage group described in chapter 5, the girls had to some extent escaped their doubly-subordinate class position, at least *in the short-term*. Eventual marriage would, if accompanied by childbirth in this area (as shorn as most others of nursery and pre-school facilities) return them to their class origins.

Youth

Let us now locate 'teenagers' in this set of social relations. In chapter 4, I reviewed the literature on youth culture research. The literature displays a tendency, current also in everyday discourse, to over-emphasise the autonomy and otherness of youth ('a world apart'), and to under-estimate the social class, gender and cultural continuities between youth and the parent cultures. To talk of 'youth' as a homogenous groups is as absurd as to talk about adults without reference to their historical context and class and gender. One as to talk about particular youth groups, e.g. from a particular social class, or section of the class, of particular gender, in particular circumstances, etc.

Bearing this in mind, we can make the following generalised definition of youth (or 'teenagers'): youth is the process of transition from a 'masculine' or 'feminine' childhood of dependence on a family of specific class character, to an adult status (or range of statuses) prescribed by the class, gender and other circumstances. The exact trajectory of that transition will depend very much upon the class, gender and other circumstances involved. Let us, for example, refer to some of the fieldwork. For the male teenagers in the section of the working class upon which I focussed, the transition is one from dependence upon the family and other institutions to independence in the labour market. The girls in this group have a more complicated trajectory – from dependence on the family and other institutions (schools, etc) through independence as young workers in a labour market relatively appreciative of young females, to a more complex and contradictory mixture of intermittent and/or part-time work in the market plus responsibility for housework and care of husbands and/or children. Such girls differ from others lower down in the working class (who I describe as 'domestics'), in that the latter tend to miss the middle phase, going fairly quickly from having a heavy housework and sibling-care responsibility in the parental home to a housework and child-care responsibility in the conjugal home. It needs to be stressed that such class/gender trajectories are characteristic of the social groups as *groups:* some individuals construct a trajectory or 'career' that differs from that characteristic for their origins and circumstances, but the group pattern generally remains. Only in those circumstances recognised as 'revolutionary' in some manner (e.g. working class rebellion, revolutionary-feminist struggles) is the group trajectory altered, through an alteration in the basis of material relations (ownership, etc) between the group and others. Such circumstances are uncommon, and did not occur within the focus of this study.

The theoretical points raised in this annexe are taken up, in the latter parts of chapter 4 of this study, as contributions to the formulation of a methodology for research into youth cultures and drinking practices therein.

NOTES TO INTRODUCTION

1. The moral panic over teenage drinking is by no means confined to Britain. In an article entitled 'New Careers for Moral Entrepreneurs', Robert Chauncey has shown the public concern over youthful drinking escalated in the United States during the 1970s, being fanned by the campaigns of the federally-funded National Institute for Alcohol Abuse and Alcoholism (Chauncey, 1980; see also Dickson, 1968-9). However Chauncey does not attempt to situate this new moral panic within any broader context of societal and political change, as will be attempted in what follows.

2. This report is quite typical of many others of the later 1970s insofar as it represents 'a "mapping together" of (previously separately-reported) moral panics in a *general panic* about social order' (Hall et al, 1978; 112). The following discussion of the panic over youthful drinking within the more general panic over social disorder and indiscipline (ibid, and Taylor, 1980) is not intended to imply that the more familiar analytic frameworks of interpretation provided by medical and social-psychological theories are irrelevant for an understanding of drink-related problems. But, as chapters 1-3 of this study will show, definitions of drink-related problems as historically produced are closely related to concerns over the fact or possibility of breakdowns in class discipline, and it is only in the last few decades that medicine and social psychology has given a gloss to those definitions.

3. Changes in the statistics collected on the basis of interventions and processing carried out by state agencies bear no necessary relation to changes in the social behaviour of the groups so processed (Cohen, 1980, Lemert, 1967, Scheff, 1966, Young, 1971). Building upon Wilkins' (1964) work, Jason Ditton distinguishes between *constructed*, *fantasy* and *book-keeping* 'crime-waves'. Constructed crime waves occur when originally non-deviant acts become redefined as deviant; fantasy crime waves when more of the acts committed are discovered; and book-keeping crime waves when more of the discovered acts are collated into the official statistics (Ditton, 1979; 11). As an increase in the statistics *may* be an effect of a 'real' increase in the prescribed social behaviour, 'but could actually refer to any of the possible rise sources, since it is always feasible that the statistics used to evidence a real rise are contaminated. Acceptance of the latter qualifier casts doubt upon our ability *ever* to 'know' that deviants are committing more crimes: in fact, it is impossible to re-read existing data to evidence a real crime rise once any credance is attached to the other type of interpretation . . .' (ibid; 11-12). The first few chapters of the present study are concerned with the historical conditions in which the categories underpinning the drunkenness statistics, and associated concepts of drink-related problems, were constructed. In relation to the possibility of a 'fantasy' crime wave (in which police arrest a higher proportion of young drinkers), the following remarks of Fogelman are useful. 'Undoubtedly the statistics for drunkenness offences by young people have shown an increase in England and Wales, in Scotland, and in other industrial societies. However, not only is it difficult to extricate the separate effects of a real increase (i.e. in drinking – ND) and of changes in police practice but also these figures tell us little about the normal drinking behaviour of the great majority of young people. Spasmodic outbreaks of horror stories in the news media do little to clarify the picture' (Fogelman, 1978; 19). It is important to recognise that Fogelman is making two points: (a) supposing that there is a section of youth in which public drunkenness occurs – changes in the drunkenness statistics may well reflect changes in police proceedings rather than changes in frequency of drunkenness amongst this group, or an enlargement of it; (b) in any event the statistics tell us nothing about drinking practices amongst the majority.

4. Labelling theory has been developed by Becker (1973), Lemert (1974), Kitsuse (1972), Scheff (1974), Schur (1971), and discussed by Akers (1967-8), Box (1971), Davis (1972), Fine (1977), Goode (1975), Hirschi (1973), and Pearson (1975). For an

application to 'alcoholism' see Robinson (1976).

5. Kenneth Plummer has advocated labelling as a sensitivising perspective useful for examining the processes whereby deviant identities may be negotiated (Plummer, 1979). See also Matza (1969); for an application in relation to cannabis, Auld (1981).

6. Reviewing the literature, Box points out that whilst working class and black youth are more likely to be convicted for delinquent activities, 'self-report studies have, on the whole, failed to reveal the significant inter-class differences implied in official statistics' (Box, 1971; 83-91). He cites Chambliss' view that 'lower class person is (i) more likely to be scrutinised and therefore to be observed in any violation of the law, (ii) more likely to be arrested if discovered under suspicious circumstances, (iii) more likely to spend the time between arrest and trial in jail, (iv) more likely to come to trial, (v) more likely to be found guilty and (vi) if found guilty, more likely to receive harsh punishment than his middle or upper class counterpart' (Chambliss, 1969; 84-86; discussed by Box, 1971; 169-210). Chambliss attributes this alleged state of affairs to organisational features of the institutions making up the legal system and, particularly, to the fact that middle and upper class persons can use their resources to protect themselves from the treatment routinely imposed upon 'ordinary' criminals. Cicourel focusses upon the development of police ideology: he reports that the police develop theories about individuals and groups, morality and immorality, good and bad people, institutions, practices and typifications of community settings, and such theories or conceptions are employed in routine ways (Cicourel, 1968; 67). This view of police ideology receives some confirmation in recent statements by sections of the police:

> Police must be prejudiced if they are to do their job properly, Mr Holland told the seminar. "Prejudice is a state of mind brought about by experience" he said. "Searches of long-haired unshaven youths carrying a pack and sleeping-bag or blanket, were the ones most likely to reveal the possession of cannabis. Similarly, searching West Indian youths wearing jeans and T-shirts, and who were hanging around pedestrian precincts and subways, often turned up handbag snatchers and muggers. That is the sort of discrimination and prejudice we want from officers. That is what clears up the crime", said Mr Holland. (Guardian, 15 September, 1981)

Recent sociological work (notably Hall et al, 1978) has emphasised the ways in which social forces outside the legal system (particularly the media and mobilisation of political sentiments) bear upon such institutional practices.

7. Scheff (1974), Hargreaves (1976), and Cohen and Young (1973), provide examples of studies predating the rise of materialist approaches (see below).

8. Marxism has been described as having two traditions within it – a 'scientific' version basing itself tightly within the political economy of *Capital* and a 'critical' version concerning itself more with the emergence of social consciousness, culture and experience as actively and purposively 'lived' (Gouldner, 1980). These traditions correspond to the 'structuralist' and 'culturalist' approaches within cultural studies (Hall, 1980b). The approach taken in this study is closest to the 'culturalist' tradition, and is further modified by selective use of feminist-materialist theory (Delphy, 1977). Whilst my approach is materialist in the broadest sense (and as defined in the annexe), it lays no claim whatsoever to the mantle of marxism.

9. This definition is most clearly elaborated in Cutler et al (1977); however this is all that is taken from the 'post-Althusserians'.

10. Chapter 2 discusses the nineteenth century expansion of social welfare policies, and their legitimisation in the dominant political philosophy of the period, with special reference to drink-related policies.

11. This is shown empirically in chapters 1 and 2.

12. See for example the work of Douglas Parker, who has adapted the structuralist

political economy of James O'Connor (1973) to the analysis of the developed capitalist state's policies vis-a-vis the production of alcohol. Parker suggests that 'irrespective of the interests or consciousness of the various classes and groups in society, what we need to understand first is that to some extent the state's expenditures must be self-financing, that is, they must expand the tax base. Therefore, as a structural necessity, the capitalist state must be committed to a program of economic growth and this may entail a fiscal policy that encourages the production and distribution of alcohol' (Parker, 1977; 6). As Parker here concedes, a 'structural necessity' to encourage growth need not necessarily imply that expansion of production of all commodities is encouraged: it follows that whether or not alcohol production is encouraged by the state at a particular time has to be established by historical investigation. Parker also suggests that 'structural necessity' is, at most, a feature of contemporary state, which has a 'relative autonomy' from social classes not enjoyed by the state in previous historical periods (ibid); and that in analysing alcohol policy in periods preceding that of monopoly capitalism it may be necessary to take into account the ideologies of dominant classes (cf. Makela and Viikari, 1977). These ideologies concern themselves not simply with fiscal matters, but also with social policy and public order issues: 'the relation of the state to alcohol is not determined objectively but is mediated by the social consciousness of different groups' (ibid; 161).

13. For sake of consistency, one text – that of Rubin, 1979 – was used for this periodisation. Rubin's history of economic ideas has the advantage of clearly spelling out the economic and political philosophies of each historically ascendent class – although, in common with other political economists, he pays scant attention to the relationship between these philosophies and the development of sexual divisions. Some compensation is made for this in chapter 2.

14. Pearson (1976), and Taylor (1971).

15. See Willis (1978; 151): 'Housework is not completion, it is maintenance of status. Cooking, washing and cleaning reproduce what was there before. Certainly in a sense housework is never completed – but neither is it as difficult or productive as masculine work is held to be.' But 'held to be' *by whom?* Contrast with Luxton (1980).

16. The ways in which the term 'working class' is used in this study, and the relation betwen 'youth' and social class and sexual divisions, are discussed in some detail in the Annexe and in chapter 4. There, 'the working class' is defined as consisting of all those who have full and effective possession of their labour power (capacity to work), which they may sell, in the labour market, for a wage, whilst not possessing their own means of production (which would allow them to sell their own products, instead of their labour). Within the working-class as so defined, distinctions can be made between those who occupy various *strata* ('levels or grades' according to the Oxford dictionary) within the market. 'Lower' strata include those who work in the lowest grades or levels of the labour market, being rewarded with the lowest wages and/or the least job-security: in sectors of the construction industry, in small manufacturing, in cleaning, and in the catering and hotel industries (into which certain ethnic minorities are disproportionately recruited). Such jobs are generally described as 'unskilled'. 'Upper' strata of the working class include a variety of relatively high occupational grades – as signified by pay and working conditions – such as the 'skilled' manual trades (entry into which is regulated by apprenticeships), and recently-developed high technology occupations such as computer programming. These strata are predominantly male. Also included at this level are those supervisory grades whose role in directing the labour of others is itself largely predetermined, routinised, and closely supervised: supervisory staff in most large shops, offices and factories exercise their powers within working conditions that have already been 'designed' (Hales, 1980) by others. (These grades should be distinguised from 'professions', making up the 'new' *middle* class, members of which

take a hand in the creation of structuring of 'the conditions for the routinised work activities of colleague-subordinates' – Johnson, 1977; 106).

Now, 'middle' strata of the working class are those grades or levels (in occupational terms) falling below the upper, 'skilled' grades (whether 'manual' or not), yet above the lowest, 'casual employment' grades. It is the service sector, which has expanded quite rapidly during the post war period, which provides the largest source of such employment. Middle strata occupations therefore include 'white collar' work in shops, offices, distribution and state bureaucracies and enterprises (but excluding lower-grade jobs in hotels and catering). Womens' employment is important in the service sector. More detailed descriptions of these strata must rest upon concrete invesitgation of particular social groups, and that empirical task is taken up in chapter 5.

NOTES TO CHAPTER 1

1. This method is outlined in the introduction, above.
2. Anno – Edw III, cap 3 (1357); and Anno – Edw III, cap 8 (1364-5). Source used throughout this chapter *Chronological Table of the Statutes* and *Statutes at Law* housed in Senate House Library, University of London.
3. Anno 5 Ric II, cap 4 (1381).
4. Anno 3 Hen VIII, cap 8 (1511-12)
6. Anno 23 Hen VIII, cap 4 (1531-2)
7. Anno 23 Hen VIII, cap 7 (1531-2)
8. Anno 5, Edw VI, cap 18 (1552)
9. Anno 2 & 3 Edw VI, cap 10 (1549)
10. Anno 25 Hen VIII, cap 7 (1533)
11. Labour shortages and inflows of foreign silver caused inflation (Rubin, 1976; 22-5).
12. Chambliss does not mention the relationship between controls on vagracy and on drinking.
13. Cited in Chambliss, 1971; 210
14. Statute of Labourers, 1350: Introduction to the Statute
15. Anno 4 & 5 Hen 7, cap II (1495)
16. Anno 4 & 5 Hen 7, cap 7 (1495)
17. Anno 3 & 4 Edw 6, cap 5 (1549)
18. Anno 5 & 6 Edw 6, cap 25 (1552)
19. Anno 1 Jac 1, cap 9 (1603)
20. Anno 4, Jac 1 & 5 (1606)
21. Anno 21 Jac 1, cap 10 (1609)
22. An ordinance for the better observation of the Lords-Day, passed on 8th April 1644
23. Passed on 28 June 1647
24. Passed on 19 April 1650
25. For a historical account of the development of English education, see Lawson & Silver (1973).
26. Board of Education (1909)
27. See Williams & Brake (1980; 45-62), also Shadwell (1903).

NOTES TO CHAPTER 2

1. This possibility is discussed in Central Policy Review Staff (1979), Royal College of Psychiatrists (1979), D.H.S.S. (1977) and Expenditure Committee (1977; 122-124).

2. See, for example, Carter, who ascribes the relative lack of success of the English temperance movement to internal conflicts between prohibitionists and those prepared to make compromises (Carter, 1933); Also Harrison (1971). The present study does not investigate American alcohol policies.

3. Mathias (1959), Levy (1951), Hawkin & Pass (1979).

4. *On Liberty*, cited by Harrison (1971; 389).

5. The concept of a block of allied classes or factions is taken from Gramsci in his Prison Netobooks (1971; 168 in the English edition edited by Hoare & Nowell-Smith).

6. Fraser (1973) provides a clear description of social welfare initiatives of the period.

7. *Hansard*, 22nd May 1846, LXXXVI, 1031, 1034.

8. The distinction between problems in the production and realisation of surplus value is clearly described by Glyn and Harrison (1980) especially pp. 6-28.

9. Westminster Gazette, 16th March, 1908; 1.

10. ibid.

11. General Manager's Report 1920, and other evidence reported in Royal Commission on Licensing (1931) reviewed in Williams and Brake (1980; 108-112).

12. 'It is our view that a prima-facie case of considerable strength has been made out in its (public ownership's) favour. We think it theoretically sound: and that experience in Carlisle has gone far to show it to be sound in practice also', (Royal Commission, 1931; 86).

13. There is a considerable technical literature on the so-called 'distribution of consumption' model of alcohol problems, the work of Lederman (1956) and de Lint (1974) being best known. The basic postulates of this *homo economicus* model are that society can be conceptualised as an aggregate of individuals; that each individual's social behaviour is determined by factors pressing upon him; that drinking practices may be conceptualised in purely quantitative terms, i.e. in terms of millilitres of ethyl alcohol imbibed; that the primary factors bearing upon levels of consumption are the costs of consumption and the consumption of other persons; and that adverse consequences of drinking are directly proportional to and directly caused by levels of consumption. Recent research by one of the model's early advocates casts some doubt on its empirical validity (de Lint, 1981). However, the model receives quite wide support from disease epidemiologists and in the World Health Organisation (W.H.O. 1980). The Home Office Research Unit has published a pamphlet critical of the mechanical nature of the model and suggesting that there is need to study cultural 'factors' said to mediate between levels of consumption and harm (Tuck, 1980; 20); this has been sharply attacked by advocates of the model ('Editorial', *Lancet*, 21 Feb 1981; 425-426 and Skog, 1981). The model suffers from severe theoretical inadequacies e.g. atomisation of the population, neglect of social class and other divisions and associated cultures and practices, neglect of the social forms of drinking practices within specific cultures, neglect of problems inherent in using medical statistics, etc – that may be summarised under the general category of positivism in social research (cf early criminological research, discussed in Taylor et al, 1974; 31-66). It nevertheless retains considerable ideological importance because it generates numberical 'data' that is used to legitimise advocacy of restrictions on alcohol production.

NOTES TO CHAPTER 3

1. Nineteenth century expansion of such measures were legitimised by the ascendance of Millian political philosophy over the political philosophies of Ricardo, Smith and other advocates of 'laissez-faire' in the eighteenth and early nineteenth centuries (discussed in the preceding chapter). It is important to recognise, however, that

welfare measures within the sphere of distribution are no more 'interventionist' than are so-called 'laissez-faire' policies, since 'laissez-faire too is a form of state regulation introduced and maintained by legislative and coercive means' (Gramsci, 1971; 160). The difference lies in the structure of the intervention: so-called 'laissez-faire' intervenes to enforce the discipline of the market economy, while welfare intervenes to complement and compensate for it.

2. The course of these struggles, alliances and compromises may be extremely complex, and can be by no means reduced to a process of subordination by capital of the working class, or males and capital of women. Contradictory demands may be made of women at any given time – e.g. support for women's domestic role within the family, and calls for women to enter wage labour within the market system and within the welfare state itself – and these contradictions may find expression in the form of welfare state services (Wilson, 1980, Deem, 1981). The issue is further complicated by the fact that capital itself is heterogeneous and does not have one single interest – indeed the split between industrial and financial capital in Britain is quite pronounced (Minns, 1981). This makes it clear that a simple model of the welfare state being a creature of capital is as adequate as the model of it as an unproblematic gain for workikng class men and women. This is probably shown most clearly in Wilson (1980).

3. The concept of rule (or 'hegomony') being underpinned by a mixture of consensus (or consent) and coercion is discussed by Gramsci in his *Prison Notebooks* (1971). The relationship between these two concepts is not one of 'balance', as if they were simply complementary and additive in character, but one of interdependency. Anderson has suggested that:

> An analogy may service to illuminate the relationship in question – provided its limits (those of any analogy) are kept in mind. A monetary system in the capitalist mode of production is constituted from two distinct media of exchange: paper and gold. It is not a summation of these two forms, for the value of fiduciary issue which circulates every day and thus maintains the system under normal conditions is dependent on the quantum of metal in the bank reserves at any given moment, despite the fact that this metal is completely absent from the system as a medium of exchange. Only the paper, not the gold, appears within circulation, yet the paper is in the final instance determined by the gold, without which it would cease to be currency. Crisis conditions, moreover, will necessarily trigger a sudden reversion of the total system to the metal which always lies invisibly behind it: a collapse of credit infallibly produces a rush to gold. In the political system, a similar structural (non-additive and non-transitive) relationship between ideology and repression, consent and coercion, prevails. The normal conditions of ideological subordination of the masses – the day-to-day routines of a parliamentary democracy – are themselves constituted by a silent, absent force which gives them their currency: the monopoly of legitimate violence by the State. Deprived of this, the system of cultural control would be instantly fragile, since the limits of possible actions against it would disappear. With it, it is immensely powerful – so powerful that it can, paradoxically, do 'without' it: in effect, violence may normally scarcely appear within the bounds of the system at all. (Anderson, 1976-7; 43)

4. Recent trends have, as noted in the introduction, been towards monetarism and disciplinary policies. This however was not the case until the early 1970s (Hall et al, 1978) although the ground was being laid in the 1960s (Hall et al, 1978; N.D.C., 1980, especially the chapter by Greenwood and Young).

5. Initially, NHS costs did fall *as a proportion of GNP* (Gough, 1975; 78).

6. Expenditure Committee (1977), and subsequent paragraphs in this chapter.

7. The clearest instance of this tendency is the growth of 'Intermediate Treatment' facilities to deal with 'children in trouble': these facilities are

intermediate between the health and law enforcement systems (see Home Office, 1968; for a critique, Pitts, 1981; and for an overview of the trend, S. Cohen's article on *The Punitive City,* 1979).

8. In Britain, a critique of these approaches to social control provided the initial programme of the National Deviancy Conference: Cohen (1971), Taylor and Taylor (1973), Taylor et al (1973).

9. There is now a consirable literature on the social production of ill-health: this is sometimes referred to as 'materialist epidemiology' (see for example Brennan and Lancashire (1978), Brenner (1976) and Doyal (1979). The main difference between this materialist epidemiology and currently dominant approaches in mainstream epidemiology is that where the latter takes one or more 'factors' pressing upon the individual, materialist epidemiology attempts to locate the health status of individuals within the whole structure of economic and social circumstances (e.g. workplace stress and hazards, shiftwork, unemployment, isolated childcare in the home, housing conditions, diet, family structure, business cycle, etc). One problem with materialist epidemiology is its tendency to reductionism: the ways in which cultures socially constructed in response to material and other conditions may mediate between material conditions and health 'outcomes' is left unexplored. Cultural explanations are contrasted against material explanations, rather than being integrated into them. (See Working Party on Inequalities in Health, 1980;153-193).

10. See Joint Committee of the Central and Scottish Health Services Councils (1964). This was set up to 'consider whether, *having regard to recent developments in medicine,* there are any fresh fields where health education might be expected to be of benefit. . . .' (p.5). 'It is not enough that the present generation of school pupils has an increasing standard of cleanliness and hygiene, however admirable is this and the endeavours by which it is achieved. The syllabus should have as its aim giving the child in broad outline an understanding of the workings of the human mind and body, the principles of good nutrition and the need for exercise, an appropriate knowledge of preventive and social medicine, and a sense of personal responsibility for his own, his family's and the community's good health' (p.73).

11. Plant et al (1979), and reviews by Budd and McCron (1981), Dorn (1981a) and Dorn and South (1983).

12. The literature on British drug education has been reviewed by Dorn (1981b).

13. The foremost temperance education agency is the Teachers Advisory Council on Alchol and Drug Education, Manchester, in receipt of funds from the temperance insurance body Ansvar (see TACADE's *Annual Reports*). This agency has been closely involved in the dissemination of Schools Council Health Education material, to be discussed below.

14. See Brian Edsell's annual *Health Education Index*.

15. These approaches have been criticised by sociologists for their neglect of the fact that individual pupils are members of social groups, and that these groups are located differently in relation to social class, sexual and other (e.g. racial) divisions in society. It has been suggested, both on the basis of empirical studies of 'progressive' teaching in schools (Sharp and Green 1975), and on the basis of theoretical analysis of the role of education in social control (Bernstein, 1977), that child-centred teaching methods that neglect the material basis of the child's experience may function to reproduce social divisions, rather than compensating for them. Sharp and Green suggest that 'the rise of progressivism and the institutional supports it receives are a function of its greater effectiveness for social control and structuring aspirations compared with more traditional educational ideologies whose legitimacy was already being questioned. Within child centred progressivism, far wider ranges of the child's attributes become legitimate objects of evaluative scrutiny and explanatory variables in the construction of success and failure. Not mere intellectual but social, emotional, aesthetic and even physical criteria are often emphasised . . .' (Sharp and Green, 1975: 225-226). By interpreting pupils differential and scholastic progress

within the framework of a commitment to respond to the existing interests and progress of individual children, as these are manifested to the teacher within the classroom, child-centred teaching fails to take into account the material inequalities which structure children's initial interests and motivations. Differential scholastic attainment of pupils is then 'explained' in terms of the differential 'readiness' of individual children, legitimising the reroduction of social class inequalities (Sharp and Green, 1975, Bernstein, 1977).

16. See for example Cowley (1977).

NOTES TO CHAPTER 4

1. CAAAL takes the form of a set of punched index cards bearing abstracts of articles published in English-language journals, and also includes some material translated from other languages. There is a copy of CAAAL in the library of the Medical Council on Alcoholism, London. CAAAL overlaps substantially with the abstracts published in alternative editions of the *Quarterly Journal of Alchol Studies*. Both sources provide good access to published material which clearly signals 'alcohol' in its title, but are relatively poor on broader sociological studies of youth in which drinking is touched upon only in passing.

2. The best-known work on development of scientific theories is probably that of Thomas Kuhn (1970), but this account of 'paradigm shifts' fails to relate the latter in any systematic manner to forces external to and inter-acting with scientific endeavour. The question of the nature and determinacy of the relation between the structure and dynamics of society-at-large and the procedures and findings of science has been a focus of active debate in the last decade; an introduction to this debate is provided by MacKenzie (1981) and the latter part of the review by Holtzman (1981).

3. Gouldner suggests that the original dynamic of Durkheim's concern with the conditions for reproduction of *moral* order was provided by 'the problem he encountered in his critique of Comte. Durkheim's polemic against Comte's argument that the division of labour induced dissensus in social beliefs had brought him to a critique of private property. Durkheim held that it was not the division of labour as such, but only the *forced* division of labour that undermined social solidarity; this division was pathological because it was controlled by outmoded institutions, including private property. At the same time, however, Durkheim also held that social solidarity was impaired by a set of moral beliefs inadequate to integrate the new specialisations – in short, by industrial anomie. He then faced the strategic decision of which of these two impairments of modern social order he would analyse further. For various reasons, but mainly because it would bring him into an uncomfortable convergence with the socialists, Durkheim backed away from the problem of the forced division of labour and, instead, concentrated on anomie; which is to say, upon the *moral* conditions necessary for social order' (Gouldner, 1971; 250). Durkheim found it difficult 'to resist the conclusion that *anything* that produced consensus, restraint and order was intrinsically moral' (ibid; 252). Such a sociology is evidently well-attuned to historically-generated concerns about drink and indiscipline, and to the search for *any* morality that will serve to underpin temperance. 'Order, in short, becomes the fundamental basis in terms of which the moral itself is conceived' (ibid).

4. It has been argued that Durkheim's assumption of homogeneity in primitive society is incorrect (Clarke, 1975-6).

5. Merton's critique of American society and his analysis of deviance therein revolves around the postulation of a gap between the aspirations generated by a system that encourages egotistical striving and achievement, and a limited and discriminating system for allocation of rewards (Merton, 1957; Taylor et al, 1973; 91-110).

6. Jesser's use of the idea of a number of linked 'systems' may give the initial appearance that this work is influenced by that of the American systems theorist, Talcott Parsons (1951). Any such influence appears, however, to be more semantic than theoretical, since Jesser's model is characterised by relations of unidimensional causality between independent and dependent 'variables' – whilst systems models are characterised by interdependence (Gouldner, 1971; 213-215).

7. Mary Douglas has discussed childhood and adolescence as 'anomolous states' – neither fully infant nor fully adult, neither male nor female, etc – and hence inherently disquieting (Douglas, 1966).

8. Elsewhere, Anne Thompson, Kirsten Hvidtfeldt and the present writer have argued that it is attitudes towards acting in certain ways in specified situations, rather than attitudes 'in general' that are related to social behaviour (Dorn and Thompson, 1976, Dorn et al, 1977). Any such link may result from reflections on past behaviour in closely similar situations, rather than being indicative of attitudes 'causing' social behaviour – as the branch of psychological theory known as 'attribution theory' suggests (Eiser, 1977).

9. The work of Cavan, discussed below, provides an apposite example.

10. For examples of empirical studies conducted within this perspective, see the reader *Observations of Deviance* (Douglas, 1970). Elsewhere, in *American Social Order*, Douglas characterises American society as a 'conglomerate' of separate but connected moral worlds: 'On the whole, American society appears to be primarily a social conglomerate today, just as it has always been, rather than a social system, as many social scientists have thought . . . In one sense a conglomerate is a system, that is, a system with minimal assumptions concerning the interdependency of parts' (Douglas, 1971; 275).

11. As Gouldner also says: 'Morality, for Durkheim, is that which constitutes to or is useful for social solidarity . . . such a rationale for morality would have been anathema to Weber, who saw its essential justification in the *meaning* with which it endowed life' (Gouldner, 1971; 123). The ascendancy of Weber's sociology in Germany may perhaps be due, at least in part, to the relative backwardness of that country, which was capitalised only during the nineteenth century, and then extremely rapidly; the lack of a developed middle class and of modern social institutions may have provided a situation in which the active and rapid development of new meaning systems (rather than the defence of existing moralities) seemed a priority to theorists such as Weber.

12. See for example, the collection of studies edited by Mungham and Pearson (1976).

13. The position is perhaps controversial and the theoretical considerations that support it are too lengthy and complex to be fully discussed in the text of this chapter – hence the recourse to an annexe.

NOTES TO CHAPTER 5

1. The name 'Downtown' has been used in short articles published during the course of the writing up of this report (Dorn, 1980 and 1981c), but this has been replaced by 'Servicetown' because (a) the latter term better describes the character of the area, and (b) the former term has been used by Frith to describe a dissimilar area (Frith, 1981).

2. This tendency is particularly strong in American sociology, originating in the 'Chicago School' in the 1920s and 1930s, continuing in Whyte's study of 'street corner society' in the 1940s, and expanding in the 1960s (Anderson, 1923, Whyte, 1969, Becker, 1966, Polsky, 1971). It took hold in Britain in the work of Downes (1966), Cohen (1980) and the National Deviancy Conference (Cohen, 1971, Taylor & Taylor, 1973). See Butters (1975) for a review.

3. For examples of quantitative work from a materialist perspective see Westergaard and Reisler (1975), or some of the recent work on 'materialist epistemology' (chapter 3, footnote 9). The work of Phillip Cohen (1972) and of Willis (1978) illustrate the use of qualitative methods within broadly materialist perspectives.

4. The taking-up of qualitative methods has been associated with two quite distinct (and mutually incompatible) critiques of positivism, made by phenomenology and materialism. The precise definition of positivism varies with the theoretical position from which it is being defined (see below), but it may be most generally described as an approach to empirical investigation that (i) apropriates social practices and processes as a series of 'bits' of behaviour reducable to categories that correspond to those crystallised in the research instruments used (e.g. 'psychotism' questionnaires), and/or to the concerns of agencies of social control; and (ii) aggregates instances falling into these categories, hence forming quantitative data that may be subjected to statistical manipulation with the aim of discovering correlations that may represent causal relations (cf. Taylor et al, 1973, 31-66). The phenomenological critique – closely associated with researchers such as Douglas and, in respect of drinking research, Cavan (see preceding chapter) – focusses its attack on the inability of quantitative methodology to be open to the diversity, richness and complexity of social practices. Phenomenology claims that since the categories used in quantitative research reflect the researcher's commonsense theories about the world (or the implicit assumptions and theories built into standard research instruments), and since the generalisation of these categories is unwarranted and obscures the real forms of experience and social process that they are supposed to represent, quantitative research is pseudo-scientific. Any aggregation of such data into quantitative forms, or statistical manipulation in an attempt to discover causal relationships, is quite unscientific because it mistakes the model of the world constructed by the researcher, for the actual social world. The proper task of social science is to get 'back to the phenomenon', and this is to be achieved (suggest phenomenologists) by the abandonment of all preconceptions about the object of enquiry, and by the adoption of 'naturalistic' methods that allow the researcher to get close to, and be entirely open to, the subjectivity of others and the subtleties of social interaction. Such methods, drawn from journalism, anthropology and analytical psychology, included extended (sometimes 'depth') interviews and life-history taking, group discussions, participant observation, and examination of formal and unintended records of social events.

During the past fifteen years, materialist approaches have begun to adopt many of the qualitative methods of phenomenology, but have deployed them within a quite different framework. Materialist social science agrees with phenomenology in its criticism of social science's tendency to impose upon the object of enquiry a 'grid' or set of categories drawn from another social universe (e.g. from the state's conception of 'drinking problems'); but materialism denies the possibility that any object can ever be read directly, 'naturally', without theoretical preconceptions. Were it possible to sweep away all those preconceptions related to the individual and his/her personal and political commitments, those implicit in language itself would still necessarily remain, providing the framework within which the object was constituted in thought. From this point of view, an untheorised ethnography is impossible.

Both positivism and phenomenology share the assumption that there is an object that can be grasped without benefit of theoretical assumptions: the difference is that whereas positivism assumed that quantitative manipulation of a number of 'cases' will reveal the underlying relationships betwen them, phenomenology assumes that intensive exposure to a smaller number of cases will reveal the true nature of each. As Willis says:

> If the techniques of 'qualitative' methodology mark a decisive break from 'quantitative' ones, the way in which they are *usually applied* makes a secret

> compact with positivism to preserve the subject finally as an object. Indeed, what the all-embracing concern for techniques and for the reliability of the data really shows us is a belief that the object of research exists in an external world, with knowable external characteristics which must not be disturbed.
>
> The central insistence, for instance, on the *passivity* of the *participant observer* depends on a belief that the subject of the research is really an object. The concern is to minimize 'distortion of the field', with the underlying fear that the *object* may be *contaminated* with the subjectivity of the researcher. Too easily it becomes an assumption of different orders of reality between the researched and the researcher.
>
> The insistent, almost neurotic, technical concern with the differentiation of PO from reportage and Art is also a reflection of the subterranean conviction that PO belongs with the 'sciences' and must, in the end, respect objectivity. There is a clear sociological fear of naked subjectivity. The novel can wallow in subjectivity – this is how it creates 'colour' and 'atmosphere' – but how do we know that the author did not make it all up? Indeed, in one obvious way he or she did make it all up! So the search must be for a unified object which might be expected to present itself as *the same* to many minds. The first principle of PO, the postponement of theory, compounds the dangers of this covert positivism. It strengthens the notion that the object can present itself directly to the observer . . .
>
> In fact, there is no truly untheoretical way in which to 'see' an 'object'. The 'object' is only perceived and understood through an internal organization of data, mediated by conceptual constructs and ways of seeing the world. (Willis, 1980; 89-90)

5. Use of a mix of methods in a case study has been discussed in the collection edited by Filstead (1979).

6. And, as Willis (1980; 90) has pointed out, some details of the data may offer 'surprises' to the researcher.

7. The field work reported here was conducted in the second year of the project, following an initial year of work in which literature study, theoretical orientation, and initial and exploratory interviews with pupils attending schools outside Servicetown were carried out. During the first year, taped depth interviews and group discussions in six schools were carried out. These schools, located in north-east, north-west and south-east London, spanned the range of state schooling, ranging from very working class comprehensives to a grammar school that was in the process of changing (in name, at least) into a comprehensive. The interviews and group discussions were structured around the researcher's initial interest in understanding schoolchildren's awareness of, and responses to, images of 'teenage alcoholism' then being put forward in the mass media (see my 1978 MA thesis, *Labour Market Recruitment and Youth Dependency Problems,* Middlesex Polytechnic). Two factors, however, drew the study towards its present form. In the first place, the very great complexity of the issues raised by pupils in interviews and group discussions, their explicit linking of these 'leisure' issues to questions around race, gender, and their ways of dealing with the transition from school to labour market, drew attention to the need to situate drinking practices in relation to pupils' material situation. Secondly, this conclusion was compatible with the claims of neo-Marxian theories about youth and culture, which were becoming increasingly prominent during the 1970s (see chapter 4 above).

For the main part of research, therefore, a particular area of the city was chosen for study, and a particular group of youth located within it. The fieldwork, which took place between April 1979 and March 1980, proceding in three overlapping phases. The first phase, involving desk-research and interviews with Council Planning Department staff and others, focussed primarily upon contacts with local firms taking school-leavers into employment. Fifty local firms were contacted by means of a letter and followed up by 'phone, and direct contact (involving visits and interviews) was established with twenty-two. Secondary schools were contacted in a similar manner; careers teachers were interviewed in all the local secondary schools, and other teachers and pupils in six of these schools (see text). Contact was also had with local social workers, youth workers and careers officers (it should be noted, however, that most of these were primarily concerned with lower working class youth, whilst this project is primarily concerned with the marginally more privileged). Lastly, some pupils interviewed in the schools were observed in leisure situations.

The research plans, therefore, provided for a broad view of the locality in the first place and then for successive concentrations of research focus, as illustrated in diagram N.I (overleaf).

8. The letter stated that, 'in the past, the views of employers have been somewhat eclipsed by the views of teachers, social workers, politicians and others and yet, I believe, employers can make a very great contribution to our understanding of youth and their problems.'

9. 'Excruciating noise is probably the most unpleasant sensual concomitant of industrial work. Its invocation serves to remind even those who pride themselves on their penetration of the consumer-egalitarian-liberal mythology, that not only are commodities produced under specific and determinate social conditions, but also that they are produced under specific and determinate *experiential* conditions. What is the human meaning and actual experience that lies behind our easy use of cars, cosmetics, clothes and buildings? What degree of frenzy, activity, boredom and suffering has been objectified into the thousand articles on glamorous display in the department store? Is the meaning and pleasure of these things as they are consumed any more important than the meaning of the drudge of their production? It is often forgotten that the main reality, for most people, for most of the time, is work and the sound of work' (Willis, 1979; 185).

10. Steel-making and car assembly are examples of work-processes in which large teams of men work together and collectively exercise a degree of control over the pace of the work; these (now declining) industries were amongst those employing the fathers of the 'lads' in Willis' study (See Willis, 1978).

11. All reported speech is taken from taped interviews unless otherwise stated.

12. The labour market addresses the individual workers (including the school-leaver) as an independent contract-maker and hence, according to Marxian theory, enmeshes him or her in an ideology in which the imaginary relations of equality (derived from the apparently uncoerced and equal exchange of labour for the wage) appear 'real' (Pashukanis, 1978). Whilst sources of ideology other than the labour market have also been discussed in the social sciences – for example the Oedipus complex (Weedon et al, 1980), patriarchal relations (Hartman, 1979), and Ideological State Apparatuses (Althusser, 1971) – and whilst the ideology of the labour market might not be so all-pervasive as implied by unreconstructed Marxism, this does not imply that the individualistic social relation of the wage has no significance for those engaged in the labour market. Additionally, some wage workers are engaged in particular types of work-process that accentuate their independence from other workers. This is the case in many small manufacturing firms in Servicetown: see text.

13. Erving Goffman and other interactionist sociologists have discussed facework (Goffman, 1972).

14. There are fourteen secondary schools in Servicetown containing approximately 12,000 pupils (the number is falling year by year). The smallest of these has just under 500 pupils on the rolls and the largest about 2,500. All of them are,

DIAGRAM N.1; Successive concentrations of research focus

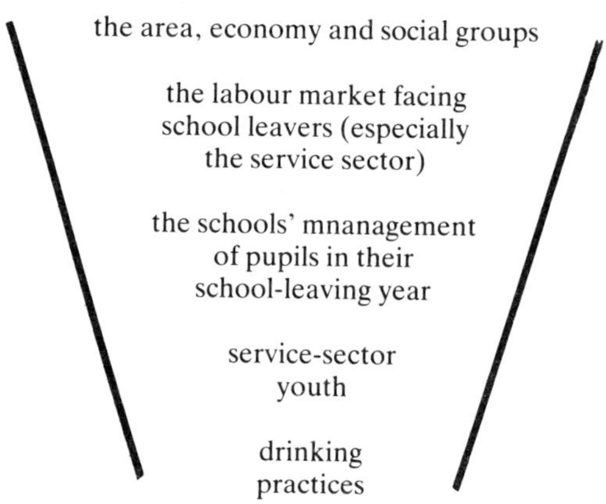

formally, comprehensives – but those which have most recently given up their grammar school pasts are quite distinguishable from the longer-established comprehensives, and there are in addition some Roman Catholic schools with a high proportion of Irish-Catholics. There are also a number of schools and units dealing with the physically handicapped, the maladjusted, and the educationally subnormal (as defined within the educational system). Conversations with teachers and children within these units helped to illuminate some aspects of the school-environments of the majority that might otherwise have been overlooked. In particular, it was a common assumption amongst teachers in 'ordinary' schools that *most* of those pupils leaving at sixteen (the majority) would obtain employment: their concern was over the quality of that employment. In units dealing with those categorised as handicapped, malajusted or subnormal, it could not be assumed that the pupils would get employment of any kind. Great importance was attached to finding these pupils jobs, and staff in these units often went to considerable lengths to set up and maintain *direct contacts* with local firms. This was in contrast to the ways in which ordinary comprehensives handled school-leaving pupils, leaving them very much to their own (or parents') devices. The careers office reckoned on interviewing each pupil in his or her school-leaving year, but several pupils interviewed apparently escaped this process (or perhaps found it forgetable). Careers teachers in ordinary comprehensives generally maintained files, but those files that I had an opportunity to examine were more concerned with pupils' aptitudes and interests than with local employment prospects. The comparison between the minority units and the ordinary comprehensives was useful in illuminating the extent to which comprehensive school-leavers are very much 'on their own' as they face the labour market.

15. Problems of control in comprehensive schools have been discussed by Hargreaves (1967) and Jackson and Marsden (1962).

16. Andrew Tolson had discussed 'the language of fatalism' (Tolson, 1977).

17. Hebdige has written of punk as essentially working class (Hebdige, 1979). His analysis seems however to be based upon a particular reading of the claims made in punk 'fanzines', rather than upon any close study of working class teenagers. In the case study area researched in the present study, street observation and discussion with teachers and youth workers were sufficient to establish that punk styles were being selectively appropriated by a number of groups throughout the class structure: whilst some of these groups were clearly lower working class in origin, others were equally clearly middle class. It would seem therefore that any characterisation of punk as a specifically working class phenomenon is unwarranted.

18. Most sociological research into girls seems to share one characteristic with research into boys: it focusses upon the lower strata of the working class. Such girls are generally portrayed as having a culture marginal to or separate from that of boys (Wolpe, 1977, Lamart, 1976, Nava, 1982). In the present study boys and girls from the middle strata of the working class participated in a shared culture – though maintaining smaller single-sex friendship groups.

19. Frith and McRobbie have discussed the ways in which popular and rock music acts as a carrier for representatives of sexuality (Frith and McRobbie, 1981). Masculinity and feminity are represented in music not simply as two monolithic stereotypes, but in various guises: masculinity as 'cock rock' (e.g. Jimi Hendrix, admired by the boys within the service sector group researched) and as 'teenybop' (in which the male appeals to be looked after, rather than demanding submission); femininity in 'sexual liberation' and in domestic-caring versions (ibid; 99-105). The music played in the pub in question was determined (a) by whoever put money into the juke-box and (b) by the disc-jockey on those evenings when the juke-box was discontinued in his favour. The service-sector entrants occasionally played the juke-box, but generally contented themselves with listening (or half-listening) to whatever records - generally drawn from the 'top fifty' – were chosen for them by others.

20. The concept of 'peer pressure' has been used in psychological and social-psychological explanations of youthful drinking (see chapter 4 above, and especially the work of Davies and Stacey, 1972 and O'Connor, 1978). And, as chapter 3 illustrates, peer pressure is the bete noire of current (affective) approaches in health education, is portrayed as an impediment to decision-making, and is blamed for encouraging alcohol consumption. The equation of round-buying with high levels of alcohol consumption seems well-established in health education – so much so that, when a short paper outlining the present study was submitted to the *International Journal of Health Education,* referees asked for reference to peer pressure to be included (personal communication trom the Editor). In contrast to this, recent observational research conducted at the University of Glasgow shows 'no evidence that round buying (by young people) is associated with higher levels of alcohol consumption' (Philip Aitken, personal communication based on initial analysis of observation data, August 1981). In the present study, attention is drawn to the possibility that the forms taken by drinking practices may differ from one social (class/gender/ethnic) group to another, and that levels of consumption result from the interaction of these forms with the variety of drinking occasions (e.g. short weekday visits to the pub, weekend 'binge', etc) that occur in particular cultures. It follows from this that any generalisation about the factors making for increased or decreased levels of consumption may be unwarranted and may obscure a variety of social processes, understanding of which should underpin health and social education.

21. Some relevant sources are the *Labour Force Sample Survey,* compiled by Eurostat (Statistical Office of the European Community) and, in the UK, *Social Trends, Regional Statistics,* and *Annual Abstract of Statistics,* all compiled by the Central Statistical Office. These statistics show that, taking the country as a whole and comparing it with other European countries, the U.K. has a relatively large service sector; and that a relatively large proportion of young women work in that sector (table N.I, column (c) – see p. 261)

Official statistics also give an indication of the extent to which adult women's labour is totally appropriated in domestic labour. In the U.K. and in other countries, housewives who do not work outside the home are described as not being 'economically active'. In some European countries the statistics also refer to a group known as 'family workers'. In these cases the head of the family is the employer, and other male family members are employees receiving part of their remuneration in the form of domestic services, which are provided by female family members who also contribute labour in other forms to the family-enterprise. These females cannot be regarded as independent agents in the labour market: they belong, with non-'economically active' housewives, to the underclass of those females who do not have full and effective possession of their labour power. In European government statistics, however, they are included in the wages labour force, and are not, therefore, included in column (d) of table N.I.

What table N.I. indicates is that in most European countries over one quarter of all young women between the ages of 14 and 24 years are employed in the service sector of the economy. Luxemburg, Denmark, the U.K., Netherlands and Germany are countries in which 30 per cent or more of young women are service sector employees. Of these five countries, however, two – Luxembourg and Netherlands – are remarkable for having higher proportion of unwaged housewives in the general population (leaving aside an additional number of 'family workers'). Only Denmark, the UK (and, to a lesser extent, Germany) induct 30 per cent or more of young women into service sector employment within the context of an economy in which the majority of married women work outside the home (as well as in it). If we regard the proportion of young women who are employed in the service sector of the economy as a measure of the extent to which the material prerequisites of service sector youth culture exist, and regard the proportion of married women who do any

Table N.1; Female Labour in EEC Countries

	(a) Proportion of young women (14-24 years) who are 'economically active' in labour market	(b) Proportion of 'economically active' young women who are employed in service sector	(c) Proportion of all young women who are service sector employees	(d) Proportion of married women of all ages who are 'housewives' are not 'economically active'
Luxemburg	46.4	83.3	37	75
Denmark	45.7	77.7	36	37
U.K.	45.3	69.1	31	40
Netherlands	36.6	82.6	30	80
Germany	44.5	66.9	30	54
Ireland	42.4	65.7	28	84
France	41.5	66.0	27	46
Belgium	37.8	66.6	25	56
Italy	30.2	45.9	14	65

Sources: all figures taken from *Labour Force Sample Survey* (Statistical Office of the European Community, 1980): Column (a) from the table 11/6, p. 84; column (b) from table 111/2, p. 94; column (c) calculated from columns (a) and (b); column (d) from table 11/8, p. 88.

kind of waged work as some indication of the beginnings of 'sex-equality' in society generally, then it may be reasonable to suggest comparative research into service sector youth cultures and drinking practices in Denmark, the UK, Germany (and perhaps other similar non-EEC countries). It should also be noted, however, that the proportion of the female population that does waged work outside the home, and the proportion of waged employment that takes place in the service sector, varies from region to region within each country (tables VII/2 and VII/5, pages 172 and 178, Statistical Office, 1980). Hence the extent to which the material prerequisites of service sector youth culture exist must vary quite substantially from region to region – and there will be local area variations, too. A variety of cultural forms, and drinking practices, might be built upon these circumstances, and region-to-region, country-to-country generalisation would be hazardous. In these conditions, we would seek to limit generalisation of the findings of chapter 5 to other inner London area.

NOTES TO CHAPTER 6

1. The emphasis upon *selective* use of media and educational resources is important. Early youth culture research tended to be based on the assumption that the media and consumption market directly shaped the social attitudes and consumption styles of youth (e.g. Abrams, 1959). This then gave way to the proposition that working class males accepted some of the themes and imagery offered in the media (e.g. 'exploit'), and incorporated them in an *exaggerated* form into their culture (Downes, 1966). Work at Birmingham has emphasised the way in which the taking up of specific 'styles' is part of a general 'working through' of the experience of upward or downward class mobility (Clarke et al, 1975). More recently Hebdige (1979) has emphasised the rejection of bourgeoise values supposedly represented in bizarre presentations of self in 'spectacular' youth cultures. Girls' cultures are, by contrast, most often described as accommodative to a future as married and as accepting of those consumer products and media themes that reinforce the role of

female dependency (McRobbie and Garber, 1975, McRobbie, 1980). It would be a mistake to attempt to generalise from any of these studies to all strata of youth. Rather, it has to be recognised that each strata of youth will have a specific relationship to the media and to the market in consumer non-durables, and that this relationship may be understood in terms of the general position of the group concerned. The appropriation of 'old-fashioned' rock music by the service-sector youth researched in the case study is a striking example of the selectivity of this relationship. For general discussions of theories of the relationship between media and its audience, see Young (1981), and for an overview with reference to alcohol, Dorn and South (1983).

2. McGuiness has conducted an econometric study, aiming to estimate changes in alcohol consumption that might have occurred in the period 1956-75 had various social and economic conditions – such as income levels, numbers of licensed premises, and level of alchol advertising – been different. He concludes that each of these conditions is positively correlated with total consumption of alcohol, but that the relation betwen total alcohol consumption and average income levels is uncertain (during the period of study). His statistical analysis assumes that the UK total population may be treated as one aggregate of individuals not clustering into specific groups (class, gender, etc) that may react in differing ways; that unwaged and dependent persons (e.g. housewives) respond to changes in social conditions in the same way as waged persons; that the relationship between changes in levels of advertising and changes in the total level of consumption is linear; that such relationships do not take differing forms at different times within the sociologically arbitrary period 1956-76; and that such relationships, observed between 1975-76, operate similarly in the 1980s. Acknowleding difficulties in enforcing a ban on advertising of alcohol, the author suggests that a reduction in advertising would cause a reduction in total alcohol consumption (p.16) and also suggests that such reduction would cause a reduction in 'excessive' drinking (McGuinness, 1979).

3. Thus for example, a change in the balance of expendible income and costs of consumption of alcohol may affect the balance between participation in episodic binge drinking ('getting paralytic' in service sector culture) and participation in more frequent but shorter round-buying occasions, rather than causing a uniform increase or decrease in both these activities. There is also the possibility that *extreme* changes in the balance of income/cost of consumption might disrupt the form of the consumption practice (e.g. might disrupt the round); but any such changes would vary from culture to culture, would depend upon each social group's responses to changes in broader material conditions (e.g. the intrusion of unemployment amongst the middle and upper strata of working class youth), and cannot be determined on the basis of empirical studies of the 'average' consumer response to dissimilar circumstances in previous decades.

4. For example, advertising themes maybe taken up insofar as one type of drink may be consumed rather than another, without affecting the form of the drinking practice (e.g. round-buying). It is interesting that the group researched seemed to have difficulty in recalling any drink advertisements that they had found particularly striking or amusing. This may reflect a lack of advertisements directed towards this group, their culture, and their normal drinking practice. Certainly, most drink advertisements shown on television during the research period seemed to appeal to either a fantasy of upper class winter sports (Martini, etc) or to butch masculinity, albeit in 'modern' garb (e.g. lagers).

5. This manual has been published in Denmark (Nortoft and Dorn, 1981) and a version is currently being prepared for publication in this country (Dorn and Nortoft, in press, Institute for the Study of Drug Dependence).

6. Extended interview with Wyn Hart, ILEA Health Education Inspector. ILEA was approached with a request for help in setting up school trials with the prototype manual *Health Careers* and, although agreeable, failed to find any schools for such

trials. This unusual outcome may reflect ambivalence over the manual, which seemed important because it represented a 'new approach', and yet problematic for this same reason. Additional problems may have been caused by the reported opposition of a D.E.S. Inspector of Health Education. At the time of carrying out the study, the D.E.S. gave financial and ideological support to the individualistic, child-centred (affective) approaches noted in chapter 3, above. In retrospect, it seems clear that classroom trials should have been arranged *directly* with a small number of schools, instead of trying to work down from the upper reaches of the educational system.

7. The work of Hilary Graham shows how a particular group (expectant mothers) regard smoking, a form of social behaviour that is 'officially' regarded as unhealthy, as an integral part of their means for coping with their domestic role and caring for the health and happiness of the family (Graham, 1976). At the institutional level, there are several quite specific conceptions of health, illhealth and the processes involved in their construction (Working Party on Inequalities in Health, 1980). Historical work has suggested how the contemporary medical discourse emerged (Foucault, 1976), but there is no evidence to suggest that this definition has a general currency amongst all social groups.

8. See for example, London-Edinburgh Weekend Return Group (1979), Carpenter (1980), ongoing meetings of the Politics of Health Group, and issues of *Critical Social Policy*.

9. For a discussion of the Manpower Services Commission and its support for 'social education', see Moos (1979). The M.S. C. is currently becoming the 'lead agency' in the state's attempt to restructure the education system, and its interventions are becoming increasingly important in the Further Education sector (ibid; 59). See also chapter II of *Unpopular Education* (C.C.C.S., 1981). There is perhaps a need now to pause long enough from the task of chacterising M.S.C schemes, and to examine the cultural forms and practises that arise amongst their youthful clients.

10. For examples of work on the informal economy see the SSRC review by South (1982). Sociological work on youth culture and delinquency has been discussed in chapter 4 above. An up-to-date introduction to feminist theory is provided by Barratt and Cockburn (1981).

11. At the present time, however, the Health Education Council seems intent on pursuing the notion of an audience without social class or sexual divisions. Although it now seems to be appreciated that different approaches may be useful in various regions of the country, the audience *within* each region still seems to be conceptualised as a community without internal divisions and distinct cultures.

12. The 'Health Education Materials Project' in the Department of Health and Welfare Education, Institute of Education, University of London, commenced in mid-1981 as a study of printed health education materials and their use at local level. This project has a feminist orientation (A. Beatty, W. Farrant, personal communications).

13. Kensington, Chelsea and Westminster Area Health Authority (Teaching) is the base for this project.

14. Reviews of the economy and forecasts of future trends are conducted by a number of academic and commercial institutions including those at Cambridge University, the London Business School, and the National Institute for Economic and Social Research. See the latter's *Review* for quarterly forecasts of movements in the domestic economy.

NOTES TO CONCLUSION

1. Recognition of the need to move on to chart drinking careers or biographies does not necessitate any return to the socio-psychological reductionism that

characterises most existing research (noted in chapter 4). There is no *a priori* contradiction between a materialist approach that situates social groups and their cultures within structures, on the one hand, and a study of individuals' biographies (and their drinking careers), on the other, as long as it is recognised that 'the science of personality is in an absolutely secondary position in relation to the science of social relations' (Seve, 1977; 446). Following this principle, Seve attempts to construct a materialist theory of personality as being structured by the 'temporal structure of all the activities (forms of labour) making up the life of the person' (ibid; 458). His analysis is however flawed by a failure to recognise forms of labour that are specific to the sexes. It has been left to non-Marxists, and in particular to followers of Freud, to discuss the relations between gender, sexuality and personality, with the result that the science of personality has been detached from that of social relations. See, for example, Lacan (1977) who seems 'to have fallen prey to the temptation to treat the most abstract/universal level of abstruction (i.e. the individual) as the most pertinant' (Hall, 1980b; 161). A more historically specific approach is provided by Foucault, who sees identity as a concept produced within a historically-specific discourse on sexuality (defining the 'child', etc – see Foucault, 1978, Weedon et al, 1980, Romano, 1981). 'It is through sex that each individual has to pass in order to have access to his own intelligibility . . . to his identity' (Foucault, 1978; 155-156). For Foucault this sexuality is a historically-specific discourse and set of practices (in the home, in schooling, etc) that confront individuals throughout their lives. Such a framework for understanding subjectivity needs, however, to be tied more closely to material facts than is done by Foucault – not only to economic development, but also to biological differences, insofar as these set limits upon activities, the 'temporal structure' of these, and hence upon personality. Development of sociological/psychological theory would necessarily be an integral part of any study of the biographies and subjectivity of individuals, and hence of research into the development of 'drinking careers'.

2. See 'Her Majesty's new opposition', *The Economist,* 281, 7214, Dec 1981, pp. 11-12.

3. Conference of Socialist Economists, London Working Group (1980) outlines some 'versions' of the A.E.S. and summarises debate around it.

BIBLIOGRAPHY

ABRAMS, M, 1959, *The Teenage Consumer*, London: Press Exchange.

ADVISORY COMMITTEE ON PREVENTION, 1977, *Report on Prevention*, London: D.H.S.S. and Welsh Office.

AITKEN, P, 1978, *Ten-to-fourteen-year-olds and Alcohol*; a Developmental Study in the Central Region of Scotland, London: HMSO.

AKERS, R, 1967-8, 'Problems in the Sociology of Deviance; Social Definitions and Behaviour', *Social Forces*, 46, (June), pp 455-65.

ALEXANDER, A, 1980, 'History of English Feminist Thought', paper presented at Communist University of London, University of London Union.

ALTHUSSER, L, 1971, 'Ideology and Ideological State Apparatuses', in *Lenin and Philosophy and Other Essays*, London: New Left Books, pp 127-88.

ANDERSON, N, 1923, *The Hobo,* Chicago: University Press.

ANDERSON, P, 1967-7, 'The Antinomies of Antonio Gramsci', *New Left Review,* 100 (Nov-Jan), pp 5-80.

ANDERSON, R, 1981, Report to the Expert Committee on Health Education, Copenhagen: World Health Organisation, unpublished.

AULD, J, 1981, *Marijuna Use and Social Control,* London: Academic Press.

BACON, M, Barry, H and Child, I, 1965, 'A Cross-Cultural Study of Drinking', *Quarterly Journal of Studies on Alchol,* Supplement, 3, pp 1-48.

BARRETT, M and Cockburn, C, 1981, 'A Quick Guided Tour round Marxist-Feminist Theory', *Head and Hand,* 8, (Summer), pp 1-2.

BEATTY, A, 1980, 'Models of Health Education', paper presented at Health Education Certifiicate Course Tutors' Workshop, 24th-26th March, Exeter.

BECKER, H, 1966, *Outsiders: Studies in the Sociology of Deviance,* Glencoe: Free Press.

BECKER, H, 1973, *Outsiders,* New York: Free Press.

BERNSTEIN, B, 1977, 'Class and Pedagogies: Visible and Invisible', in Karabel, J and Halsey, A, (eds), *Power and Ideology in Education,* New York: Oxford University Press, pp 511-34.

BLANE, T and Hewitt, L, 1977, *Alcohol and Youth. An Analysis of the Literature,* Washington: National Technical Information Service, U.S. Department of Commerce.

BOARD OF EDUCATION, 1909, *Syllabus of Lessons on 'Temperance' for Scholars Attending Public Elementary Schools,* London: HMSO.

BOARD OF EDUCATION, 1909, 922, *The Hygiene of Food and Drink,* London: HMSO.

BOX, S, 1971, *Deviance, Reality and Society,* London: Holt, Rinehart and Winston.

BRAKE, M, 1980, *The Sociolgoy of Youth Culture and Youth Subcultures,* London: Routlege and Kegan Paul.

BRAKE, T, 1981, *The Agenda for Action on Alcohol Policies,* London: Christian Economic and Social Research Foundation.

BRENNAN, M and Lancashire, 1978, 'Association of Childhood Mortality with Housing Status and Unemployment', *Journal of Epidemiology and Community Health,* 32,1, (March), pp 28-33.

BRENNER H, 1976, *Estimating the Social Costs of National Economic Policy. A report to the Joint Economic Committee of U.S. Congress,* Washington: U.S. Government Printing Office.

BREWERS SOCIETY, 1980, *UK Statistical Handbook for 1979,* London: Brewing Publications.

BUDD, J and McCron, R, 1981, 'Health Education and the Mass Media: Past, Present and Future', in Leathar, D, Hastings, G and Davies, J, (eds), *Health Education and the Media,* Oxford: Pergamon, pp 33-44.

BUTTERS, S, 1975, The Logic of Enquiry of Participant Observation', *Working Papers in Cultural Studies,* 7/8, (Summer), pp 242-53.

CARTER, H, 1933, *The English Temperance Movement – A Study in Objectives,* London: Epworth.

CARPENTER, M, 1980, 'Left Orthodoxy and the Politics of Health', *Capital and Class,* II, pp 73-98.

CARTWRIGHT, A, Shaw, S and Spratly, T, 1978, 'The Relationship Between Per Capita Consumption, Drinking Patterns and Alcohol Related Problems in a Population Sample', *British Journal of Addiction,* 73, pp 237-46.

CAVAN, S, 1966, *Liquor License: An Ethnography of Bar Behaviour,* Chicago: Aldine.

CENTRAL CONTROL BOARD, 1981, *Alcohol: its action on the human organism, London: HMSO.*

CENTRAL POLICY REVIEW STAFF, 1979, Alcohol Policies, London: Cabinet Office, (unpublished), reprinted and published 1982 as *Alcohol Policies in United Kingdom,* Stockholm: Sociologiska instutionen, Stockholm universitet.

CENTRAL STATISTICAL OFFICE, 1980, *Social Trends,* London: HMSO.

CENTRE FOR CONTEMPORARY CULTURAL STUDIES, 1981, *Unpopular Education,* London: Hutchinson.

CHAMBLISS, W, 1969, *Crime and the Legal Process,* New York: McGraw-Hill.

CHAMBLISS, W, 1971, 'A Sociological Analysis of the Law of Vagrancy', in Carson, W and Wiles, P, (eds), *Crime and Delinquency in Britain,* London: Martin Robinson, pp 206-18.

CHANCELLOR OF THE EXCHEQUER, 1980, *The Government's Expenditure Plans* 1980-81 to 1983-84, Cmnd 7841, London: HMSO.

CHAUNCEY, R, 1980, 'New Careers for Moral Entrepreneurs: Teenage Drinking', *Journal of Drug Issues,* 1, (Winter), pp 45-70.

CHRISTIAN ECONOMIC AND SOCIAL RESEARCH FOUNDATION, 1980, *Chief Constables' Reports, England and Wales, and Scotland. Part One, Drink Offences,* London: C.E.S.R.F.

CLARKE, J. Hall, S, Jefferson, S and Roberts, B, 1975, 'Subcultures, Cultures and Class: a Theoretical Overview', in *Working Papers in Cultural Studies,* 7/8, (Summer), pp 9-74.

CLARKE, M, 1975-6, 'Durkheim's Sociology of Law', *British Journal of Law and Society,* 3, 2, (Winter), pp 246-55.

CICOUREL, A, 1968, *The Social Organisation of Juvenile Justice,* New York: Wiley.

COHEN, A, 1955, *Delinquent Boys: the Culture of the Gang,* Chicago: Free Press.

COHEN, P, 1972, 'Subcultural Conflict and Working-Class Community', *Working Papers in Cultural Studies,* 2, pp 9-27.

COHEN, S, (ed), 1971, *Images of Deviance,* Harmondswoth: Penguin.

COHEN, S, 1979, 'The Punitive City', *Contemporary Crises,* 3,4, pp 339-63.

COHEN, S and Young, J, 1973, *The Manufacture of News: Deviance, Social Problems and the Mass Media,* London: Constable.

COLEMAN, J, 1961, *The Adolescent Society,* New York: Free Press.

CONFERENCE OF SOCIALIST ECONOMISTS LONDON WORKING GROUP, 1980, *The Alternative Economic Strategy,* London: C.S.E. Books and the Labour Co-ordinating Committee.

CORRIGAN, P and Corrigan, V, 1979, 'State Formation and Social Policy Until 1871', in Parry, N, Ruskin, M and Satyamutrio, C, (eds), *Social Work, Welfare and the State,* London: Edward Arnold, pp 1-20.

CORRIGAN, P and Frith, S, 1975, 'The Politics of Youth Culture', *Working Papers in Cultural Studies,* 7/8, (Summer), pp 231-42.

COWARD, R, 1980, 'Feminism and Pscyhoanalysis', paper presented at Communist University of London, University of London Union.

COWLEY, J, 1977, 'Education about Alcohol – We Have Been This Way Before', *Royal Society of Health Journal,* 97, 1, (February), pp 26-8.

CRITCHER, C, 1979, 'Sociology, Cultural Studies and the Post-war Working Class', in Clarke, J, Critcher, C and Johnson, R, (eds), *Working Class Culture,* London: Hutchinson, pp 13-40.

CUTLER, A, Hindess, B, Hirst, P and Hussain, A, 1977, *Marx's Capital and Capitalism Today,* London: Routledge and Kegan Paul.

DAVIES, J and Stacey, B, 1972, Teenagers and Alcohol: *A Developmental Study in Glasgow,* London: HMSO.

DAVIES, N, 1972, 'Labelling Theory in Deviance Research: A Critique and Reconsideration', *Sociological Quarterly,* 3, (Fall) pp 447-74.

DAVIS, W, 1964, 'A Cross-Cultural Study of Drunkenness', unpublished A.B. Theses, Cambridge, Mass: Harvard University.

DEEM, R, 1981, 'State Policy and Ideology in the Education of Women, 1944-1980', *British Journal of Sociology of Education,* 2, 2, pp 131-43.

De HAES, W and Schurrman, J, 1975, 'Results of an Evaluation Study of Three Drug Education Methods', *International Journal of Health Education,* 18, 4, Supplement, (Oct-Dec), pp 1-16.

De LINT, J, 1974, 'Epidemiology of Alcoholism: the Elusive Nature of the Problem, Estimating the Prevalence of Excessive Alcohol Use and Alcohol-related Mortality, Current Trends and the Issue of Prevention', in Kessel, N, Hawker, A and Chalk, H, (eds), *Alcoholism: A Medical Profile,* London: Edsell, pp 75-108.

De LINT, J, 1981, 'The Influence of Much Increased Alcohol Consumption on Mortality Rates: The Netherlands Between 1950 and 1975', *British Journal of Addiction,* 76, 1, (March), pp 75-84.

DELPHY, C, 1977, *The Main Enemy,* London: Womens Research and Resources Centre.

DELPHY, C, 1980, 'A Materialist Feminism is Possible', *Feminist Review,* 4, pp 79-105.

DEPARTMENT OF EDUCATION AND SCIENCE, 1968, *A Handbook of Health Education,* London: HMSO.

DEPARTMENT OF HEALTH AND SOCIAL SECURITY, 1976, *Priorities for Health and Personal Social Services in England,* London: D.H.S.S.

DEPARTMENT OF HEALTH AND SOCIAL SECURITY,1981, *Drinking Sensibly,* London: D.H.S.S.

DEPARTMENT OF HEALTH AND SOCIAL SECURITY, 1981, 'Jenkin Calls for More Collaboration to Fight Alcoholism – Build on the Common Ground', (Press Release, July 21st), London: D.H.S.S.

DICKSON, D, 1968-9, 'Bureaucracy and Morality: An Organisational Perspective on a Moral Crusade', *Social Problems,* 16, pp 143-57.

DITTON, J, 1979, *Contrology,* London: Macmillan.

DORN, N, 1980, 'Alcohol in Teenage Cultures: a Materialist Approach to Youth Cultures, Drinking and Health Education', *Health Education Journal,* 39, 3, pp 67-73.

DORN, N, 1981(a), 'Communication with the Working Class Requires a Recognition of the Working Class: A Materialist Approach', in Leathar, D, Hastings, G and Davies, J, (eds), *Health Education and the Media*, Oxford: Pergamon Press, pp 59-72.

DORN, N, 1981(b), 'Social Analysis of Drugs in Health Education and the Media' in Edwards, G and Bush, C, (eds), *Drug Problems in Britain: A Review of Ten Years,* London: Academic Press, pp 281-304.

DORN, N, 1981(c), 'Youth Culture in the UK: Independence and Round Drinking', *International Journal of Health Education,* 4, 2, (April-June), pp 77-82.

DORN, N et al, 1977, 'Problems and Rewards of Evaluation of European Drug Education; First Report of the Study Group for Evaluation of European Drug

Education and Policy', Paris: Unesco, mimeo.

DORN, N and Thompson, A, 1976, 'Research into Expressions of Attitudes about Drugs – What use is it?' *United Nations Bulletin on Narcotics,* 28, 2, pp 19-35.

DORN, N, Thompson , A and Hvidtfeldt, K, 1977, *The DEDE Report, Technical on the Drug (legal and illegal) Education Development and Evaluation Project,* London: Institute for the Study of Drug Dependence.

DORN, N and South, N, 1983, *Message in a Bottle. Theoretical Overview and Annotated Bibliography on the Mass Media and Alcohol,* London: Gower.

DOYAL, L, 1979, *The Political Economy of Health,* London: Pluto Press.

DOUGLAS, M, 1966, *Purity and Danger,* London: Routledge and Kegan Paul.

DOUGLAS, J, 1970, Observations of Deviance, New York: Random House,

DOUGLAS J, 1971, *American Social Order,* New York: Free Press.

DOWNES, D, 19676, *The Delinquent Solution: A Study in Subcultural Theory,* London: Routledge and Kegan Paul

EISER, R, 1977, 'Smoking and Attribution Theory', paper presented at Conference on Social Psychology and Medicine, Institue of Psychiatry, London.

ENGELS F, 1969, *The Condition of the Working Class in England in 1844,* Harmondsworth: Penguin.

ENGELS, F, 1970, 'Feuerbach and the End of Classical German Philosphy', in Marx, K and Engels, F, *Selected Works,* vol. 3, Moscow: Progress, pp 335-60.

ENGELS, F, 1972, *The Origin of the Family, Private Property and the State,* New York: Pathfinder Press.

FILSTEAD, W, 1979, *Qualitative Methodology,* Chicago: Free Press.

FINE, B, 1977, 'Labelling Theory: An Investigation into the Sociological Critique of Deviance', *Economy and Society,* 6, 2, (May), pp 166-93.

FINE, B, 1979, 'Law And Class' in National Deviancy Conference/Conference of Socialist Economists, (eds), *Capitalism and the Rule of Law,* London: Hutchinson, pp 29-45.

FINN, D, 1982, 'There's Work to be Done? The Manpower Services Commission and Youth Unemployment', in Henderson, J, (ed), *Working for Capital,* London: Routledge and Kegan Paul, (in press).

FIRESTONE, S, 1979, *The Dialectic of Sex: the Case for Feminist Revolution,* London: The Womans Press, and 1971, London: Jonathan Cape.

FOGELMAN, K, 1978, 'Drinking Among Sixteen-year-olds', *Concern* (Journal of the National Childrens Bureau, London), 29, (Autumn), pp 19-25.

FOOT, C, 1956, 'Vagrancy Type Law and its Administration', *University of Pennsylvania Law Review,* 104, pp 603-51.

FOUCAULT, M, 1976, *The Birth of the Clinic,* London: Tavistock.

FOUCAULT, M, 1977, *Discipline and Punish,* London: Allen Lane.

FOUCAULT, M, 1978, *The History of Sexuality. Volume I: An Introduction,* London: Allen Lane.

FRASER, D, 1973, *The Evolution of the British Welfare State,* London: Macmillan.

FRITH, S, 1981, *Downtown: Young People in a City Centre,* Leicester: National Youth Bureau.

FRITH, S and McRobbie, A, 1981, 'Rock and Sexuality', in Dale, R, Esland, G, Fergusson, R and MacDonald, M (eds), *Politics, Patriarchy and Practice,* Lewes,: Falmer Press, pp 97-111.

GATHERER, A, Parfit, J, Porter, E and Vessey, M, 1979, *Is Health Education Effective?* London: Health Education Council.

GLASER, B and Strauss, A, 1968, *The Discovery of Grounded Theory,* London: Weidenfeld and Nicholson.

GLYN, A and Harrison, J, 1980, *The British Economic Disaster,* London: Pluto Press.

GOFFMAN, E, 1972, *Interaction Ritual,* Harmondsworth: Penguin.

GOODE, E, 1975, 'On behalf of Labelling Theory', *Social Problems,* 22, 5, (June), pp 570-83.

GOUGH, I, 1975, *The Political Economy of the Welfare State,* London: Macmillan.

GOULDNER, A , 1971, *The Coming Crisis of Western Sociology*, London: Macmillan.

GOULDNER, A, 1976, *The Dialectic of Ideology and Technology,* London: Macmillan.

GOULDNER, A, 1980, *The Two Marxisms,* London: Macmillan.

GRAHAM, H, 1976, 'Smoking in Pregancy: the Attitudes of Expectant Mothers', *Social Science and Medicine,* 10, pp 399-405.

GRAHAM, H, 1979, 'Prevention and Health: Every Mother's Business. A Comment on Child Health Policies in the 1970's, in Harris, C et al, (ed), *The Sociology of the Family: New Directions for Britain. Sociological Review Monograph 28,* pp 160-85.

GRAMSCI, A, 1971, *Selections from the Prison Notebooks,* London: Lawrence and Wishart.

GREENWOOD, A, 1920, *Public Ownership of the Liquor Trade,* London: Leonard Parsons.

GREENWOOD, V and Young, J, 1980, 'Ghettoes of Freedom: An Examination of Permissiveness', in National Deviancy Conference, (eds), *Permissiveness and Control,* London: Macmillan, pp 149-74.

GUSFIELD, J, 1966, *Symbolic Crusade: Status Politics and the American Temperance Movement,* Urbana: University of Illinois Press.

HALEVY, E, 1928, *The Growth of Philosphical Radicalism,* reprinted 1971, London: Faber and Faber.

HALL, R and Butcher, L, 1981, 'Against Our Selves: Why Women Against Rape couldn't join a march through Soho', London: Women Against Rape (mimeo).

HALL, S, 1980(a), *Drifting into a Law and Order Society,* London: Cobden Trust.

HALL, S, 1980(b) 'Cultural Studies: two paradigms', *Media, Culture and Society,* 2, 1, (January), pp 57-72.

HALL, S, Critcher, C, Jefferson, T and Roberts, B, 1978, *Policing the Crisis: Mugging, the State, and Law and Order,* London: Macmillan.

HARGREAVES, D, 1967, *Hightown Grammar,* Manchester: University Press.

HARGREAVES, D, 1976, 'Reactions to Labelling', in Hammersley, M and Woods, P, (eds), *The Process of Schooling,* London: Routledge and Kegan Paul, pp 210-7.

HARRISON, B, 1971, *Drink and the Victorians,* London: Faber and Faber.

HARTMAN, H, 1979, 'The Unhappy Marriage of Marxism and Feminism: Towards a More Progressive Union', *Capital and Class,* 8, (Summer), pp 1-33, revised and reprinted in Sargent, L, (ed), 1981, *Women and Revolution,* London: Pluto.

HAWKER, A, 1978, *Adolescents and Alcohol,* London: Edsall.

HAWKINS, K and Pass, C, 1979, *The Brewing Industry,* London: Heinemann.

HEBDIGE, D, 1979, *Subculture. The Meaning of Style,* London: Methuen.

HILL, C, 1972, *The World Turned Upside Down,* Harmondsworth: Penguin.

HIRSCHI, T, 1973, 'Proceedural Rules and the Study of Deviant Behaviour', *Social Problems,* 21, 2, pp 159-73.

HIRST, P, 1979, *On Law and Ideology,* London: Macmillan.

HOLLINGSHEAD, A, 1949, *Elmtown's Youth,* New York: Wiley.

HOLTZMAN, E, 1981, 'Science, Philosphy and Society: some recent books', *International Journal of Health Services,* 11, 1, pp 123-49.

HOME OFFICE, 1968, *Children in Trouble,* London: HMSO.

HOME OFFICE, 1979, *Offences of Drunkenness England and Wales 1978,* London: Home Office.

HORTON, D, 1943, 'The Functions of Alcohol in Primitive Societies: A Cross-cultural Study', *Quarterly Journal of Studies in Alcohol,* 4, pp 199-320.

HOUSE OF COMMONS EXPENDITURE COMMITTEE, 1977, *Preventive Medicine, Volume 1, Report,* London: HMSO.

JACKSON, B and Marsen, D, 1962, *Education and the Working Class,* London: Routledge and Kegan Paul.

JAHODA, G and Crammond, C, 1972, *Children and Alcohol: A Development Study in Glasgow,* London: HMSO.

JENKS, J, 1979, 'Health Education – The Myth of Consensus', *Monitor* (newsletter of the Teachers' Advisory Council on Alcohol and Drug Education, Manchester), 52, pp 8-10.

JESSOR, R, Graves, T, Hanson, R and Jessor, S, 1968, *Society, Personality and Deviant Behaviour,* New York: Holt, Rinehart and Winston.

JESSOR, R and Jessor, S, 1977, *The Web of Time: a Developmental Study of Problem Behaviour in Youth,* New York: Academic Press.

JOHNSON, R, 1979, 'Culture and the Historians' and also 'Three Problematics: elements of a theory of working class culture', in Clarke, J, Critcher, C and Johnson, R, (eds), *Working Class Culture,* London: Hutchinson, pp 41-44 and 210-37.

JOHNSON, T, 1977, 'The Professions in the Class Structure', in Scase, R, (ed), *Industrial Society: Class, Cleavage and Control,* London: George Allen & Unwin, pp 93-110.

JOINT COMMITTEE OF THE CENTRAL AND SCOTTISH HEALTH SERVICES COUNCILS, 1964, *Report* ('Cohen Report'), London: HMSO.

KITSUSE, J, 1972, 'Deviance, Deviant Behaviour, and Deviants: Some Conceptual Problems', in Filstead, W, (ed), *An Introduction to Deviance,* New York: Markham, pp 233-43.

KLAUSNER, C, 1964, 'Sacred and Profane Meanings of Blood and Alcohol', in Kluckhohn, R, (ed), *Culture and Behaviour,* New York: Free Press.

KUHN, T, 1970, *The Structure of Scientific Revolutions,* Chicago: University of Chicago Press.

LACAN, J, 1977, *Ecrits. A Selection,* London: Tavistock.

LAMART, A, 1976, 'The Sisterhood', in Hammersley, M and Woods (eds), *The Process of Schooling,* London: Routledge and Kegan Paul, pp 152-9.

LAWSON, J, and Silver, H, 1973, *A Social History of Education in England,* London: Methuen.

LAWTON, D, 1980, *The Politics of the School Curriculum,* London: Routledge and Kegan Paul.

LEATHER, D, Hastings, G and Davies, J, (eds), 1981, *Health Education and the Media,* Oxford: Pergamon.

LEDERMAN, S, 1956, *Alcohol, Alcoolisme, Alcoolisation,* Paris: Presse Universitaire de France.

LEMERT, E, 1967, *Human Deviance, Social Problems and Social Control,* New York: Prentice-Hall.

LEMERT, E, 1974, 'Beyond Mead: The Societal Reaction to Deviance', *Social Problems,* 21, 4, pp 457-68.

LEVY, H, 1951, *Drink – an Economic and Social History,* London: Routledge and Kegan Paul.

LONDON BOROUGH OF SERVICETOWN, 1978, *Development Plan,* Servicetown: London Borough of Servicetown.

LONDON-EDINBURGH RETURN GROUP, 1979; *In and Against the State,* London: London-Edinburgh Return Group/Publications Distribution Co-op.

LUXTON, M, *More Than a Labour of Love: Three Generations of Women's Labour in the Home,* Toronto: Women's Press.

McCLELLAND, D, Davis, W, Kalm, W, Wanner, E, 1972, *The Drinking Man,* New York: Free Press.

McCRON, R, 1980, 'Mass Media Campaigns in Health Education: A Critical Overview', unpublished, pp 13.

McCRON, R and Budd, J, 1979, 'Mass Communications and Health Education', in Sutherland, I, (ed), *Health Education; perspectives and choices,* London: George Allen and Unwin, pp 199-216.

McGUINNES, T, 1979, *An Econometric Analysis of Total Demand for Alcoholic Beverage in the UK 1956-1975,* Edinburgh: Scottish Health Education Unit, (folio), pp 24.

McKENZIE, D, 1981, 'Notes on the Science and Social Relations Debate', *Capital and Class,* 14, pp 47-60.

McROBBIE, A, 1980, 'Settling Accounts with Subculture Theory: a Feminist Critique', *Screen Education,* 34, (Spring), pp 37-50.

McROBBIE, A and Garber J, 1975, 'Girls and Subcultures: an Exploration', *Working Papers in Cultural Studies,* 7/8, (Summer), pp 209-22.

MADDOX, G, 1962, 'Teenage Drinking in the United States' in Pittman, D and Snyder, R, (eds), *Society, Culture and Drinking Patterns,* New York: Wiley and Sons, pp 230-245.

MAKELA, K and Viikari, M, 1977, 'Notes on Alcohol and the State', *Acta Sociologica,* 20, pp 155-79.

MAKENHAM, P, 1980, *Youth Unemployment: an Examination of Youth Unemployment Using National Statistics, Research Paper no. 10*, London: Department of Employment.

MALOS, E, (ed), 1980, *The Politics of Housework,* London; Allison and Busby.

MARX, K, 1959, *Capital,* (3 volumes), London: Lawrence and Wishart.

MARX, K, 1969, *Theories of Surplus Value,* (3 volumes), Moscow: Progress.

MARX, K, 1979, 'Thesis on Feuerbach', supplement to Marx and Engels, *op cit,* pp 121-3.

MARX, K and Engels, F, 1970, *The German Ideology,* London: Lawrence and Wishart.

MASS-OBSERVATION, 1943, *The Pub and the People,* London: Boyers.

MATHIAS, P, 1959, *The Brewing Industry in England,* Cambridge: University Press.

MATHIAS, P, 1979, *The Transformation of England,* London: Methuen.

MATZA, D, 1969, *Becoming Deviant,* New Jersey: Prentice-Hall.

MATZA, D and Sykes, G, 1961, 'Juvenile Delinquency and Subterranean Values', *American Sociological Review,* 26, pp 712-19.

MERRIT, A, 1980, 'The Nature and Function of Law', *British Journal of Law and Society,* 7, 2, (Winter), pp 195-214.

MERTON, R, 1957, *Social Theory and Social Structure,* New York: Free Press.

MIDDLEMAS, K, 1979, *Politics in Industrial Society,* London: Andre Deutsch.

MILL, J, 1921, *Principles of Political Economy with Some of their Applications to Social Philosphy,* London: Green and Co.

MILLER, W, 1958, 'Lower Class Culture as a Generating Milieu of Gang Delinquency', *Journal of Social Issues,* 15, pp 15-9.

MILLIBAND, R, 1972, *Parliamentary Socialism,* London: Merlin.

MINNS, R, 1981, 'A Comment on "Finance Capital and the Crisis in Britain"', *Capital and Class,* 14, (Summer), pp 98-109.

MITCHELL, J, 1974, *Pscyhoanalysis and Feminism,* Harmondsworth: Penguin.

MOOS, M, 1979, 'Government Youth Training Policy and its Impact on Further Education', stencilled Occasional Paper 57, Birmingham: Centre for Contemporary Cultural Studies.

MUNGHAM, G and Pearson, G, 1976, 'Introduction: Troubled Youth, Troubling World', in Mungham, G and Pearson, G, (eds), *Working Class Youth Cultures,* London: Routledge and Kegan Paul, pp 1-9.

MURODCK, G and McCron, R, 1976, 'Youth and Class: the Career of a

Confusion', in Mungham, G and Pearson, G, (eds), *Working Class Youth Cultures,* London: Routledtge and Kegan Paul, pp 10-26.

NAVA, M, 1980, 'Gender and Education', *Feminist Review,* 5, pp 69-78.

NAVA, M, 1982, '"Everybody's Views Were Just Broadened". A Girls Project and Some Responses to Lesbianism', *Feminist Review,* 100, (Spring), pp 37-60.

NATIONAL DEVIANCY CONFERENCE, (eds), 1980, *Permissiveness and Control*, London: Macmillan.

NATIONAL YOUTH BUREAU, 1981, *Youth and Society* (whole journal issue on Social Education), 50, (January).

NAVARRO, V, 1978, *Class Struggle, the State and Medicine*, London: Martin Robertson.

NORTOFT, B and Dorn, N, 1981, *Sundhedskarrier (Health Careers)*, Copenhagen: Komiteen for Sundhedsoplysning (Committee for Health Education).

OAKLEY, A, 1974, *The Sociology of Housework*, London: Martin Robertson.

O'CONNOR, James, 1973, *The Fiscal Crisis of the State*, New York: St. Martin's Press.

O'CONNOR, Joyce, 1978, *The Young Drinkers: A Cross-National Study of Social and Cultural Influences*, London: Tavistock.

OPEN UNIVERSITY HEALTH CHOICES TEAM, 1980, *The Good Health Guide,* London: Harper and Row for the Open University in association with the Health Education Council and the Scottish Health Education Unit.

PARKER, D, 1977 'Alcohol Control Policy and the Fiscal Crisis of the State', *Drinking and Drug Practices Surveyor*, 13, (December), pp 3-6.

PARKER, H, 1974, *View from the Boys*, London: David and Charles.

PARSONS, T, 1942, 'Age and Sex in the Social Structure of the United States', *American Sociological Review,* 7, pp 604-16, reprinted 1954 in his *Essays in Sociological Theory*, Chicago: Free Press.

PARSONS, T, 1951, *The Social System,* New York: Free Press.

PARSONS, T, 1954, *Essays in Sociological Theory*, Chicago: Free Press.

PASHUKANIS, E, 1978, *Law and Marxism: a General Theory*, London: Ink Links

PEARSON, G, 1975, *The Deviant Imagination*, London: Macmillan.

PEARSON, G, 1976, '"Paki-bashing" in a North East Lancashire Cotton Town', in Mungham, G and Pearson, G, (eds), *Working Class Youth Cultures,* London: Routledge and Kegan Paul, pp 48-81.

PERRY, L, 1979, *Women and Drug Use: an Unfeminine Dependency*, London: Institute for the Study of Drug Dependence, (leaflet).

PETTY, W, 1963, 'Political Arithmetic', in Hull, C, (ed), *The Political Writings of Sir William Petty*, (Volume 1), New York: Kelly.

PITMAN, D, 1967, 'Drinking Patterns and Alcoholism: A Cross-Cultural Perspective', in Pitman, D, (ed), *Alcoholism,* New York: Harper and Row, pp 3-20.

PITTS, J, 1981, 'From Rock-Climbing to Rock-Breaking: Thatcherism and Young Offenders', Occasional Papers in Criminology and the Sociology of Deviance, No. 1, Enfield: Middlesex Polytechnic.

PLANT, M, Pirle, F and Kreitman, M, 1979, 'Evaluation of the Scottish Health Education Unit's 1976 Campaign on Alcoholism', *Social Psychiatry,* 14, 1, pp 11-24.

PLUMMER, K, 1979, 'Misunderstanding Labelling Perspectives', in Downes, D and Rock, P, (eds), *Deviant Interpretations*, London: Martin Robertson, pp 85-121.

POLSKY, N, 1971, *Hustlers, Beats and Others*, Harmondsworth: Penguin.

POWELL, R and Clarke, J, 1975, 'A Note on Marginality', *Working Papers in Cultural Studies*, 7/8, (Summer), pp 223-30.

PROTZ, R, 1978, *Pulling a Fast One*, London: Pluto Press.

ROBERTS, B, 1975, 'Naturalistic Research into Subcultures and Deviance: An Account of the Sociological Tendency", *Working Papers in Cultural Studies*, 7/8, (Summer), pp 243-252.

ROBINSON, D, 1976, *From Drinking to Alcoholism: A Sociological Commentary,* London: Wiley.

ROBINSON, D and Henry, S, 1977, *Self-help and Health*, London, Martin Robertson.

ROMANO, C, 1981, 'Michel Foucault's New Clothes', *Village Voice*, 26, 18, (April-May), pp 1 and 40-2.

ROOM, R, 1976, 'Ambivalence as a Sociological Explanation: the Case of Cultural Explanations of Alcohol Problems', *American Sociological Review,* 41, (December), pp 1047-65.

ROSE, H and Rose, S, (eds), 1976, *The Political Economy of Science,* and *The Radicalisation of Science,* London: Macmillan.

ROWBOTHAM, S, 1973, *Hidden From History,* London: Pluto.

ROWBOTHAM, S, 1979, 'The Women's Movement and Organising for Socialism', in Rowbotham, S, Segal, L and Wainwright, H, (eds), *Beyond the Fragments*, London: Merlin Press, pp 21-156.

ROYAL COLLEGE OF PSYCHIATRISTS, 1979, *Alcohol and Alcoholism: Report of a Special Committee of the Royal College of Psychiatrists*, London: Tavistock.

ROYAL COMMISSION ON LICENSING, 1931, *Evidence to a Report of the Royal Commission on Licensing (England and Wales) 1929-31*, London: HMSO.

RUBIN, I, 1979, *A History of Economic Thought*, London: Ink Links.

RUSCHE, G and Kirchheimer, O, 1968, *Punishment and Social Structure,* New York: Russell and Russell.

SCHAEFER, J, 1973, 'A Hologeistic Study of Family Structure and Sentiment', PhD dissertation, New York: State University of New York.

SCHAPS, E, Di Bartolo, R, Palley, C and Churgin, S, 1978, *Primary Prevention Research: A Review of 127 Program Evaluations. PYRAMID Project Report to National Institute for Drug Abuse,* Washington: Department of Health Education and Welfare, mimeo. Revised and reprinted, 1981, 'A Review of 127 Drug Abuse Prevention Programs', *Journal of Drug Issues*, 11, 1, pp 17-43, (references deleted).

SCHEFF, T, 1966, *Becoming Mentally Ill: A Sociological Theory,* Chicago: Aldine.

SCHEFF, T, 1974, 'The Labelling Theory of Mental Illness', *American Sociological Review*, 39, (June), pp 444-52.

SCHMIDT, W and De Lint, J, 1972, 'Causes of Death of Alcoholics', *Quarterly Journal of Studies on Alcohol*, 33, pp 171-85.

SCHOOLS COUNCIL HEALTH EDUCATION PROJECT, 1977, *All About Me* and *Think Well* (including 'Deadly Decisions') Teaching Packs, London: Nelson.

SCHUR, E, 1971, *Labelling Deviant Behaviour*, New York: Harper and Row.

SEBESTYEN, A, 1980, 'Women Against the Demon Drink', *Spare Rib,* 100, (November), pp 22-7.

SEGAL, L, 1979, 'A Local Experience', in Rowbotham, S, Segal, L and Wainwright, H, (eds), *Beyond the Fragments,* London: Merlin Press, pp 157-210.

SEVE, L, 19777, *Man in Marxist Theory; and the psychology of personality*, Sussex: Harvester Press.

SHADWELL, A, 1903, *Drink, Temperance and Legislation*, London: Longman's, Green and Co.

SHARP, R and Green, A, 1975, *Education and Social Control: A Study in Progressive Primary Education*, London: Routledge and Kegan Paul.

SKOG, O, 1981, 'Alcoholism and Social Policy: are we on the right lines?', *British Journal of Addiction*, 76, (September), pp 315-21.

SOUTH, N, 1982, 'The Informal Economy and Local Labour Markets', in Laite, J, (ed) *Bibliographies and Reports on Local Labour Markets and the Informal Economy,* London: Social Science Research Council.

STATISTICAL OFFICE OF THE EUROPEAN COMMUNITIES, 1980,

Labour Force Sample Survey, Luxemburg: Office for Official Publications of the European Community.

STEWART, M, 1976, *Keynes and After*, Harmondsworth: Penguin.

STULL, D, 1975, 'Hologeistic Studies of Drinking: A Critique', *Drinking and Drug Practices Surveyer* (Social Research Group, University of California), 10, pp 4-10.

TAYLOR, I, 1971, 'Soccer Consciousness and Soccer Hooliganism', in Cohen, S, (ed), *Images of Deviance,* Harmondsworth: Penguin, pp 134-64.

TAYLOR, I, 1980, 'The Law and Order Issue in the British General Election and Canadian Federal Election of 1979: Crime, Populism and the State', *Canadian Journal of Sociology*, 5, 3, (Summer), pp 285-311.

TAYLOR I and and Taylor L, 1973, *Politics and Deviance*, Harmondsworth: Penguin.

TAYLOR, I, Walton, P and Young, J, 1973, *The New Criminology*, London: Routledge.

THANE, P, 1978, 'Women and the Poor Law in Victorian and Edwardian England', *History Workshop*, 6, (Autumn), pp 7-28.

THERBORN, G, 1976, *Science, Class and Society*, London: Verso.

THOMPSON, E, 1980, *The Making of the English Working Class*, Harmondsworth: Penguin.

THURMAN, C, 1981, 'The Structure and Role of the Alcoholic Drinks Industry', London Brewer's Society, unpublished mimeo.

TIMES NEWSPAPERS, 1960, *Beer in Britain*, London: Times Publishing Company.

TIMPANARO, S, 1975, *On Materialism,* London: New Left Books.

TOBIAS, J, 1979, *Crime and Police in England 1700-1900,* London: Gill/Macmillan.

TOLSON, A, 1977, 'The Language of Fatalism', *Working Papers in Cultural Studies*, 9, pp 147-54.

TUCK, M, 1980, *Alcoholism and Social Policy* (Home Office Research Study No. 65), London HMSO.

ULLMAN, A, 1958, 'Socio-cultural Background of Alcoholism', *American Academy of Politics and Social Science, Proceedings*, 315, pp 44-54.

VAIZEY, J, 1958, 'The Brewing Industry', in Cook, P and Cohen, R, (eds), *Effects of Mergers,* London: Allen and Unwin, pp 397-400.

WANDER, M, 1978, 'The Small Group', in Wander, M, (compiler), *The Body Politic. Womens Liberation in Britain*, London: Stage 1, pp 107-15.

WEEDON, C, Tolson, A and Mort, F, 1980, 'Theories of Language and Subjectivity', in Hall, S, Hobson, D, Lowe, A and Willis, P, (eds), *Culture, Media, Language,* London: Hutchinson, pp 195-216.

WESTERGAARD, J and Reisler, H, 1975, *Class in a Capitalist Society*, London: Heinemann.

WHITEHEAD, P and Harvey, C, 1974, *'Exploring Alcoholism: an Empirical Test and Reformulation', Journal of Public Health and Social Behaviour,* 15, pp 57-65.

WHYTE, W, 1969, *Street Corner Society*, London: University of Chicago Press.

WILKINS, L, 1964, *Social Deviance*, London: Tavistock.

WILLIAMS, P and Brake, T, 1980, *Drink in Great Britain 1900-1979*, London: Edsel.

WILLIS, P, 1978, *Learning to Labour: How Working Class Kids Get Working Class Jobs*, London: Saxon House.

WILLIS, P, 1979, 'Shop Floor Culture, Masculinity and the Wage Form', in Clarke, J, Critcher, C and Johnson, R, (eds), *Working Class Culture*, London: Hutchinson, pp 185-200.

WILLIS, P, 1980, 'Notes on Method', in Hall, S, Hobson, D, Lowe, A and Willis,

P, (eds), *Culture, Media, Language*, London: Hutchinson, pp 88-95.

WILLMOTT, P, 1966, *Adolescent Boys of East London*, London: Routledge and Kegan Paul.

WILSNACK, S, 1977, 'The Impact of Sex Roles on Women's Alcohol Use and Abuse', in Greenblatt, M and Schuckit, M, (eds), *Alcoholism Problems in Women and Children,* New York: Grune and Stratton, pp 37-63.

WILSON, E, 1980, *Only Half Way to Paradise,* London; Tavistock.

WILSON, E, 1981, 'Psychoanalysis: Psychic Law and Order', *Feminist Review,* 8, (Summer), pp 63-78.

WILSON, G, 1940, *Alcohol and the Nation*, London: Nicholson and Watson.

WILSON, P, 1980, *Drinking in England and Wales,* London; Office of Population Censuses and Surveys.

WOLPE, A-M, 1977, *Some Processes in Sexist Education*, London: Women's Research and Resources Centre.

WORKING PARTY ON INEQUALITIES IN HEALTH, 1980, *Inequalities in Health*, London: Department of Health and Social Security.

WORLD HEALTH ORGANISATION EXPERT COMMITTEE ON PROBLEMS RELATED TO ALCOHOL CONSUMPTION, 1980, *Problems Related to Alcohol Consumption: Technical Report 650,* Geneva: World Health Organisation.

WRIGHT, E, 1978, *Class, Crisis and the State*, London: New Left Books.

YOUNG, J, 1971, *The Drugtakers,* London: MacGibbon and Kee/Paladin.

YOUNG, J, 1973, 'The Myth of the Drug Taker in the Mass Media', in Cohen, S and Young J, *op cit*, ppp 350-59.

YOUNG, J, 1981, 'Beyond the Consensual Paradigm: a Critique of Left Functionalism in Media Theory', in Cohen S and Young, J, (eds), *The Manufacture of News, Deviance, Social Problems and the Mass Media*, (revised edition), London: Constable, pp 393-440.

AUTHOR INDEX

Note. Co-authors are indexed as such: hence, Blane and Hewitt, rather than under Blane (alone), or Hewitt. But when an author has written alone *and* with others, s/he is so indexed (for example – McCron, *as well as* Budd and McCron).

ends

SUBJECT INDEX

Note. Only terms not listed on the *Contents* page are included below. (Hence, for example, 'Round system' is not indexed as such since it carries several entries in the *Contents*, under chapter 5). To identify passages discussing sociological approaches associated with particular theorists, see the *Author Index*, above.